Rhinecliff

A HUDSON RIVER HISTORY

The Tangled Tale of
Rhinebeck's Waterfront

Published by

Black Dome Press Corp.
1011 Route 296
Hensonville, New York 12439
www.blackdomepress.com
Tel: (518) 734-6357

First Edition Paperback 2009

Library of Congress Cataloging-in-Publication Data

Philip, Cynthia Owen.
   Rhinecliff : the tangled tale of Rhinebeck's waterfront : a Hudson River history / Cynthia Owen Philip.
   — 1st ed. pbk.
      p. cm.
   Includes bibliographical references and index.
   ISBN-13: 978-1-883789-62-6 (trade paper)
   ISBN-10: 1-883789-62-1 (trade paper)
   1. Rhinecliff (N.Y.)—History. I. Title.
   F129.R43P47 2009
   974.7'33—dc22

                          2008045422

Front cover painting: *Hudson River from Ponckhockie* by Joseph Tubby (1821–1896), oil on canvas, 18" × 30", circa 1880. Collection Friends of Historic Kingston, www.fohk.org or www.friendsofhistorickingston.org. Gift 2008 from Mr. and Mrs. John N. Cordts. This view shows Rhinecliff on the right with a white structure on the shore.

Design: Toelke Associates

Printed in the USA

10 9 8 7 6 5 4 3 2 1

Rhinecliff

A HUDSON RIVER HISTORY

The Tangled Tale of
Rhinebeck's Waterfront

CYNTHIA OWEN PHILIP

BLACK·DOME

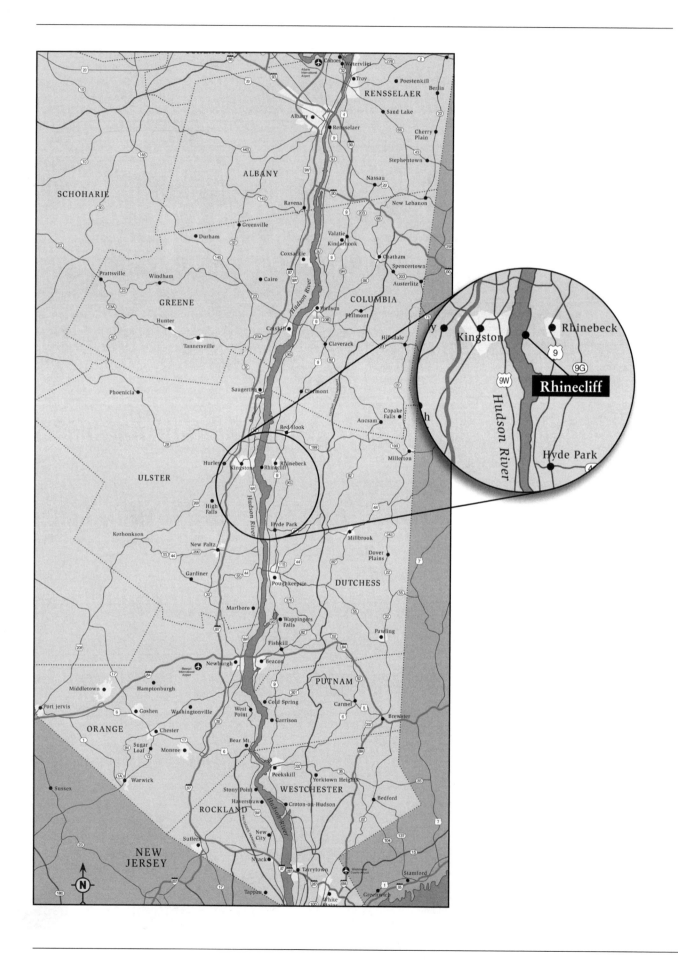

Contents

Acknowledgments

First, I'd like to thank the hamlet and all its inhabitants from the Native Americans and the Kipsbergen Kips to those who have come here more recently and, like me, a Rhinecliffer for thirty years, are new-comers. I have been happy in this always surprising place.

As always in such an endeavor as this book, the list of those who have made it possible is wide and deep. But I would especially like to thank old-timers Bill and Ruby Allen, Harry and Anne Heywood, Betty and the late Don Cole, the late Ray Dedrick, Elinor Van Etten, Mary Denu and Allan Coon. They have shared their memories, observations and photographs as well as their unstinting support. Newcomers Jack Dierdorff, Alonzo Smith and the late Pat Hayes did, too. Steven Mann stood by the whole way. Terry Eargle gave me a boost, just when I needed it. The Rhinebeck Historical Society, the Museum of Rhinebeck History, the Senate House Museum and the Dutchess County Historical Society were immeasurably important resources, as were the Starr Library and our own Morton Memorial Library. The Friends of Historic Kingston graciously gave permission to use their beautiful painting of the stretch of river between Rondout and Rhinecliff as the front cover illustration.

Without the technical expertise of Cynthia Baer, this book would have been scantily illustrated; she has been a patient and cheerful support throughout the project. Peter Bradford stepped in with his meticulous scanning when the rush to completion was almost overpowering. So did Sean Thompson. Those who provided or took photographs were generous beyond all expectations; they are noted in the captions.

Proofreaders Matina Billias, Natalie Mortensen and Ed Volmar had their work cut out for them. Among other faults, I cannot spell. Steve Hoare, my editor, and I were on the same page; his comments have been immensely energizing. Debbie Allen, publisher of Black Dome Press, is the one who with infinite faith and steadfastness actually brought this work to fruition. I should also like to thank Wint Aldrich, John Cronin and Nancy Kelly for their thoughtful reading of the manuscript and their very kind words.

Finally, as writing is a solo and often lonely occupation, I thank my family and long-suffering friends for providing good advice and much-needed moments of comic relief. In short, I think of this book as a group effort. However, all errors and omissions are, of course, my own.

Prologue

In the late 1970s I was working in New York City as a freelance writer. In a fit of either exuberance or desperation — probably both — I decided I needed a small place in the country with easy public transportation to the city. My one close friend in northern Dutchess County didn't miss a beat when I asked about the area. "Rhinecliff is the place for you," was the immediate response. "I know you'll love it." I was rather surprised. Some years before when I was visiting in the neighborhood, the only comment about Rhinecliff was that it was down-at-the-heels and rowdy. "Go take a look," my friend insisted. Well, the lucky end of this story is that, within two weeks, I found exactly the kind of house in the kind of community I was looking for. I have been as happy as a goldfinch in a ripe mulberry tree ever since.

What first attracted me to this small waterfront hamlet was its extraordinary location. It is high on the east bank of the great Hudson River, opposite Kingston. Although no longer the great water highway between New York, Albany and on to Lake Erie that it once was when the Erie Canal was in operation, the river still carries an impressive array of heavy freight and a delightful jumble of pleasure boats. The huge tows and tankers are reminders of its former industrial might. The sailboats, motorboats, iceboats, kayaks and canoes, dancing with the wind and tide or struggling against them, are the latest version of the recreational delights the river has always offered. The hamlet's backdrop, the ancient multilayered, multihued Catskill Mountain range, has been beloved throughout its long history by painters, writers, and residents, and heralded for its spectacular sunsets and horrendous Rip Van Winkle storms.

The hamlet's up-and-down topography — a series of steeply ascending rocky cliffs interspersed with swales and a few fine fields — is full of surprises. Most of the houses are close together but, because all are placed where the land dictates rather than on a grid, each has its own distinct personality. Individually they are not grand, but they give the hamlet an intimacy that contrasts perfectly with the expansiveness of its setting.

As I walked from the railroad station to my house that spring, enveloped by the scent of old lilacs and the whishing sound of the rolling Hudson, Rhinecliff spoke to me of gritty steadfastness and independence. It was these characteristics, I now know, that compelled me to ferret out its long history. The task has been a fascinating one that became even more absorbing when, as a former regional planner, I realized that many other waterfront settlements share similar elements — a post road, a major railroad, commercial fishing, dictating terrain, tolerant churches, very old houses, multi-generational old-timers, increasing numbers of newcomers, some commuters, converted one-room schoolhouses, a tradition of kids entertaining themselves and a pride of place and heritage. Every waterfront community has its own special history, of course, but scratch the surface and their shared characteristics are greater than their differences. This is what has made writing this book such a fascinating adventure.

1

The First Settlement

Kipsbergen

The first thing I discovered about Rhinecliff is that the hamlet was not called by that name until 1851, when the name "Rhinecliff" was given to a much smaller subdivision laid out to take advantage of a station stop on the new Hudson River Railroad. The settlement was then more than 150 years old.

It was in the summer of 1686 that four Kingston Dutchmen acquired two parcels of land from Native Americans of the great Lenape tribe, who had been hunting, fishing and making tools there for at least 8,000 years. Gerrit Aartsen, Arie Roosa and Jan Elting received the first and larger parcel from Aran Kee, Kora Kee and Kreme Much. Soon afterward, their friend, Hendrickus Kip, secured for himself and his brother Jacob a smaller adjacent parcel from Anamaton, Ankony and a sachem, Calycoon. Together the parcels encompassed 2,200 acres on four miles of waterfront.

In exchange for this land, the partners gave "Six Buffaloes, Four Blankets, Five Kettles, Four Guns, Five Horns, Five Axes, Ten Kans of Powder, Eight Shirts, Eight Pairs of Stockings, Forty Fathoms of

Wampum or Sewan,* Two Drawing Knives, Two Adzes, Ten Knives, Half Anker of Rum, and One Frying Pan." (That array of goods may seem eclectic, but it reflected Native Americans' appreciation of European manufactured goods, as well as their own media of exchange.) Beginning in the northwest corner, marked by a large blazed oak, the boundary ran from the Hudson River directly eastward to what would become Hog Bridge on the old Post Road (just west of the Village of Rhinebeck). It then followed the Rhinebeck Kill and the great Landsman Kill in a long bow until it again reached the river at its southwest corner.

Few stretches of land in the Hudson Valley were as beautiful or as promising. High bluffs overlooked the wide river teeming with shad, sturgeon, herring, bass, eels, mussels and clams. Three depressions made places to launch boats. Scattered throughout its heavy forests, replete with game, were cleared patches on which the Native Americans had planted corn and squash. The Landsman Kill offered several fine mill sites. The Hudson River provided a straight route to the markets of New York, 100 miles to the south and already a port of international significance. Sixty miles to the north was Albany, a premier destination for the fur trade and with trails heading west along the Mohawk River Valley.

It may seem surprising that the Native Americans relinquished their ancestral lands so easily and so cheaply. However, their concept of land ownership was radically different from that of Europeans. Unlike the great Dutch jurist Grotius, who wrote, "Property is something that is called ours," they did not believe an individual or even a tribe could possess land. It belonged to the Great Spirit. In their view, what they enjoyed was the ephemeral use of the land.

Seven Native American points, a drill and a grinder unearthed on the Kipsbergen patent. Painting by Alvin Wanzer, 2007.

If they did not use it, they could trade it with other tribes or, in case of war, lose the use of it to the enemy. As far as the Native Americans were concerned, the Dutchmen, with their ritual exchange of European tools and clothing along with some rum, had merely gained the right to live on the land.

By 1686 these Native Americans should have known better, but, as with all peoples, fundamental

---

*Sewan or wampum, along with grain and beaver skins, was one of the principal mediums of exchange: twelve white beads or six black beads equaled one stuyver or one-half guilder; six guilders equaled one English pound. Wampum was usually sewn into belts of six or more feet.

Although this petroglyph has long been associated with the Kipsbergen partners' 1686 acquisition of their land from Native Americans, it is now thought to be far older. Photograph 1930, courtesy of Wilderstein Preservation.

now the Wilderstein estate, but evidence is mounting that the pictograph is of much earlier origin.)

In 1688 the Dutchmen received affirmation of their acquisition in the form of a patent granted by James II, to whom the Dutch had ceded their land in New York in 1664. The patent was signed, with his "lysense, consent and approbation," by the provincial governor, Thomas Dongan. The document had undergone a two-year round-trip to England, because British laws decreed that the Crown was the "fountain of all real property and from this source all titles are to be derived." In boilerplate terms, the king's signature gave the patentees, their heirs and their assigns forever "all meadows, woods, marshes, waters, hunting, hawking, fishing and fowling and all other profits, advantages, commodities and emoluments to the said parcel of land." The annual quitrent to the Crown was "eight bushels of good, sweet merchantable winter wheat" in perpetuity.

Kip Forebears

It was the fourth major settlement on the Hudson River — only Albany, New York and Kingston preceded it — and it was the first on the river's east bank. Only the Kips settled on the patent. For this reason the whole 2,200 acres were given the name Kipsbergen. The main motive of the other partners' acquisition was either speculation or a means of providing for their many children.

Just who were these Dutch Kips? Originally the family was from Kype in the Brittany region of France. Like so many others, they had probably

beliefs die hard. Equally instrumental was the fact that wars against other tribes and Europeans, as well as smallpox epidemics and access to liquor, had so reduced them that they had become semi-itinerants and were ready to move on. Moreover, they must have known and trusted the Dutch partners, especially Hendrickus and Jacobus Kip, whose New York City–based father, Isaac Kip, had established a relationship with them through trading. Whatever their principal motivation, the six Native Americans made their marks on the conveyance papers. (Some claim they memorialized the exchange with a pictograph cut into a rock on the waterfront of what is taken refuge in the United Netherlands for religious reasons because, once there, they converted from Roman Catholicism to Protestantism. At that time the Netherlands was the most civilized country in Europe, enjoying what is known as its Golden Age. It was the home of such immortals as Rembrandt, Vermeer and Leibniz. Equally important, it was tolerant of all religions and cultural traditions, its welcome extending to Jews, Muslims and even Gypsies. Dutch was the language of world trade, but in their homes all residents of the Netherlands freely spoke the tongue of their birth.

It is claimed that an early Hendrickus Kip was one of the company that sent the explorer Henry Hudson to find the elusive Northwest Passage to the spice islands of the Far East. If so, it may well have been that Hendrickus's son who immigrated to New Amsterdam with a wife and five children in 1637. Why he risked all and left such a flourishing world center for a shabby Dutch West Indies Company outpost established just over a decade before is not known. Perhaps tales swapped by his father and his friends of the Hudson River Valley's abundance had stirred him. Or maybe he was fleeing the collapse of the Tulip Mania that occurred in February of the year he and his family set sail.*

In any case, this first new-world Kip was thought to have been a tailor in Holland — a valued craft in that fashion-conscious country — so it is likely that he arrived on the shores of New Amsterdam, as New York was then called, with more than a few guilders in his pockets. What he found there was a port in the making on the East River, guarded by a fort within which were the director's mansion, an erstwhile parade ground, a barracks for sixty soldiers, six workshops and a wooden church. Huddled around it were the remains of rotting cabins built by the first arrivals and a sprinkling of comparatively decent houses, including a bakery, a plethora of grog shops, a small house for a schoolmaster and another for a midwife.

The settlement — and indeed the entire colony of New Netherland—then belonged to the Dutch West India Company, whose overriding interest was in trading rather than in establishing a permanent community. Moreover, the company had sent ne'er-do-wells to govern it. By the time the Kips arrived, it was in deplorable condition. The fortress was in disrepair. No more than 250 men were capable of bearing arms. The dirt streets and pathways were filled with refuse and foraging animals. Of four windmills, only two were operable — a gristmill and a sawmill. The few outlying farms produced more weeds than crops. The population consisted mainly of male fortune hunters. A surprisingly low percentage was Dutch. An equally surprising high percentage was African or Caribbean blacks, some slave, a few free. A Tower of Babel mix, it is said that at least eighteen languages were spoken there.

Gradually, the settlement became more organized. It took a great leap forward when, in 1647, the strict, wily, one-legged Petrus Stuyvesant (Petrus, the Latin form of Pieter, signified higher education) descended upon it as the Director General of New Netherland (as well as of Curaçao, which he had previously governed). By then, Hendrickus Kip had acquired a farm on which he grew tobacco and hops for beer — both absolute necessities for the population's sense of well-being — near a bridge that crossed De Heere Gracht, the great canal that bifurcated the settlement. Kip had also earned a reputation for strong-minded individualism; he was one of the few who protested the brutal slaughter of Native Americans in the confrontations of the early 1640s. Despite that stance,

*The Tulip Mania was a wild and engulfing speculation in which otherwise worthy burghers squandered their fortunes to buy one rare tulip bulb.

he was appointed one of the Council of Eight — prominent citizens who, with the director general, ruled the fast-growing town. In 1653, when the settlement became a city with its own government, the Kips were among the elite families who became Grand Burghers.

Although the city prospered under Stuyvesant, it was by no means secure from British harassment. Well-ensconced in New England, the British, in fact, claimed the Dutch colony as their own on the basis of prior discovery. They had already settled thirteen towns on Long Island, in contrast to the Dutch West Indies Company's five. Moreover, Wiltwyck, as Kingston was then called, had a significant number of British settlers. (The interest of the first Wiltwyck settler, Thomas Chambers, may well have been mixed, for he was "an English soldier of fortune employed by the Dutch.") In 1664 the British took definitive action. They sent four frigates and two thousand troops, first to Brooklyn, then to Staten Island, and finally through the Narrows to New Amsterdam itself. With a crumbling fortress and only a handful of soldiers, Director General Stuyvesant could do nothing but surrender.

The highly practical Dutch took their conquest in stride. The mild Articles of Capitulation permitted them to keep their religion, language, contractual agreements and their traditions of women's rights and children's equal inheritance. Although the city and province were renamed New York, after James the Duke of York, now its master, the freeholders of the city continued to govern themselves. The main stricture was that the Dutch must take an oath to the British monarch. Most, including the Kips and Stuyvesant, who became the governor of British New York, did so.

Hendrickus Kip's eldest son, Hendrickus (II), who had married the daughter of Stuyvesant's first counselor, lived near the busy port and was a *schepens* (or alderman) of the city. (To keep the Hendrickuses and Jacobuses straight, they will be numbered according to their generations in America.) Hendrickus's second son, Jacobus (II), was appointed secretary of the council of the colony and was also a *schepens,* honored positions he continued to fill under the British. A successful brewer, he acquired a large farm on the Kingsbridge Road, in the area on the East River known today as Kips Bay, and built a fine homestead of imported brick there. Iron numerals proclaimed the year 1665 from each gable. The Kip coat of arms, featuring a demi-griffon holding a cross, was carved in stone above the door. Enlarged in 1696, its dining room ran the width of the building, with windows overlooking the bay on the east and the meadows adorned with plum, peach, apple and pear orchards on the west. (It has been claimed that one of the pear trees, imported by Petrus Stuyvesant to the old fort, was moved to the Kip farm where it lived to be over 230 years old. The property remained a social focal point of New York City for almost two centuries. It was the last of the Dutch *bouweries* when it was demolished in 1851.)

Hendrickus's youngest son, Isaac (II), was a sloop captain who traded with fast-growing Kingston and the flourishing fur-trading post, Albany, bringing to those local burghers the vast array of European imports — wine, watches, fine fabrics, lace, books, tools and Dutch clay pipes — they needed or simply wanted. Farmers in the city and on Long Island were growing good tobacco, as was he, so he undoubtedly sold that upriver, too, for Dutch women as well as their men were inveterate smokers. On the return trip to New York, he carried grains for bread, oats for horses and lumber for builders, some of which would be trans-shipped to the West Indies and even to Europe. It was Isaac (II) who sired the Hendrickus (III) who would eventually found Kipsbergen.

When not trading, Isaac (II) lived on Stone Street, so-called because it was the first in New Amsterdam to be paved. He also owned a lot by the East River water gate on what is now the northeast corner of Pearl and Wall streets. His fence was so near the defensive wall that the city ordered him to remove it so the passage to the port area could be widened. When Isaac (II) failed to convince his neighbor to sell him a piece of his garden so he could build a handsome house on his water gate lot, Isaac sold that property to the city. He then sold his lot in a sheep pasture on De Prince's canal — a branch off de Heere Graft — to his brewer brother, Jacobus (II), who already possessed the lots on either side of it. Having divested himself of his property in the city's center, Isaac (II) bought a large farm on the Hudson River in the Harlem section of Manhattan. By the time his son Hendrickus (III) left the city for Kingston, the Kips were spread about the whole island of Manhattan. They were, and would remain, a distinguished, top-ranking family there.

From Kingston to Kipsbergen

No one knows when and why Hendrickus (III) made the move to Kingston, but records of the late 1670s show him well-established there as a man of property. Nor is it known why he left what must have been a comfortable life in that bustling town and took his family across the river to an unhewn and potentially unsafe place. Perhaps it was the same spirit of adventure that had sent his forebear to New Amsterdam, augmented by the opportunity to acquire a substantial amount of land at virtually no expense to himself and his much younger brother, Jacobus (III), who was then, like their father, a sloop captain.

Still, Kingston was an attractive place to be and must have been hard to leave. After New York and Albany, it was the third most populous settlement in the entire province and had three times as many inhabitants as any other in Ulster County. (The first census, in 1703, would count 406 males and 159 females above the age of ten years, 207 male children, 146 female children and 91 Negroes.) Located two miles inland of the port (called Esopus), many of Kingston's dwellings were substantial. Along the creek, which paralleled the river, the superb agricultural land could be double-cropped. In the mountains were endless timber forests. Kingston had become an important source of commodities for New York City.

A saving grace would be that the Kips' removal to the east side of the river did not necessitate separation from Kingston life. On the contrary, crossing the river was easy and their ties remained close. They continued to possess property and do business in Kingston, and to attend its Dutch Reformed church. Moreover, the Kips' fellow patentees still lived there.

It is not known when Hendrickus (III) built the stone homestead on his new land. The lintel over the doorway, now preserved in the Rhinebeck post office, bears the inscription "HK AK 1700." ("AK" are the initials of his wife Annetje.) But this date could have signaled an important expansion, rather than a first building. Whatever the case, it is

Hendrickus Kip built the first house in the settlement circa 1698. The Beekman, Livingston and Heermance families, subsequent owners, greatly enlarged it. The original part of the house is on the right in this postcard circa 1908, courtesy of Harry Heywood.

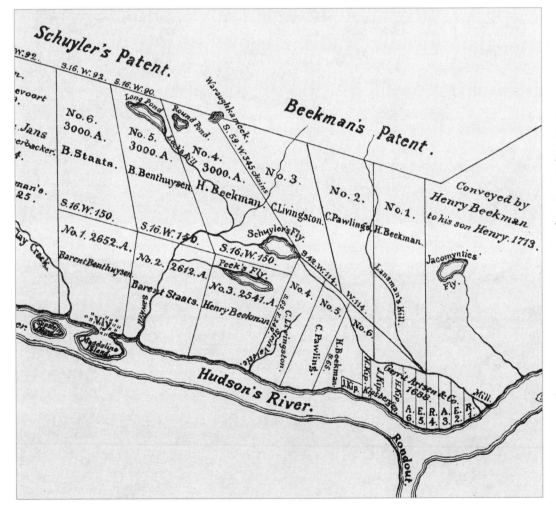

The earliest known map of the Kipsbergen patent (lower right). The map is useful, too, for marking the hamlet's encirclement by the Beekmans who married into the Pawling and Livingston families. Courtesy of the Dutchess County Historical Society.

doubtful that the house started out as a single room to be added onto as the family grew — a Dutch homebuilding tradition in the Hudson River Valley — for Hendrickus (III) and Annetje already had their three children: a grown boy, a twelve-year-old boy and a young girl. Moreover, they were quite prosperous. His father had died, leaving the large farm in northern Manhattan, and Annetje's father, who died when she was young, had left her a small inheritance. Furthermore, Hendrickus (III) had accumulated a significant amount of property in Kingston. The sale of a lot in 1695 characterizes him as being "late of Kingston," so it is entirely possible that he had already moved to the east bank of the Hudson by that time. At any rate, the original structure could have been built as soon as Hendrickus (III) received his patent, for he had acquired his land separately and, unlike his partners, would divide it only with his brother.

Jacobus Kip, Hendrickus's younger brother and also a patentee, built the stone section of his house at the ferry landing circa 1708. The wooden section was added to make it a tavern, and the porch was added still later. It has recently been spruced up with a geometrical railing. Photograph by Alan Coon, 2007.

For some unknown reason, it was not until 1702 that the division of the land among the other patentees took place. Arie Roosa, Roeleff Elting (in place of his deceased father) and Gerrit Aartsen split their parcel into six equal lots, numbering them from the Landsman Kill on the south end to the Kips' southern border on the north. Roosa took lots one and four, Elting two and five and Aartsen three and six, a Dutch way of equalizing the quality of land each received, with a drawing made for order of choice. At the same time, Hendrickus (III) divided his land with his brother following a variation on that pattern. He took two-thirds of his half on the most southerly end, upon which his house stood. The property extended from Aartsen's northern boundary (where a small watercourse dribbles down into a pool at end of the railroad station parking lot today) and went north to the Native Americans' Sepasco trail

Jan Kip's house, built circa 1715. This is also known as the Abraham Kip house. Jan sold the house in 1716 to his Uncle Jacobus, whose youngest child, Abraham, would inherit it. Photograph by Alan Coon, 2007.

(Rhinecliff Road). Jacobus took his full acreage on the other side of the trail. (Later maps show the brothers as sharing the trail's river landing.) Hendrickus's remaining third was a long thin strip abutting Jacob's parcel. All the partners retained an interest in the valuable mill sites along the Landsman Kill.

Sometime before 1708, Jacobus (III) built a one-room stone house on the waterfront with that date cut into the stone in an original wall. He probably immediately enlarged it, because he and his wife Rachel Swartwout, the daughter of Wiltwyck's first *schout* (chief official, combining the offices of sheriff, prosecutor and tax collector), already had seven of their nine children. Having reached his forties, Jacobus (III) had retired as a sloop captain. He now began running an informal ferry to Esopus. The ferry is thought to have been fashioned from hollowed-out buttonwood logs and propelled by sails and oars.

Hendrickus Kip (III) died in 1713. In true Dutch fashion he left each of his children a third of his property. Hendrickus (IV), the younger son, received the homestead. The land west of it with riverfront went to his daughter Catholyntie. She and her husband Matthys Sleght, an important political figure in Kingston, may have already built a stone house on it, for they already had three of their nine children. The eldest son, Jan, was given a parcel above his uncle's on the Sepasco trail. There, by 1715, he had built a sturdy one-room stone house. He would not live there for long, however; in 1716 he sold it to his uncle Jacobus (III), probably because of poor health, and moved with his wife Lysbet Van Kleeck and their five children to a property next to her family's place at Poughkeepsie. When Jan died in 1719, he bequeathed the remainder of his Kipsbergen land to his brother and sister. That same year Hendrickus (IV) deeded his portion to Catholyntie, adding significantly to the property she already owned and, perhaps, increasing her acreage to equal that of her brothers in accordance with the wish of their father and Dutch tradition.

All this time, Jacobus (III) had been steadily increasing his holdings. In 1706 he bought from William Traphagen of Kingston twenty-four waterfront acres outside the patent, north of his brother's second lot. In 1714 and 1719 he added to it a hefty 390 contiguous acres bought from Hendrickus Beekman of Kingston. With four stone houses, much of the arable land surrounding them cleared and drained, as well as the ferry connection to Kingston, the Kips had transformed the wilderness into a distinctive settlement.

The Eltings, Aartsens and Roosas, who continued to live in Kingston, were not idle. Like most settlers, they were busy buying and selling real estate. What is worthy of note is that all their transactions involving their Kipsbergen land took place within the circle of their own families. The only break was when Arie Roosa sold Hendrickus Beekman of Kingston the six-acre mill site at the mouth of the Landsman Kill. There is no record of how Roosa persuaded the other partners to agree. It may well have been connected with Beekman's sale of Jacomyntie's Vly to Elting's heirs, which took place at the same time.

The patentees had believed that the Vly, a large and exceptionally fertile meadow across the Landsman Kill, was included in their exchange of goods for land with the Native Americans, only to discover that it was a part of the patent procured by Beekman in 1697. And Beekman himself had laid claim to most of Kipsbergen. Whatever the case, selling the mill site was a foolish thing to do. Losing control of it would have crucial repercussions. Mills were known to be an extremely valuable asset — a rare source of ready money — and, as the patentees must have known, the two other watercourses within their patent were incapable of producing sufficient power to run a wheel. Beekman constructed his dam and put up his gristmill immediately. The mill is thought to have been the first in Dutchess County.

While these transactions were taking place, the governing of the county was becoming more organized and more local. In 1713 the provincial legislature ordered that county

Site of the first mill on the Landsman Kill, located near where the stream enters the Hudson River. The mill site was bought by Judge Henry Beekman from the patentees in 1706. The mill was located where the man is standing and was operated by an overshot wheel. Beekman required all his tenants to grind their grain there. Photograph 1910, courtesy of Wilderstein Preservation.

elections be held to choose one freeholder as supervisor, two as assessors and two as collectors. No record remains of who they were, but as Kipsbergen comprised a tenth of the still-scant county population — 46 of 445 persons, to be exact — and all the heads of household were freeholders, it can be supposed that at least some Kips were elected. In 1717 the northern Dutchess County boundary was moved to just below the great Livingston patent in Columbia County, and Dutchess County was divided into three wards — North, Middle and South. There was no question Kipsbergen would become the site of the North Ward's elections. It was its primary political and social center.

By that time, however, the Beekman family had entered into the life of the settlement with force.

2

Enter the Beekmans

The settlement at Kipsbergen continued to prosper in the first decades of the eighteenth century. Hendrickus's and Jacobus Kip's children married, most often among Kingston families, and begat succeeding generations who in turn intermarried, sometimes with cousins. The population steadily increased through marriages and births, and settlement was encouraged by the liberal inheritance traditions and land sales within the patentees' extended families. For instance, Matthys Sleght of Kingston came to Kipsbergen by way of his marriage to Hendrickus Kip's daughter, Catholyntie; Hendrickus Heermance by his marriage to Gerrit Aartsen's daughter; Laurens Osterhout by his to Roosa's daughter. The new families made the most of the settlement's orientation toward the river, trading with Kingston, Albany and New York. They farmed, using oxen for logging and plowing and horses for transportation. They fished, both to feed their families and commercially. They were weavers, carpenters and wheelwrights. Hendrickus Kip, the patentee, had become a cooper. When he died, he left his valued tools specifically to his eldest son, Jan, who in turn passed them on to his son. Jacobus continued to run the ferry between Kipsbergen and Esopus. It operated mainly on demand, rather than as a scheduled service, because most of the residents owned their own boats.

Into this idyllic, close-knit setting marched the Beekmans, great landowners who would play a decisive role in the evolution of Kipsbergen. In 1697, Hendrickus Beekman had received a royal patent for 84,000 acres in the southeastern section of Dutchess County where the towns of Beekman, Pawling, Dover, Unionvale and the northeastern half of LaGrange now are; it is significant to the story of Rhinecliff only for the income and prestige Beekman gained from it. At the same time, however, Beekman gave seven Native Americans sixty pounds for 21,766 acres between the lands of Pieter Schuyler and Henry Pawling in the northern section of the county. The purchase made him the largest landowner in Dutchess County. (A young boy reportedly said of him: "If there is really land on the moon, Mr. Beekman must own it.") The latter parcel included the land that would become the inland town and the Village of Rhinebeck. Because it surrounded Kipsbergen, its impacts on that settlement began immediately and would increase decade by decade. In fact, the impacts of these land acquisitions continue to affect the hamlet today.

It was Hendrickus Beekman's father Wilhelmus who founded the family fortunes in America. Born of Dutch parents of considerable status who emigrated to the United Netherlands via Sweden and Germany, Wilhelmus came to New Netherland in 1647, ten years after the Kips. He had the good fortune to cross the ocean on the same ship as Petrus Stuyvesant, the vigorous director general of New Netherland and the Caribbean dependencies. The friendship Wilhelmus formed with him during their five months' voyage would be of lasting value.

Wilhelmus quickly acquired land in Harlem on the northern frontier of Manhattan. In 1649 he made a love match with Catalina de Boogh, the daughter of a wealthy Albany trader. Hendrickus, the eldest son of nine children, was born in 1652. The following year, Wilhelmus was appointed by Stuyvesant to be one of New Amsterdam's five original *schepens*. To be closer to the city, he moved his family south to a farm at Corlear's Hook. They moved again when Stuyvesant appointed him Orphan Master, an important position in Dutch society for it monitored the debits and credits of new widows whose husbands had died without a will and saw that proper guardians were appointed for the children. Although Wilhelmus did not serve long in the post, he built a house not far from the city's protective wall on the north side of today's Chatham Square. At the same time, he acquired a brewery, a flour mill and some slaves. He was well acquainted with the Kips, living near them and serving with them as *schepen* and alderman, on juries and eventually on the Governor's Council. A respected man of the city (although he was accused of smuggling and of not paying the tax on beer he brewed and consumed in his family), he was recognized for his energy, intelligence and, not least of all, his friendship with Stuyvesant.

In 1658, Stuyvesant sent Wilhelmus south to govern the newly conquered colony of Swedes on the Delaware River. It was a difficult job in an isolated location, but he was right for it because he was acquainted with the Swedish language and customs. During his stay there, he dealt with threats from the British in Maryland, lack of provisions for his militia and drunkenness among the Native Americans as well as the Swedes. After a taxing five years, his incumbency ended with a complicated, internal power struggle that, in essence, he lost. Forced to seek another post, he did not ask for a position in the city, as might have been expected. With a large and expensive family, as he wrote his faithful friend Petrus Stuyvesant, he could not afford to live there. Rather, in June 1664 he transferred to Wiltwyck, as Kingston was then called, to be its *schout*. This top job gave him jurisdiction over all the land between New Amsterdam and Fort Orange, the northern outpost that would soon be called Albany.

As Wilhelmus Beekman quickly discovered, Wiltwyck did not lack for turmoil. The Second Esopus War with the Native Americans had begun in 1663 and carried into 1664. Then, only two months after Wilhelmus's arrival in Wiltwyck, Stuyvesant handed the province over to the British. Wilhelmus swore allegiance to the British king and simply became sheriff of what was now called Kingston, with duties essentially the same as *schout*, except that he was now responsible to the governor. Paid with a percentage of the fines, fees and taxes collected, Wilhelmus made a good thing of his position. He brought both men and women to court for such infringements as evading the liquor taxes, outright smuggling, not paying bills, not castrating bulls and stallions, fisticuffs, wife beating, stealing bedding from laundry lines and, as always, wage and property disputes. Using "vile and foul language" was forbidden behavior, too; a woman named Aeltje was fined 100 guilders for yelling at the plaintiff the equivalent in Dutch of "Kiss my ass." Wilhelmus pocketed up to two-thirds of the fines collected. He also slivered a percentage off bounties on wolves — a scourge to keepers of pigs, calves and other livestock. In addition he was paid fees for witnessing and proving wills.

Nor was Beekman hesitant to sue in his own behalf. One such case involved his claim for twenty-one whole beaver skins from a man who still owed him that amount from a sale of Negroes; he was awarded twenty beavers, the equivalent of around 160 guilders. (That at least some part of Beekman's income came from trading slaves seems unquestionable, for New York was a major market; it has been estimated that 20 percent of the city's fast-growing population was slaves — Stuyvesant himself owned at least forty — and slaves were already being shipped upstate.) Another suit involved a thief who had broken into his house and stolen a keg of wine, a sword and a pistol; that man got away. Beekman was also a defendant in personal actions having to do with smuggling and property encroachment.

At the same time, Beekman was responsible for the settlement's safety. It had been stockaded, but the "savages" never ceased to be regarded as a threat. They were useful as trading partners, but even in peaceful times Beekman enforced laws prohibiting settlers from offering Native Americans a place to spend the night within the stockade, as well as laws prohibiting selling them liquor. When quartering soldiers in settlers' homes became necessary, quarreling between Dutch residents and English soldiers was never-ending; often it disintegrated into stabbings. As the court was in session every two weeks, and many extraordinary sessions were called, Beekman more than earned his keep.

In 1670, Wilhelmus was relieved of his duties with thanks for having fulfilled them so well. He returned to New York where, with proceeds from his work as *schout* and sheriff and from the sale of his Chatham Square and Corlear's Hook properties, he bought a large farm with a brew house, two mills, an orchard and a fine piece of meadowland in the area now traversed by Beekman Street. He resumed his role as a city potentate, becoming an alderman in 1678 and deputy mayor in 1680.

In 1683, Thomas Dongan, the governor who would give the Kipsbergen partners their patent, arrived in New York. He carried instructions from the Duke of York — soon to inherit the throne as James II — to create an assembly of eighteen men, elected by freeholders, to help govern the province. Empowered to discuss and pass laws about virtually anything, subject only to veto by the governor or the duke, the fledgling representative Assembly, of whom only a handful were Dutch, convened that October. Although the names have been lost, Beekman, as one of the most experienced and popular of the ruling elite — if not the most affluent — was probably elected, as he would be to the Assembly of 1684.

Its first work was to approve the Charter of Liberties that ensured the assembly would receive revenue from several import duties to support its work. Broadcast to the city's inhabitants, called together by a trumpet fanfare, the charter also gave citizens civil rights such as trial by jury. Equally important, it gave them some protection from Crown-imposed taxation. To bolster the city's position as the source of financial power, it secured various monopolies for certain of its residents. For instance, a provision that may well have benefited Wilhelmus and his merchant friends, but was a thorn in the flesh of Hudson River Valley farmers, required that all flour bound for foreign ports be bolted (sifted) in the city. In addition, it stipulated that only freemen who had lived there for at least three years could trade upriver. For his work on forwarding the charter and the commercial privileges, Dongan received a "gift" of 300 pounds from the grateful merchants.

Judge Hendrickus Beekman

Meanwhile, Wilhelmus's eldest son, Hendrickus, was carrying on for him in Kingston as a merchant trader, among other things. With his excellent connections not only in New York, but also through his many cousins in Albany, Hendrickus's business flourished. Following in his father's footsteps, he, too, was elected to the Provincial Assembly, representing Ulster and Dutchess counties. (At that time, they were administered as a single entity.) As assemblyman, he helped fortify Albany against Native American incursions. Put on the committee to reorganize the judiciary, he did such a good job that he was appointed Ulster County's justice of the peace, a powerful, enlightening office wherein he presided over countless property issues as well as the usual hair-raising domestic disputes. For this work he is known as Judge Beekman.

Judge Beekman would serve in the majority of assemblies; only his death in 1716 would cut off his political career. During his tenure, he worked to repeal the very act requiring flour for export to be sifted and packaged in New York City that his father had been instrumental in passing. This endeared him to his constituency, the farmers and provision agents who detested that measure. Equally important, he vigorously campaigned in the struggle to wrest still more home rule from the representatives of the Crown. Laying foundations for the coming split with Britain, one of this movement's clarion calls was "no taxation without representation."

In addition, Judge Beekman was an ardent member of the socially powerful Dutch Reformed church. He encouraged the baptism of Negro, Mulatto, and Indian slaves. (Of the ninety-one slaves in Kingston, many were his.) However, at the same time, he served on a committee that espoused laws giving masters the right to punish slaves at their discretion, stopping short only of killing them, prohibiting slaves from gathering together without the permission of their masters, and authorizing towns to employ a "Common Whipper." These laws also prevented slaves from testifying in any court whatsoever and, finally, asserted that baptism in no way implied emancipation. Such oppressive laws suggest that the judge, too, was engaged in the well-entrenched and lucrative slave trade. Whatever the case, his proposal for church leniency was not an attempt to make slaves' lives more bearable. Rather, it was a protest against the inroads the British were making on Dutch culture, one form of which was advancing the power of the Anglican sect.

In all this work, one of the judge's great, but seldom noted, strengths in both his business and his political life was that Dutch, still the lingua franca of global trade, was his first language. Like his father, he also managed adequately in English and probably in German and French, too. All were spoken in Kingston in this period, and it was useful to have at least a smattering of the Native American languages as well.

In his private life, the judge was a land speculator, as was almost every man — and many a woman — who could scrape a few stuyvers or sewan together. Already possessing considerable holdings in Ulster County, the judge obtained patents for the two tracts of land in Dutchess County. He did not settle on these properties, however, but continued to reside in Kingston when he was not in New York City attending sessions of the assembly or pursuing his own business and pleasure. Nor did he actively draw settlers to them. But he did buy the Kipsbergen partners' gristmill site, an indication that he was contemplating founding a farming community there.

Even when his father Wilhelmus died in 1707, Judge Beekman did not move to his Rhinebeck patent. Nor did he try to settle it. But, in 1706, in a small attempt to entice a few homesteaders, he sold to William Traphagen, wheelwright of Kingston, the 210 acres of meadow, marsh and upland north of the Kips' land. At the intersection of the Sepasco trail and the recently built Queen's Highway (it was not called the King's Highway until George I succeeded Queen Anne in 1715), the parcel ran westward to the Hudson River and was bounded in three directions

by Beekman woodland. Traphagen then sold Jacobus Kip twenty-four acres of the parcel that was contiguous to his land. And, in 1714, Beekman would sell Jacobus eighty-nine acres adjacent to the Traphagen parcel and, a little later, the high land east of it.

It is interesting that these sales and the earlier purchase of the gristmill site mark the first records of the Beekmans' paths having directly crossed with the Kips'. Obviously, within such a small population, they must have met in Kingston. It is all the more surprising because their families had been acquainted from the time the Beekmans set foot on Manhattan soil. However, even in small societies there are hierarchies. As members of the Provincial Assembly, the Beekmans were undeniably on the top of the heap. With their large land holdings, they were allied with the patroons, especially the Livingstons, who had parlayed 2,600 Columbia County acres "bought" from Native Americans in 1683 and 1684 into 160,000 acres by the time their patent was granted in 1686 by the same governor who granted the Kipsbergen patent. (The patroonships were of Dutch origin, begun in 1628 when Van Rensselaer acquired 700,000 acres surrounding Fort Orange. The British — such as the Livingstons — who had the right connections followed suit. Still, the preponderance of the Livingston land was of uncertain title. Nevertheless, its sheer magnitude gave the family the social and political leverage they sought.) Moreover, Judge Beekman's three children intermarried with the Livingstons: Hendrickus to Janet Livingston, daughter of the nephew of the first lord of Livingston Manor; Cornelia to Gilbert Livingston, the fourth son of the lord; and Catherine to Johannes Rutsen, whose connections to the Livingston family were more distant, but nevertheless contributed to the Beekmans' station in the charmed circle of the most elite, most powerful and most self-assured families in the province.

The Palatine Leaseholders

In 1713, suddenly realizing he must put a significant body of settlers on his land in order to satisfy the requirements of his large patent, Judge Beekman did so by importing indentured Palatine Germans from the Livingston manor. Refugees from epidemics, famines and interminable wars in their homeland, the Palatines had initially made their way to England, from whence 2,500 were sent to New York under contract with the Crown to work off their passage by producing tar, pitch and turpentine for the Royal Navy, then being enlarged in anticipation of war with Spain and France. In 1710 many of these Palatines had been sent to Robert Livingston to help populate his land. He needed them, for he also was obliged to settle more than the five very poor tenant families living there to make good his already suspect patents. Hoping for a doubly profitable venture, Livingston promised the Palatines, in exchange for their labor, a third of a loaf of bread and a quart of cheap beer for each person daily, plus a small amount of meat three times a week. Not incidentally, he was reimbursed from Crown funds for these necessities.

Unfortunately, the naval stores scheme failed miserably. Not only were the Germans, originally vintners and farmers, total strangers to the work of making tar, but the trees were

The Palatine Cemetery is located at the intersection of the present-day Routes 9 and 9G. The first Lutheran church, built of logs, was nearby. Its language was German. Later, the Palatines would build a large stone church a short distance to the north on Route 9. It stands today. Photograph by Alan Coon, 2007.

a poor species and grew in small patches. Moreover, supervision was either erratic or punitive. In the fall of 1713, the Crown abandoned the project and Livingston left the Palatines to their fate. They were ravaged by cold, hunger and disease. When Beekman offered them a chance to return to farming, thirty-five of the families accepted. They became his tenants, settling on subdivided land centered at Wey's Crossing on the Queen's Highway. (The place is marked today by the little graveyard where Routes 9 and 9G cross, a small early-eighteenth-century farmstead, and the Lutheran Church and its parish house.)

The importance to Kipsbergen of the Palatines' arrival on Beekman's grant lay in their numbers — around 147. In Kipsbergen at that time, there were only sixty-four inhabitants and two slaves. Thus, virtually overnight, Beekman acquired a population well over twice Kipsbergen's size. However, unlike Kipsbergen properties, which were freeholds, Beekman would only lease his land to the new settlers. Following the semi-feudal patroon system, these settlers could seldom look forward to attaining the status of freeholders. Rather, their lot was to be perpetual tenants, paying yearly quitrents either in money or, more often, in produce or in labor: grain, fowls and hogs, work on manor roads or in the fields. Moreover, they relinquished their mining and milling rights to the patroon. Should they choose to sell their leaseholds, they were obligated to give the patroon the right of first refusal and as much as a third of the worth of whatever improvements they had made. If they fell behind on their quitrents, he could toss them out. This happened infrequently, but many tenants became enchained by debt. The Palatines were accustomed to oppression in their native lands, however, and were not immediately frightened by the confining aspects of Beekman's imposed tenantry. Quite simply, they were glad to be saved from starvation.

Colonel Henry Beekman

Judge Beekman died suddenly in 1716. No will or inventory exists, but he was rich. A good Dutchman, his three children shared in his inheritance. His widow, the daughter of a Swedish man-of-war captain, was to enjoy life-use of it. But, the following year, in a deed that begins with the formula "for pure love, tender and motherly affection," she gave the children her rights in the judge's real estate holdings, except for the Kingston house and its outbuildings, the corn mill in Kingston, the rents on the settled land in Dutchess County and the house and brewery in New York City.

Colonel Henry, as historians call him to distinguish him from his father the judge, was born in 1688. Even at that late date his first and, throughout his life, more fluent language was Dutch. But he was thoroughly at ease in English; he even adopted the anglicized form of his name, except with family and old friends. By the time his father died, he was participating fully in the life of Kingston and New York City. Through the prestige his father and grandfather had bestowed on him, as well as his own exertions, he was prepared to become a leader in his own right. However, rather than Ulster County, his political base would be Dutchess County. In 1723 he would pay sixty-nine pounds, the highest tax in the North Ward of Dutchess County. Jacobus Kip followed with fifty-five pounds. Then came Jacobus's nephew-in-law, Matthys Sleght, with thirty-two pounds. Altogether, these three accounted for 15 percent of the tax collected.

Year after year, from 1724 to 1758 when he retired, Colonel Henry Beekman occupied one of Dutchess County's two seats in the Provincial Assembly. In that job he persistently promoted New Yorkers' trade with upstate Native Americans and the right of the assembly to pursue its work free from interference by the governor. At the same time he took care of common local issues — the elimination of wolves, the preservation of deer, the prevention of forest fires, the extension of roads, the care of the poor and the upgrading of horse and cattle breeds.

Colonel Henry's home life was less prosperous. His wife, Janet Livingston, died in 1724 shortly after their daughter Margaret was born. Soon afterwards, he married Gertrude Van Cortlandt. The marriage added that powerful clan to his intimate connections and brought him her splendid inheritance, which, according to British law, he controlled. But apparently she was as disagreeable as Janet had been merry; the new union produced no issue. Then tragedy struck again and yet again. The colonel's older daughter died. His only son, also named Henry, who had been sent to Holland for schooling, died there. This left him with just one child, Margaret, who was brought up in Brooklyn by her maternal aunt. The silver lining was that she would marry Judge Robert Robert Livingston, a cousin. They would provide Henry with eleven strong-minded grandchildren.

In 1726, the year of his second marriage, Colonel Henry acquired the Kip homestead from Hendrickus Kip (IV) in exchange for excellent farmland in what would become Red Hook. The colonel considerably

enlarged the house. Although his duties as assemblyman and also as sheriff of New York City, a position to which he was appointed in 1728, kept him in the city much of the time, he occupied the house at least seasonally until he died in 1776.

There were several reasons why Colonel Henry would have wanted this Kip property. Together with the mill site on the Landsman Kill, it gave him a pincer on Kipsbergen. Looking ahead to the development of his political career, he may have felt he needed property there as an underpinning. Although his Palatine tenants far outnumbered Kipsbergen residents, Kipsbergen was where the freehold voters were. Moreover, its proximity to a major local landing on the Hudson gave him easy access to Kingston, Albany, New York City, and even to his properties in southern Dutchess County. At that time, river transportation was far more convenient and comfortable than bumping along the dusty or muddy and almost always rutted King's Highway. With its flourishing shipping and its easy connection to Kingston, it was also the liveliest settlement in northern Dutchess County.

Then, too, there may have been an ongoing rivalry between the New York Kips and the Beekmans that expressed itself upriver. The Kips had come to New Amsterdam ten years earlier than the Beekmans, and the many who still lived there wielded significant social and political power. In Ulster County, on the other hand, the Beekmans had steadily drawn ahead. Henry may have wanted the house to demonstrate the superior standing his family had attained in Dutchess County. Social status, in those days, was largely measured by ownership of land, and Beekman had already amply demonstrated his acquisitive hand. In fact, he had originally laid claim to the entire Kipsbergen patent. That claim failed, but he insisted that Jacomyntie's Vly was included in his father's patent. That this may have been at least a gray area is borne out by

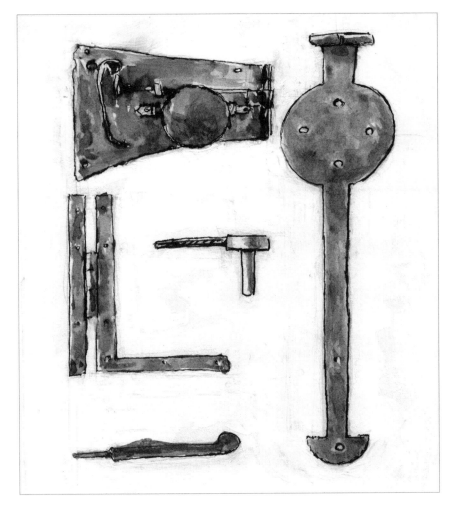

Hardware unearthed from the ruins of the Hendrickus Kip homestead, burned in 1910: a door hinge, a door lock, an L-hinge, a pivot and a knife handle. Painting by Alvin Wanzer, 2007.

the fact that, at the same time as he bought the homestead, Beekman forever renounced his spurious claim to all the Kipsbergen patentees' land.

Nevertheless, it is surprising that the Kips let their homestead go out of the family. True, Hendrickus (IV) would exchange it for first-rate farmland, but up to that time the Kips had kept their property in the family. Whether Beekman brought pressure to bear will probably never be known, nor will it be known whether the Kips ever regretted selling it. With this sale, however, the Kipsbergen Kips gave both tangible and symbolic precedence to the Beekmans. It would not be the Beekman family's last incursion into Kipsbergen.

The Dutch Reformed Church

In 1730, Colonel Beekman's land holdings were increased to 100,000 acres by his Van Cortlandt father-in-law's death. Buttressed by this windfall, he set about effecting a great change in the social aspects of his Rhinebeck property as well as in those of Kipsbergen. He gave two acres of land on the King's Highway between the Sepasco trail and his most recent gristmill on the Landsman Kill for a Dutch Reformed church. Intended to draw

The Dutch Reformed Church was built by Colonel Henry Beekman as an anchor for his settlement on the Flatts — the present Village of Rhinebeck. Beekman also wished to woo the Kipsbergen population from the Kingston church they had faithfully attended. The service was in Dutch until the 1770s. This is the second church, built in 1807. It has a vigorous congregation today. Courtesy of the Dutch Reformed Church of Rhinebeck.

the Kipsbergen community into his orbit, it was also a real estate development, for the colonel gave the church forty-three acres for its maintenance. This was lotted up and offered first as leaseholds; when that approach was not entirely successful, individuals were allowed to buy it. John A. Kip and Solomon Van Steenburgh, both with Kipsbergen origins, each bought a lot on the King's Highway. (The church still collects very small quitrents on much of the property.) The settlement that grew up there became known as the Flatts because, unlike so much of the surrounding land, especially in Kipsbergen, it was, indeed, flat.

The church deed with its provisos paints an excellent portrait of the times, as well as the colonel's Christian morality and his business acumen. The church land must be used only for a church, school, meetinghouse, or chapel; no wine, rum, brandy, beer, cider, or other spirits, and no merchandise of any kind could be sold there; if not soon improved with a meetinghouse, it would revert to him. The first lay governors were Kipsbergen men: the elders were Jacobus Kip and Hendrickus Heermance, and the deacons were

The grave marker of a Van Etten descendant, perhaps a soldier in the Revolutionary War. Van Ettens still live in the hamlet. Photograph by Cynthia Hewitt Philip, 2007.

Jacobus Van Etten and Dr. Isaac Kip. Kipsbergen families would, in fact, outnumber town families serving in these positions until the Revolutionary War, for the Palatines, comprising the preponderance of Rhinebeck residents, attended the Lutheran church at Wey's Corners where the service was in German. For eleven years the Rhinebeck church was interwoven with the Kingston Dutch Reformed Church through a sharing of ministers. As in Kingston, preaching at the new church was in Dutch. The first record of the use of English would be when Clarissa Kip was baptized in 1776.

Despite the church's new cemetery, many Kipsbergen families preferred to inter their dead either in Kingston or in Kipsbergen's burial ground, called Evert Van Wagenen's Kerkhoff, which lay on a rise between the dwellings of Evert Van Wagenen and Matthys Sleght. In 1750 the Van Wagenen family formally deeded the two acres forever "for all the neighborhood that shall be willing to lay or be buried" there, and to improve it "with all the commodities" necessary for its proper use. In his little history of Kipsbergen, published in the local newspaper in 1894, historian Edward M. Smith reported fifteen stones still readable. They bore the names of Kips, Van Ettens, Van Wagenens, Heermances, and Radcliffs, all families still flourishing in the hamlet at that time. The earliest stone then existing was marked "O.V.W. 1724." Barent Van Wagenen was buried there in 1732. Hendrick Heermance's marker is engraved "1750 DEB 2 MEI IS HM BEGRAVE" (loosely translated, this states that he was buried on May 2, 1750); his wife, Sara Van Etten Heermance, a granddaughter of Gerrit Aartsen, was buried there the previous year. Today only a few gravestones remain. But the clarity of the beautifully engraved red sandstone markers is as clear as if they had been placed there yesterday.

3

The Enveloping Precinct of Rhynbeck

In 1738 the British established the precinct of Ryn Bek, with the Palatine settlement at Wey's Corners as its center. When Kipsbergen residents learned that their land was absorbed within the new precinct's boundaries, it could only have been an enormous shock. They retained their freeholder status, including their right to sell their land to whomever they pleased, but the voting place was removed to Wey's Corners. Kipsbergen, for political purposes, was now under Beekman's thumb.

It is easy to suspect that Colonel Beekman, fundamentally conservative, temperamentally relentless and endowed with the arrogance of his inherited position among the province's landed aristocracy, had long cherished a plan for controlling Kipsbergen. His purchase of Schuyler property to the north and the Hendrickus Kip homestead, followed by his giving land for the Dutch Reformed Church, were possibly his first moves in drawing the settlement into his semi-feudal orbit. Although in lighthearted moments he referred to himself as "an old Esopus farmer," he was well aware that he possessed the social, political and commercial underpinnings to make the takeover seem an inevitable event.

If this was his ambition, it can be said that he succeeded only in part. Kipsbergen residents did not give up their deep-rooted, Dutch sense of independence. While the Palatines would become tied to tenant farming and rarely ever left their own near surroundings, Kipsbergen was firmly river-oriented. In multiple ways Esopus and Kingston, rather than the Beekman settlement, would remain Kipsbergen's outside source of commercial and social vitality. Moreover, the Kips continued to be connected to New York City by their families and their shipping enterprises, and thence to the wider world. When, in 1881, "upstreeter" Edward M. Smith commented on the absorption of Kipsbergen by Rhinebeck in his history of Rhinebeck— "And this was the last of Kipsbergen, the 'High Dutchers' having become too many for the 'Low Dutchers'"—he got it wrong. It most certainly was not the last of Kipsbergen. The only thing true about that prejudiced remark was the tribute Smith paid to the church as a force in governing society.

Kipsbergen grew as a transportation hub. In addition to the improved Sepasco trail that led to New England and the King's Highway, today's River Road provided a land connection with the Dutch river settlements of Hoffman's Landing, now called Tivoli, and of what would become Barrytown and Annandale — then Schuyler land with great estates served by leasehold tenants. Although Beekman guided the Palatines' shipping to family-controlled Shultz's landing, north of Kipsbergen, the Kips' Long Dock remained the center of trade. The Kips improved their wharf and ran a far more organized ferry service than they had in the haphazard early days. Moreover, Abraham, Jacobus's youngest child, who now lived in Jan's house, enlarged it to use as a tavern. It quickly became the place for local residents to meet and discuss whatever was on their minds, as well as the drop-off point for mail and merchandise. There, travelers bringing news and gossip from places outside the area could get food and drink as well as rudimentary sleeping accommodations.

Abraham was also the current custodian of the east-west ferry run. In answer to the need for more efficient service, he teamed up with Moses Cantyne of Kingston, who ran the west-to-east ferry, to seek an exclusive right for their routes from the British Crown. Endorsed by King George II, the impressive grant runs to fourteen foolscap pages. It notes that Jacob Kip had built the wharf; that the Kips had been carrying passengers for more than fifty years, and Moses Cantyne for ten years; and that no ferry existed north of Newburgh — forty miles distant — or south of Albany — sixty miles distant. With the proviso that no person would be prohibited from carrying themselves and their goods in their own canoes, the two men were given a monopoly covering two miles on either side of their landings. The yearly tax was five shillings, to be paid at the Custom House in New York City every Lady Day, May 1. From November 1 to March 1, when ice was expected to close the river, they would be under no obligation to carry persons or goods; but if, during this period, they were able to make their way through the ice floes, they could double their fees. They could also double them during regular months after eight o'clock at night. Finally, they were required to run two boats and to avoid unreasonable delay to passengers.

The following fees were imposed: a man and a horse, two shillings, six pence; one person, one shilling; a footman, nine pence. Freight rates indicate customary trade — a calf or hog, six pence; a sheep or lamb, four pence; a pail of butter, two pence; a tub of butter, four pence; a bushel of salt or grain, one penny; a hundredweight of iron or lead, nine pence; a loaded wagon, six shillings. Business was brisk. The ferry would operate under this exclusive right, with similar fares, for the next two hundred years.

Abraham Kip died two years later at the age of forty. As his wife, Eliza Pruyn, and two small sons had predeceased him, his only heirs were Amelia, eight years old, and Jacob, six years old. His will, which categorizes him as a yeoman, gives an extraordinary picture of Dutch family life at that time. Stating that he was weak in body, he went on to provide for his business and his entire household.

> To my son Jacob I give my Great Bible and my gun. The rest of my estate I leave to Jacob and Amelia when my son is of age, or if dead to his brothers and sisters. [There were no more children.] My executors are to rent out my house and farm and lands and also the Ferry across Hudson's River to a good husbandman that will keep the same in good order, and also that always a good Ferry boat and proper attendance be kept agreeable to the Patent granted for said Ferry. All household stuff, horses, cattle etc are to be sold at public vendue and the money put at interest to sure persons, or for building a storehouse. And as my servant and negro slaves have behaved faithful and obedient, it is my will that my servant, during the time limited by his indenture, and my negroes, Peggy and Robin, shall be hired to some honest persons, as they shall like best, and if possible that Peggy and Robin may be both at one house, and my old wench Bett shall have liberty to choose any good family that will take and keep her for victuals and clothes. My wench Diana I would have live in the family where my children live. Lastly I beg favor of my dear mother-in-law and my brother-in-law, Johannes Pruyn, to take my children and not let them want for victuals and clothes. ...

Meanwhile, marriages with Kipsbergen families and Kingston families continued as before, steadily increasing the population of Kipsbergen, although making it complicated to keep track of them. For instance, Dr. Isaac Kip, the grandson of Jacobus (III), married his cousin Rachel, daughter of Jacobus and Klaartje Van Wagenen. The bond with the Heermance family made when Annatje (Aartsen) Van Wagenen married Hendrickus Heermance was reinforced when her sister Neeltje married his brother Andries, and then further solidified when another of Jacobus's grandsons married Catholyntie Heermance, and his granddaughter married Nicholas Heermance. The Van Steenburghs came in when Jacobus's (III) grandson Pieter married Maria Van Steenburgh, and his granddaughter Rachel married Timothius Van Steenburgh. Sarah, another granddaughter, married William Radcliff of Kingston. The Kips also married into Rhinebeck families. Jacobus J. Kip, for instance, married Arent Traphagen's widow; it was through her that he acquired the land on which, sometime around 1769, he built the tavern fronting on the King's Highway that is the nucleus of today's Beekman Arms.

But the marriage that would have the most significant long-range impact on Kipsbergen, though perhaps not so noted at the time, was that of Colonel Beekman's only surviving child, Margaret, to Judge Robert Robert Livingston, grandson of the first lord of the manor, a cousin and also an only child. It took place in 1742. Theirs may have been a marriage of convenience, the uniting of two powerful landed clans, but it was a remarkably contented household, increasing almost yearly until there were eleven children, only one of whom did not live to maturity. Although the family resided at Clermont, Livingston's seat at the Lower Manor, Margaret maintained a close relationship with her father and with Rhinebeck. She remained a staunch supporter of the Dutch Reformed church there, even though her Scots-descended husband was an Anglican. She also stuck to many of the Dutch traditions. Keeping

Margaret Beekman Livingston (1724–1800), c. 1795. Gilbert Stuart (1755–1828), oil on canvas, 36 ¼ × 27 ⅞. Asset: CL.1981.56.a. Clermont State Historic Site, Germantown, N.Y., New York State Office of Parks, Recreation and Historic Preservation. The sole heir of her father, Colonel Henry Beekman, and the defacto heir of her husband and cousin, Judge Robert Robert Livingston, Margaret Beekman remained at heart a capable and shrewd Dutch woman until the day she died.

her maiden name, she was known for most purposes as Margaret Beekman. Like her father she was equally fluent in English and Dutch.

Colonel Beekman continued to operate in the thick of politics, his position now enhanced by being even more closely interwoven with the Livingston power structure. His chief political lieutenant was his nephew, Henry Livingston, who lived in Poughkeepsie. Gilbert Livingston, a brother-in-law, was his business partner as well as a fellow assemblyman. Having become the leading spokesman of the assembly, Beekman adamantly refused to be intimidated by the Crown's attempts to rein it in. Supported as he was by a circle of tight-knit elites, his main interest was enlarging his prerogatives. It was not difficult to do. As assemblyman, Beekman was entitled to appoint all county officers not directly appointed by the Crown, such as sheriffs, militia officers, judges and coroners. Like most patronage, it was lucrative, and the colonel was no laggard when it came to receiving "rewards." He also used his influence and money to swing elections for those positions that were not appointed. Through Henry Livingston, he lavished cider, wine, bread, beef, pork and bacon on his constituents before election days. Moreover, although it was no longer governed together with Dutchess County, old ties also placed Ulster County in Beekman's hand. To round off his close connections, the chief justice of the province, James DeLancey, was his nephew. The popular DeLancey, who maintained a racecourse on his estate, would become lieutenant governor, a position that gave him even more political power.

In 1758, Colonel Henry, then seventy years old, retired from the Assembly, purportedly to devote himself to personal affairs. He retained significant political muscle, however, by passing on the two Dutchess County seats he controlled to Henry Livingston and to his grandson Robert Robert Livingston. Their solidarity would be vital in 1766 when artisans and tenant farmers joined forces and rose up against the oppressive dominion of the great landowners. That disturbance was quickly put down, but it stubbornly kept raising its belligerent head.

The American Revolution

The Revolutionary War was long in coming, but come it did. In the Hudson River Valley its way had been amply prepared by the first settlers' insistence on control of the purse by the Assembly, rather than by the faraway Crown or its representatives. Strictly speaking, the war only grazed Kipsbergen. Six Kips, two Radcliffs, one Van Steenburgh and one Van Wagenen are singled out in the Dutch Reformed graveyard as veterans of that war; Captain Jacobus Kip, Dr. Isaac Kip, Major Andrew Kip and Captain Benjamin Van Steenburgh were among the officers. How much military action they saw is not known. However, General Richard Montgomery, a Marylander married to Margaret Beekman's eldest daughter Janet Livingston, became a local, indeed a national, hero. Montgomery marched off to Quebec from the Flatts, where he and his bride were temporarily living while building their handsome mansion Grasmere on land bordering the Landsman Kill given to them by Janet's grandfather Beekman. Shot dead in the initial assault on the citadel, Montgomery was the first general in the war to perish. Henry Beekman Livingston, Montgomery's brother-in-law, who had joined him in the campaign, was said to have performed with some valor there and at the battles leading up to Saratoga. If so, they seem to have been Henry's last decent acts.

Rather than fight, Margaret Beekman's eldest son, Robert Robert Livingston, used the conflict to forward his political career. During the war he established first his state, then his national position. Although he was not at heart a true revolutionary, he sided with the cause; he was what has been termed a conservative nationalist. Like the other great landowners, he feared that if the British were victorious, Parliament might extinguish his grant or change the system of leaseholds that formed the basis of his social and economic well-being. Moreover, he and this elite band confidently expected that, with the Americans' victory, the power exercised by the British under colonial rule would devolve directly to them.

Robert R. Livingston's role in the founding of the nation was impressive. Only thirty-three years old, he was the leader of New York's delegation to the Continental Congress and as such was appointed, along with the seasoned Benjamin Franklin, John Adams, Thomas Jefferson and Roger Sherman, to draft the Declaration of Independence. There is question of how profound his contribution was; he himself did not boast of any and almost certainly would have, if he could have. Nevertheless, he, or his position in the most powerful of the colonies, was thought important enough to be thus rewarded.

Livingston's most strenuous work was devoted to helping frame the state constitution. Although it was actually written by John Jay, it clearly reflected Livingston's aristocratic beliefs. The Declaration of Independence was incorporated into the document,

but the final state constitution paid little heed to the principle of equality. The government was divided into two houses, the Assembly and the Senate. Prosperous tenants as well as freeholders were allowed to vote for the Assembly, as could artisans, merchants and tradesmen of New York and Albany, but the Senate became a stronghold for landed interests. Only freeholders whose property brought in a sizable income annually could vote in Senate elections. Moreover, voting was by voice, providing ample opportunity for intimidation. The land system, with its leases and quitrents, was left intact. Primogeniture, too, remained. Finally, and most important to Livingston and his friends, the constitution provided that nothing in it was to be construed as affecting the grants of land made by the Crown before October 1775. This guaranteed that the great landlords would continue to control their fiefdoms. In no way did the state constitution provide comfort for leaseholders. Nor was there much in it for the small freeholder.

While Livingston was performing these labors, a profound change took place in the family. His Livingston grandfather died in 1775. His father succumbed to a sudden fever later that same year. At that time, Margaret was keeping vigil at the bedside of her own father, who was dying slowly and painfully of a mortified foot. Colonel Beekman died in January 1776. Devastating as were these deaths to the entire family, which was still mourning General Montgomery, the fact that Margaret's husband died before her father gave her control of vast Beekman holdings and, because she was a strong-minded Dutch woman, more than a little de facto control of her husband's property. Together, they made her the most powerful woman in New York State and, perhaps, in all of America.

What the inhabitants of the Kipsbergen section of Rhinebeck thought about the war is not known. As freeholders and traders their viewpoint was entirely different from either tenant farmers or the great landowners. In practical ways they actually benefited by the war. During its early days, twelve American frigates built in Poughkeepsie were sent for rigging to Kingston. Given the close connections, some Kipsbergen men must have earned good wages fulfilling the contracts.

Kipsbergen joined, too, in the burst of pride and the flurry of patriotism generated when Kingston briefly became the seat of state government after the British occupied New York City. That euphoria disappeared in a cloud of smoke, however, when on October 16, 1777, a British force anchored off Esopus intent on destroying Kingston, the "Nursery for almost every villainy in the country," according to Major General John Vaughan, commander of the attacking forces. Kingston men bravely defended the hastily fortified redoubt for one morning before the British overcame them and burned the prosperous town building by building, until all that was left standing were two houses, one barn and charred remains. An estimated three thousand people were homeless, many of them destitute. It has been said that Barent Van Wagenen, who witnessed the fire from the Kipsbergen bluffs, also saw a British force land in the hamlet and then march north along the road to Hoffman's Landing. It is more probable, however, that the marauders went by boat directly to Hoffman's Landing, where they burned Hoffman's mill as well as the Livingstons' mills, houses and outbuildings, including Margaret Beekman Livingston's Clermont. What is certain is that on October 23 the British ships lay off Kipsbergen, but did no harm there. On orders to return to the environs of New York City — some say so that the admiral could speed on to visit his Philadelphia mistress — they simply sailed downriver the next day.

By the time the fleet departed, General Horatio Gates had won the battle of Saratoga. As the British had hoped to split New England off from the provisions raised in New York's Mohawk and Esopus valleys, provisions on which the local populations also depended for food, their defeat was a major turning point in the war. Flush with victory, General Gates taunted General Vaughan, the perpetrator of the destruction in Ulster and Dutchess counties, declaring, "Should your Further conduct be delineated by such Horrid Barbarity, our utmost efforts may prove ineffectual to preserve you from the resentment of a justly incensed people." The British did not enter the area again.

So great was sympathy for the Kingston victims that charity rolled in from surrounding towns and even surrounding states. Robert R. Livingston granted the ravished town three thousand acres of his rough Hardenburgh patent, pleading he could not send money or provisions because his tenants were refusing to pay rents. During the turmoil, his mother had escaped to Salisbury, Connecticut, and then to the Kip homestead in Rhinecliff, which she had just inherited. But, in true form, she soon returned to Clermont, where she lived in her rebuilt farmhouse while she restored her ruined garden and supervised the reconstruction of her house. To do this work she had to secure exemptions from military duty for her workmen. The following letters from Margaret to Governor George Clinton show how neatly the great landowners were able to manage.

Claremont 19 Nov^{rr} 1778

Sr
As you were so Obligen as to indulge
me with an exemption from Military
Duty for my workmen, who were
employed in Building my farm House, I
am incouraged to request the Same favor
for those to be imployed in rebuilding
my late Dwelling House — Many hands
must nessessarily be ingaged as the
House is pretty large, Such as Masons

Carpenters Brick Burners Labourers &
Stone & Lime Breakers and Burners ...
my Daugh[s] can bring up the Certificate
as they propose waiting upon Mrs.
Clinton, to whom I beg you'll be pleased
to present my Best Respects

> I am
> Your Excel[ys]
> Humble Servant
> Marg[t] Livingston*

As Governor Clinton did not reply quickly enough
to suit her, she wrote again in three weeks: "I am
Very unhappy in being obliged to trouble your
Excellency with my scribble, but nessity compels
me as I cannot get workmen without an Exemption
from Military Duty." Apparently she got her men,
for the house was rebuilt during the war. (It is worthy of note that work on the farmhouse began during the winter of 1777 and 1778, while General
Washington and his troops were suffering from cold
and hunger at Valley Forge.)

In the war years ahead, it was through embargoes that the British harassed Hudson Valley farmers and tradesmen most acutely. In addition, the
American army seized their produce and animals
to feed its hungry soldiers. Some local residents
turned to trading with the enemy; despite the risk,
the profits that could be made by supplying New
York City, then exploding with refugee Tories as
well as thousands of British troops, were allur-
ing. Many in the Hudson Valley, in fact, were convinced that if the British prevailed, their lot might
be improved, for when it occurred to the great
landowners to notice them at all, it was usually
with fear that their disaffection would lead to an
uprising similar to that of 1766.

The Saga of Henry Beekman Livingston and Nancy Shippen

At last, in January 1783, the British admitted defeat.
However, the revolutionary army was not entirely at
peace. Angry that Congress had failed to deliver the
pay and pensions they had been promised, a group of
officers met at Newburgh hoping to foment an insur-
rection. General Washington went there to calm tem-
pers. On the way back from Albany, he took the time
to pay a call on Henry Beekman Livingston, who
had taken over the Kip homestead at Kipsbergen.
Although this wayward Livingston may have acted
courageously in the Quebec battle, he had recently
displayed such erratic, mean-spirited and even vicious
behavior, that it is hard to believe the general went out
of his way to congratulate him on his bravery. What is
far more probable is that, in an unheralded act of personal generosity, Washington stopped at Kipsbergen
on the way to Kingston as a discreet ambassador of
goodwill on behalf of Margaret Beekman.

The saga of Henry Beekman Livingston and
Nancy Shippen is a dismal one with no good ending, but it is worth telling as a facet of Kipsbergen
life that would continue in various forms during their
family's fifty-year ownership of the Kip homestead.
In 1781, Nancy, the giddy eighteen-year-old daughter of Washington's good friend Dr. William Shippen
of Philadelphia, had been snatched from the bosom
of her great love, a French diplomat, and married to
Henry Beekman Livingston in what might politely
be called a marriage of convenience; her father needed
money to keep up the family's high standard of living, and Livingston possessed it. After the perfunc-
tory ceremony, her father took her from Philadelphia
to her mother-in-law's house at Clermont. Having
been greeted most civilly there, she was delivered
to her husband in Kipsbergen. Within a year Nancy

---

*Clermont State Historic Site, Germantown, New York. New York State Office of Parks, Recreation and Historic Preservation.

produced a daughter, named Margaret after her grandmother, but called Peggy. In that time she also discovered her husband was profligate as well as emotionally erratic and abusively jealous. It was well known that he had sired many illegitimate children in the surrounding countryside. At one point he threatened to gather them all up and take them, together with Nancy's child, to Georgia. Nancy, accustomed to the charmed life she had led in Philadelphia, could not bear the loneliness and fear visited upon her and, with the blessing of her mother-in-law, returned to her father's roof, leaving Peggy with her father, as she was legally required to do. Margaret Beekman saw to it that her granddaughter was raised at Clermont under her sharp eye. Friends of the family did what they could to help by carrying letters and verbal messages back and forth, and by interceding for Nancy and her daughter whenever a ray of hope presented itself. Washington's visit may well have been one such attempt at reconciliation. If so, it was fruitless.

The situation was never resolved. When Margaret Beekman Livingston died in 1800, she left Peggy a handsome bequest, apparently what her mother would have received if she had remained with Henry. Henry, who, legend relates, was so mentally deranged that he plowed his acres in satin coat and silken hose, died in 1831. Towards the end of their lives, the mother and daughter lived either together or in mental institutions. Nancy died in 1841 at age seventy-eight, her letters from the French diplomat close by her. The Kip homestead was sold to John Armstrong Jr., a Rhinebeck lawyer and Livingston descendant who had been given custody of Peggy's affairs. Armstrong then sold the homestead to Andries J. Heermance, to whom he had previously rented it. Hence, it is today referred to as the Kip-Beekman-Heermance property; the Livingston incumbency is left out. Peggy died utterly incompetent at age eighty-three, her bequest having been squandered by Armstrong. She was buried in the same grave as her mother in a cemetery on the outskirts of Philadelphia.

The Federal Period

With the peace, the great landlords of the Hudson River Valley returned unmolested to their neo-feudal ways. They had strong tools to help them. One was the state constitution. Another was that the Senate, which appointed the major state officers, rewarded Robert R. Livingston with the Chancellorship of the Courts, an immensely powerful position in the state and, in fact, the national hierarchy. A third was the even more onerous lease law, written by Alexander Hamilton, that tied tenant farmers ever more firmly to the great landowners' soil. (Hamilton, born out of wedlock in the Caribbean, had married into the immensely rich and powerful Van Rensselaer/Schuyler clan. There is no question that he was a brilliant thinker. Nevertheless, it is possible to think of this work as the price he paid for his bride.) In addition to an annual rent of ten to fourteen bushels of winter wheat, four fat fowls and a day's work with horse and wagon, a tenant must promise to use the land for agricultural purposes only. Wood was added to mineral and mill rights as reserved to the landlord. Worse still, a tenant could not sell his land, only the unaltered lease, and this only by giving the landlord up to a half of what he had gained from his improvements. Such a lease was genially termed an "incomplete sale." Moreover, when a leaseholder died, a fee was demanded for the reassignment of the lease. In other words, from generation to generation, tenants shouldered all the obligations of land ownership, as well as the burdensome yearly rent, and yet received only a fraction of the worth of any improvements they had made. The self-satisfaction of the great landlords had seldom been higher.

Moreover, their political ascendance was made visible to the entire country when George Washington became the first president of the United States. The ceremony took place at Federal Hall on the corner of Broad and Wall streets in New York City, the national government's temporary home. Chancellor Robert R. Livingston, New York State's rising star, administered the oath of office. A telling note is that while Livingston dressed in a full suit of fine black cloth, the usually impeccably dressed president-elect wore a simple homespun suit.

Yet, looking beneath the surface on a trip through the state to report on its agricultural progress, the Englishman William Strickland remarked that, although the great proprietors lived extremely well off the work of their tenants, they were careless stewards of their land. Their interest in it seemed to him limited to squabbling among each other over who possessed the mill rights, which were, as they had always been, one of their few sources of hard money. Still, in 1793, Chancellor Livingston was a major force in founding the Society for the Promotion of Agriculture, Arts and Manufacturing in New York. He was also an early experimenter with gypsum, shipped from Nova Scotia, to improve his clay-laced soils.

The Rising Middle Class

Artisans, professional men and freeholders who could move about saw their lives improve in the years after the war, however. Stagecoach service between New York City and Albany along the Post Road (formerly the King's Highway) was begun in 1785. The time it took to travel the entire length in a covered wagon drawn by four strong and able horses was advertised as three days. From New York, connections could be made to Philadelphia. The price was expensive — four pence a mile, or about eight dollars for the whole route — but for those who could pay, it was worth it. Although far from comfortable, it was vastly more reliable than travel by sloop, which was subject to the vagaries of the wind when the river was open, and nonexistent when ice closed it. Rhinebeck gained much excitement and some prominence because the first night's stop on the southward trip was at its tavern. Moreover, mail was delivered to the town by the stage twice a week.

Spurred by such progress in land transportation, Rhinebeck was organized as a town in 1788, perhaps coincidentally exactly one hundred years from the year the Kipsbergen partners received their patent. Hamlet men became the town supervisors. Peter Cantine was the first. William Radcliff, Peter Cantine Jr. and Andrew Heermance followed. However, Kipsbergen was steadily falling behind in its population of voters. After 1805, inland men took over until 1830, when Kipsbergen resident Isaac F. Russell served for two years.

In contrast, Kipsbergen's growth was slow, occurring mainly by marriages and births and by sale and subdivision of property among relatives and friends. One such transaction is described in a 1789 survey map of the division of land jointly held by William Radcliff and Moses Cantine Jr. (Spellings varied in those days: Cantine was now spelled with an "i" instead of a "y," and sometimes Radcliff ends with an "e" or a "t.") The fact that Radcliff became one of the proprietors of the ferry monopoly through his marriage to Sarah Kip, a granddaughter of Jacob Kip, and that Cantine Jr., who became the other proprietor of the ferry when his father died that year, was married to a Radcliff, made for an amicable transaction. Dividing it in the old Dutch way, Cantine took the Jacobus Kip homestead. William Radcliff, who already owned Abraham's place, took the almost fifty-acre parcel surrounding it. They shared the dock. Each took equal parts of a thin, vacant, forty-six-acre east-west lot that spanned Kips Kill. They also took equal parts of an even skinnier lot, also vacant, that went from the river to the lower road to Red Hook (River Road). This they divided in the middle, Radcliff taking the riverfront portion, Cantine the road front portion.

Of interest also is a map on which icons for houses are sketched, some with owners' names written beside them. Going along "the road from the ferry to the Flatts," there is the three-chimney Jacobus Kip homestead by the river, now in the possession of Moses Cantine Jr.; it has a major addition, and across the road is a structure that looks like a barn or a storehouse. Abraham Kip's house, originally the Jan Kip homestead, also has three chimneys and is noted as the William Radcliff house; directly below is a small house, with no owner noted. Dr. Isaac Kip's ample two-chimney house is at the intersection of the lower road to Red Hook and the road to the Flatts. There is an unidentified house west of the Red Hook Road. Other houses existed that are not on the map. They are Roeloff Kip's house built in 1735 overlooking the river north of Long Dock, and the house of Gerardus Lewis on fifty acres, in the vicinity of Hog Bridge.

By 1797, according to Thompson's map of Rhinebeck Precinct, there were six houses along the road to Red Hook. The Jacob Kip house had become an inn, and the storehouse Abraham had anticipated in his will is by the dock. There are three houses along the river between Long Dock, now called Radclift's Landing, and Shultz's landing on the north, and six houses between Radclift's Landing and the Landsman Kill. Inland are four houses between the Post Road and what is today Kelly Street and Morton Road. Including Dr. Isaac Kip's house, there are six along the road to Red Hook and two along the Rhinebeck road north of the ferry road. Kip's Inn is shown on the Post Road, north of the road from the ferry. (That it is now on the south side of the ferry road is because of a change in the alignment of that road.)

It is difficult to estimate the population of Kipsbergen at this time, because they are melded together in Rhinebeck precinct. However, the village on the Flatts pulled steadily ahead of the hamlet, probably because the Post Road provided year-round transportation and the mill sites along the Landsman Kill offered opportunity for diversified industry. Nevertheless, by including slaves in its categorization of household members, the 1790 census offers some indication of how prosperous or how busy the various residents were. For instance, Henry Beekman Livingston and Andries Heermance lead all the rest with eleven slaves each. Then comes Moses Cantine with nine, several probably

"Linwood" was built circa 1794 by Thomas Tillotson, who had been the Surgeon General of the Continental Army, and his wife Margaret Livingston, who bought the land in the southern tip of Kipsbergen from patentee descendant Matthias Van Etten. Linwood's panoramic view sweeps south to the distant Shawangunk Mountains. Photograph 1870s, courtesy of the Rhinebeck Historical Society.

employed in running the ferry. Jacobus Kip has six; Pieter Heermance and Isaac Kip each have five. A.G. Heermance, Sarah Van Steenburgh and William Radcliff have three each; Jacobus Radcliff has two. The Van Wagenens and Van Ettens have no slaves.

The Encompassing Great Estates

Margaret Beekman's control over both her husband's and her father's property brought about profound changes in Kipsbergen's land-ownership patterns. Faithful to her Dutch heritage, she saw that each of her children was set up on a handsome estate. In 1787, following her instructions, eight of her ten living children drew lots for their acreages, the exceptions being Janet, who had Grasmere from her

Beekman grandfather, and her errant son, Henry Beekman Livingston, who had already been removed from the pool by Beekman's leaving him the Hendrickus Kip homestead. Otherwise, either by design or by chance, her sons ended up on Livingston land and her daughters on Beekman land. Attracted by the beauty of its waterfront, Margaret, Catherine and Gertrude bought outright or exchanged their Beekman inland properties for land in Kipsbergen. Together with Janet's Grasmere, these properties almost encircled the hamlet. The only breaks in the loop were Lot 3 in the middle section, which would soon be taken over by a grandchild, and the Kip-owned north end, minus, of course, the homestead.

Margaret, the second Livingston daughter, was married at the Dutch Reformed church on the Flatts in 1779 to Dr. Thomas Tillotson of Maryland, the Surgeon General of the Continental Army. Shortly afterwards, Tillotson bought what remained of Lot 1 and part of Lot 2 from Matthias Van Etten, who had inherited it from his father. The property possessed one of the most panoramic views in the valley, across the Hudson to the lower Catskills and a long sweep downriver to the distant Shawangunks. In 1794 they built a handsome brick house, called Linwood because of its magnificent linden trees. For the rest of their lives, they made Linwood a center of aristocratic hospitality. (When Tillotson died in 1832, nine years after Margaret, he would leave it to their youngest son.)

Catherine, the third daughter, met Freeborn Garrettson, also a Marylander, while he was visiting the Tillotsons. A prominent circuit-riding Methodist minister, Garrettson helped establish that sect in the northeastern United States. They were married in 1793. In 1795 he acquired 160 acres of land in Lot 2 from Johannes B. Van Wagenen, in exchange for Catherine's lands in the eastern part of town. They built a comfortable wooden dwelling called Wildercliff, so-named, perhaps, because the Native American pictograph memorializing the partners' purchase was on their waterfront. Described by a contemporary as "a home for the Lord's people; strangers were welcomed as brethren," it, too, had a glorious downriver view. (Garrettson died in 1827, and after Catherine's death in 1849, Wildercliff was passed on to their only child Mary, a dwarf of great intelligence and charm. She lived there until she died in 1879, carrying on her parents' tradition of good works and open hospitality.)

Like Catherine, Margaret's fourth daughter, Gertrude, had received land east of the King's Highway in the settlement of Wurtemburg. She and her husband, Morgan Lewis, did not live on this inheritance. Rather, in 1790, they built a mansion in Staatsburg. At the same time, however, they also forged a strong link to Kipsbergen. Lewis had bought the Beekman mill at the mouth of the Landsman Kill, and now obtained from Johanes Van Wagenen the right to erect a dam on the kill to run the mills and the factory he would build on its south side, in the area eventually called Fox Hollow. It was their daughter and son-in-law who, in 1809, would buy Lot 3, the land that would become Ellerslie.

In 1795, Catherine Livingston and her husband Freeborn Garrettson, a renowned circuit-riding Methodist minister, exchanged with patentee descendant Johannes Van Wagenen the inland property her mother Margaret Beekman had given her for 160 acres north of the Tillotsons. Catherine and Freeborn called their comfortable wooden house Wildercliff, probably because the Native American petroglyph was on the property. The wings are a much later addition. The house has been handsomely restored. Photograph 1905, courtesy of Wilderstein Preservation.

The relevance of these Livingston holdings to Kipsbergen was that they established a two-level society — that of the manor-born, who were often absent in New York City where they had both houses and relatives, and that of the freehold-born, who lived in the hamlet full-time and had gradually lost touch with their city kin. The two groups had scant contact. Although neighbors, an unbridgeable social gap existed between their disparate worlds. For the next two hundred years, these estates would provide jobs as artisans, farmers, gardeners and sometimes house servants to Kipsbergen residents. At the same time they would form a noose around the hamlet, separating it even more decidedly from the rapidly growing Flatts.

4

Transportation Revolutions

The turn of the century ushered in an era of transportation revolutions that would transform America and, indeed, the entire world. For Kipsbergen this transformation began in 1802 with the opening of the Salisbury Turnpike, a toll road that ran from Long Dock to Salisbury, Connecticut. Its tollhouse was located where Kips Kill crosses the old Sepasco trail (the site of the present Town of Rhinebeck garage). Unlike the four-foot-wide Native American trail that wended its way from the river to New England avoiding hills as much as possible, and which the Dutch had slightly widened to accommodate their wagons (Route 308), the turnpike ran as straight as possible, like the Roman roads of England. At least part of the impetus for building the turnpike may have come from Robert R. Livingston, for he had long claimed Salisbury, Connecticut, and its iron deposits as an integral part of the Livingston grant. His claim was ultimately unsuccessful, but at least the hard turnpike surface, although steep, was some improvement over the rutted dirt of the widened Native American trail route. Moreover, it opened up marginal farmland and settlements along its route. Its life as a toll road was brief, but it still exists as a rural thoroughfare.

Not so the entirely novel form of travel launched on the Hudson River in 1807 — that long-pursued invention, steam navigation. It was the product of the brain of Robert Fulton, a Pennsylvania-born artist and inventor, and of the monopoly for steam navigation on the Hudson River possessed by Robert R. Livingston. Its impact was global and lasting. The two men had met in Paris, where Livingston was the United States minister plenipotentiary to France and Fulton was trying in vain to sell to the reluctant Napoleon Bonaparte his system of submarine warfare, which he was convinced would end conflict at sea and thereby promote free trade. When Fulton learned that Livingston had once launched a full-scale steamboat with disastrous results, but had obtained the monopoly, he happily signed a contract making him Livingston's partner. Fulton developed a small prototype and, in August 1803, he confidently demonstrated it on the Seine River before the whole of Paris. He even gave rides in two towed boats to the enraptured scientific community. (One such scientist was the then-elderly Louis Antoine de Bougainville, a renowned navigator who gave his name to the popular tropi-

cal flower.) Interestingly, Livingston was not there to share the triumph. He had taken his family to Switzerland for a little vacation, perhaps to escape James Monroe's having taken over his role in negotiating the Louisiana Purchase, but equally possibly because he was afraid the experiment would fail and his stature would be further compromised.

Three years would go by while Fulton continued to promote his ultimate marine weapon, this time in England. There, he succeeded in blowing up a brig, only to have his "torpedoes" refused as cowardly. Nevertheless, the British paid him enough money to buy a steam engine made to his specifications from the renowned manufacturers, Bolton and Watt, and to make the initial payments on the boat that would make good his and Livingston's exclusive steam navigation rights on the Hudson River.

Back in America in December 1806, Fulton fetched his engine out of storage and engaged New York's foremost shipwright, Charles Browne, to make the hull. By midsummer she was ready to go.

This early farmhouse on the Salisbury Turnpike settlement at Cases' Corners had been altered to accommodate a store and Essolene station in the 1930s when this photograph was taken. It has since been restored as a house. Courtesy of Gary Hobson.

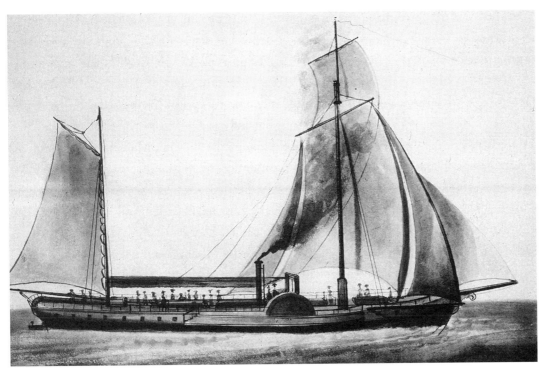

Robert Fulton's inventions relied in part on his also being an artist. Having developed his skill at mechanical drawing, he was able to design on paper and thus was not forced to build expensive full-scale models. This is an 1809 sketch of The North River Steamboat *that secured him and Livingston the monopoly for steam navigation on the Hudson River. It was customary to use sail as well as steam late into the nineteenth century. Courtesy of the U.S. Naval Academy Museum.*

Having tinkered with the completed boat for just one afternoon, Fulton demonstrated her perfection before the New York City populace. On Sunday, August 16, he took her from the East River shipyard through the swirling waters of the Battery to a berth near what is now 12th Street. Aboard were eminent New Yorkers, all invitees of Livingston who, however, remained securely at Clermont.

The very next day at one o'clock in the afternoon, *The Steamboat*, as she was called because there was no other vessel like it in the world, started on her historic 150-mile run to Albany, again before an immense, but heavily doubting crowd. Bets were on that the entire absurdity would blow up or be claimed by the devil himself. Only Fulton, a ship captain versed in the river's vagaries, and a stoker were on board. After a brief interlude in which Fulton adjusted the engine, the boat steamed through the afternoon and the moonlit night without mishap. Stunned river men were frightened out of their wits. To them she was a satanic fire-spitting gristmill miraculously rolling along regardless of wind, tide or current. Late morning the following day, *The Steamboat* rounded the bend and cruised by Kipsbergen. At precisely one o'clock she dropped anchor at Robert R. Livingston's Clermont. She had covered the 110 miles at over four miles an hour.

Great was the celebration Livingston reportedly put on. Although he had not seen fit to journey to New York to wish Fulton godspeed, it was with the delight of a pleasure outing that he, his son-in-law, and a visiting English prelate joined him the next morning for the comparatively short run to Albany. In this segment *The Steamboat* raised her speed to five miles an hour. After a handsome reception by the still half-believing Albanians, she began her return trip, stopping only at Clermont to let off the satisfied Livingston contingent. Two intrepid Frenchmen, the distinguished forester Francois Andre Michaux and the botanist Andre Parmentier, were the only passengers stalwart enough to risk the much longer trip to the city. Perhaps they had witnessed the splendid showing Fulton's model had made on the Seine four years earlier and knew better than anyone that they were witnesses to an international historic event. At every riverbank settlement, crowds greeted her passing with brass bands and waving handkerchiefs. The entire garrison at West Point marched down to the waterfront and sent up loud and repeated huzzahs. Again with no breakdown, her speed maintained an average of five miles an hour all the way to New York. "Fulton's Folly" became Fulton's triumph. As the British prelate reported: "In her the mind is free from suspense. Perpetual motion authorizes you to calculate on a certain time to land; her works move with all the facility of a clock; the noise when on board is not greater than that of a vessel sailing with a good breeze."

Almost immediately Fulton began scheduled, on-time service between New York City and Albany. Now registered as the *North River Steamboat*, she picked up passengers and limited freight from river landings, including Long Dock in Kipsbergen. Although trade embargoes protesting British impressments of American sailors, followed by the War of 1812, forced a serious decline in commercial shipping, it did not deflect passengers' enthusiasm for steamboats. To the fleet were added the *Car of Neptune* and the *Paragon*. Each a little faster and far more luxurious than her predecessor, they set the standard for the great day liners and night boats to come. Unfortunately, the gardens planned at Red Hook to assure the highest quality produce for their dining rooms never came to be, for Fulton suddenly died of pneumonia in February 1815. He was given the most splendid funeral accorded to a civilian in New York City to that date. (It was after his death that the *North River* began to be called *The Clermont*, probably at the instigation of Livingston's sons-in-law who had inherited Livingston's portion when he died in 1813.)

However, Fulton's steamboat empire, which included boats on Long Island Sound, the southern ports and the great Mississippi system, continued until the United States Supreme Court, in its *Gibbons vs. Ogden* decision of 1824, found that state monopolies prevented free interstate commerce. This landmark case placed all navigable waterways in the nation under the jurisdiction of the federal government, at last fostering true competition.

The impact of steam freight and passenger boats on Hudson River landings was literally immeasurable. Although not entirely displacing the swift, world-roaming clipper ships or the handsome Hudson River sloops for over another hundred years, steamboats offered reliable speed that permitted scheduled arrivals and departures. A gentleman with a business appointment in Albany or New York City could be confident of being there on time. Accommodations became ever more luxurious. Speed increased. In fact, speed became such a fixation that, to increase power, captains ordered safety valves closed down, causing boilers to explode, boats to catch fire, and passengers and crew to die from drowning or burns. (It is noteworthy that, although he was ambitious and driving, no boilers exploded while Fulton was alive.) Still, few passengers gave up the convenience and delight of traveling by steamboat or the efficiency of sending packages for express delivery. In 1838 the arrival of Cunard's Great Western Steamship, which departed from Bristol, England, and arrived at New York City just fourteen days later, would tie the United States to Europe indissolubly.

The Erie and the Delaware and Hudson Canals

The Erie Canal, another feat of engineering that advanced transportation dramatically, was completed in 1825. It, too, had international as well as national importance, although its impact did not prove as long-lasting as the steamboat's. Stretching from just above Albany to Lake Erie, the canal linked the port of New York, via the Hudson River, to the Great Lakes and, through them, to Canada and to the vast interior reached by the Mississippi River system. In New York it brought the agriculturally rich northwestern section of the state within easy shipping range of New York City, whose soaring population demanded ever more provisions, building materials and the infinite variety of other goods needed by artisans and householders. The canal reinforced that city as the nation's first port

and its capital of finance. With cutting-edge industry flourishing in the new towns along the canal's route, New York retained its status as the most powerful state in the nation. How immediately successful the Erie Canal was can be measured by the fact that its tolls paid off its immense cost within seven years.

However, the canal was a mixed blessing to mid-Hudson River landings. It destroyed the area's preeminence in growing grain. Grain from the extraordinarily fertile Midwest could now be directly shipped to New York City, not only for its own consumption, but for worldwide distribution. It was only secondarily that the canal's great prestige and the huge boost it gave to the state's economy gradually filtered down to the old Hudson River communities.

It was, in actuality, the smaller Delaware and Hudson Canal, begun in 1825 and opened in 1828, that would have the greater impact on Kipsbergen. The Delaware and Hudson Canal Company's purpose was to bring Pennsylvania coal to New York City, Albany and western New England. Starting in the Pennsylvania coal fields, the loaded boats passed over a series of railed inclined planes — boat-lifting devices invented thirty-five years earlier by none other than Robert Fulton, but powered by steam rather than water — to the canal's headwaters at Honesville, Pennsylvania. From there, the 108-mile canal made its way from an almost thousand-foot elevation with help from 109 locks to its sea-level terminus at Esopus, or as it was now called, Rondout. There the canal company bought the docks of an early shipper and set up offices for a long, successful stay. In the week of November 11, 1835, for instance, ninety-three barges laden with 2,810 tons of coal, and sixty-nine others with general cargo arrived at the burgeoning port. By 1837 the crush of steam-propelled barges and passenger boats, together with sailing sloops and schooners, had become so great that the federal government

Shipping became so heavy at Rondout that, in 1837, two lighthouses were built to replace former primitive and erratic aids to navigation — the Esopus Meadows Lighthouse at the southern approach to the creek and the Rondout Lighthouse at its mouth. This postcard is of the second Rondout Lighthouse, built in 1867. Courtesy of Harry Heywood.

built the Rondout Lighthouse to guard the entrance to the creek. In the next year its twin, the Esopus Meadows Lighthouse, was built to warn boats of the extensive mudflats at the southern approach. The flashes of the powerful lights and the deep sound of the foghorns became part and parcel of residents' lives on both sides of the river.

Former canal diggers and immigrants fleeing the potato famine in Ireland swarmed to Rondout looking for whatever work they could find. Together with a sprinkling of Germans, they created a shantytown around the docks called New Dublin. As trade and population swelled, so too did the cash boxes of local merchants who provided everything the workers needed, from flour, pork, mackerel and salt for packing fish to warm caps and cloth capes. The principal clothing emporium even carried fur and silk hats for the gentry who lived up the hill. A fanning mill was added to the saw and cotton mills already established. A school was opened in 1831. The fine Mansion House hostelry, a project of the canal's chief engineer, James McEntee, opened in 1832. A Roman Catholic church was built in 1837. And there was, of course, a proliferation of bars and saloons — by casual count, fifty of them legal and far more of them illegal. Rondout became, in essence, a rowdy company town, with owners and managers living on the heights and workers down by the waterfront.

Kipsbergen, too, benefited directly from the Delaware and Hudson Canal, for it strengthened the hamlet's position as a transportation hub. Coal

to be sold in nearby east-bank towns and western Connecticut and Massachusetts was unloaded at the developing Slate Dock. A short distance south of Long Dock, the Slate Dock was downhill from the Hendrick Kip homestead and located on Catholyntie and Matthys Sleght's land. ("Slate" is, undoubtedly, a corruption of the name Sleght, although some insist the dock was named after the stone quarried in the southeastern outskirts of town.) Steamboats stopped there for passengers and produce. By 1842 it was flourishing so well that the Slate Dock Company attempted to buy Long Dock and put it out of the freighting business. However, a rival group of Rhinebeck men, intending to run a freight boat every other Tuesday, got in ahead of them and bought Long Dock with the intention, they said, of preventing a monopoly. The ultimate outcome was that Long Dock continued to be the ferry terminus, and passenger steamboats picked up and dropped passengers there, too. But Slate Dock garnered the preponderance of freighting. For instance, the *Milan*, a barge towed by the steamer *R.L. Stevens*, left the dock for New York City on Tuesdays and Fridays carrying lumber, lime, plaster, coal, salt, flour and ale, and returned the following day with a wide range of sundries and luxuries for area farmers and townspeople.

In reality, the community needed both docks at this time, for ferry use was steadily increasing. The ferries were not rowed nor sailed, nor were they yet propelled by steam. Rather, horses toiling round and round gave the paddlewheels their power. Peter and James Radcliff, linked to the Kips and Cantines by marriage, now ran the ninety-year-old ferry monopoly in both directions. It consistently proved a fine moneymaker.

As Kipsbergen's ties with Rondout strengthened, whatever tenuous relationship it had with inland Rhinebeck flagged. Although Kipsbergen resident Isaac F. Russell was town supervisor from 1830 to 1832, one might say Kipsbergen turned its back on Rhinebeck, for it had always been far easier to get to Rondout by boat than to trudge the two miles uphill to the Flatts. To inland residents, Kipsbergen was virtually a foreign territory. It had little to attract them. Their use of the ferry and the passenger boats was at best sporadic, and their freighting needs could be taken care of by an agent or a carter. As a result, there was scant socializing between the two communities. Kipsbergen remained what it had been from the beginning: "the land over against the Rondout creek." Yet, even when Rhinebeck village set an example by incorporating as a separate municipality, Kipsbergen did not take the steps necessary to follow suit. It remained, perhaps out of self-important complacency, a part of the town.

The Estates

During these busy times of transition, there was much building of new and refurbishing of old estates. Henry James Kip of Albany was drawn to Kipsbergen, both because he was a descendant of the original settler, Jacob Kip, and because his wife Sarah was a descendant of the Palatine Berghs of Rhinebeck who had married into the Sleght and Radcliff families. In 1832 he bought most of Jacobus's land — the ferry landing was retained by Jacobus's successors — and named it Ankony after one of the Native Americans whose land Hendrickus Kip had acquired. Henry J. Kip built a handsome Greek Revival mansion for his family and developed a model gentleman's farm on the surrounding fields. That land has remained in cultivation to this day.

Ten years later, William B. Kelly, a New York merchant, bought Ellerslie. This was the great estate bought by Maturin Livingston and his cousin and wife Margaret, the daughter of Gertrude Livingston and Morgan Lewis and the granddaughter of Margaret Beekman Livingston. They had built a fine house of their own design on the highest point of land, two hundred feet above the river with spectacular views overlooking Margaret's aunts' houses — perhaps one of the site's attractions — and named the property Ellerslie. However, within two years of keeping house on her own, Margaret so longed for the comforts of her family's mansion in Staatsburg that she and her husband abandoned Ellerslie and went to live there. A merry-go-round of owners followed. One James Thompson bought it in 1816 and added over a hundred acres to the property. When he died ten years later, he left it to his son who, shortly afterwards, decamped to sunny Italy with his Livingston wife, having sold Ellerslie to one James Warwick. Warwick lost it in the 1837 financial panic to one William Platt. Finally, in 1842, William B. Kelly bought it from Platt for $42,000. It would be his full-time home.

Ellerslie had fallen into good hands. Kelly, a second-generation Scotch-Irishman whose family had come from Ireland with the famous revolutionary Robert Emmet, had retired in his thirties from the most prosperous dry-goods businesses in New York City. A straight shooter, Kelly knew how to plan ahead and how to implement plans. With customers in all the major cities of the United States, it was he, for instance, who established a system of grading his agents that would eventually develop into Dun and Bradstreet. When the Great Fire of 1835 engulfed his storehouses along with the entire business district south of Wall Street, he quickly understood that even the richest insurance companies would not be able to honor their policies. His fellow businessmen refused to believe him or to realize, as he did, that no new bricks would be made until the following spring. Instead of joining the throng keening over their losses, he scouted out bricks still available along the Long Island Sound coast. Needless to say, his new storehouses were open to receive shipments well before his competitors'.

At the same time, although Kelly lived in the fine house he had built on fashionable Washington Square, he spent his leisure hours helping those whom many of his wealthy friends deemed hopeless. Among the boards on which he served were the Colored Orphan Asylum and the Deaf and Dumb Asylum. He was active as well in the workers' savings bank movement.

In 1836 William Kelly's older brother John, who had been tending the family business in Europe, died; it was a great shock, even in those days of high death rates, because he was only thirty-two years old. Soon afterwards, William and his younger brother Robert turned their business over to their employees. Robert married Arietta Hutton of

Henry James Kip of Albany was drawn to Kipsbergen because he was a descendant of patentee Jacobus Kip. Moreover, Henry's wife, Sarah Bergh, had Palatine as well as Dutch ancestors. A house built by one of her ancestors was still standing on the original grant in 1832 when Henry bought Jacobus's land, except for the ferry landing, and built their noble Greek Revival house there. They called the place Ankony, after one of the Native Americans from whom the initial parcel was acquired. The new Kip family would live there as gentlemen farmers for the next hundred years. Photograph 1940s, courtesy of the Rokeby Collection.

William B. Kelly's Ellerslie was remodeled with help from his friend Richard Upjohn, an Englishman whose breakthrough success was Trinity Church at the head of Wall Street in New York City. Woodcut circa 1870s, collection of the author.

Grasmere, a farm south of Slate Dock in Kipsbergen. (This is not to be confused with Janet Livingston Montgomery's Grasmere. The fashion for romantic house names in the early nineteenth century apparently included duplications.) As William, himself, was about to be married, it must have been then that he started looking for property nearby and found Ellerslie.

Stimulated by the semi-mythic rendering of the valley's splendid scenery by its great artists — Thomas Cole, Asher B. Durand, Thomas Doughty and their circle — and by the great strides being made in farming techniques, Kelly set out to make Ellerslie one of the finest country seats in America. He hired the great architect Richard Upjohn to restore and enlarge the Livingstons' decaying mansion by adding, among other things, a new south façade graced with double fluted Doric columns. Kelly gradually increased the property from 400 to 800 acres, 500 of which were a park surrounding the house. He established a scientific farm on an even grander scale than Ankony's. Stocked with imported Guernsey and Jersey cows, it possessed a full array of outbuildings, for many of which Kelly was the architect. Soon he was shipping 700 to 800 tons of hay from his wharf — the one built by Morgan Lewis to serve his Wurtemburg tenant farmers. To fertilize Ellerslie's marginal soils, Kelly erected a storage building at the dock for the great

Andrew Jackson Downing, the most popular — and still revered — American landscapist of the 1840s, divided his creations into the more wildly romantic "Picturesque" and the more sedate "Beautiful." He praised Kelly's Ellerslie as "one of our finest examples of high keeping and good management, both from an ornamental and an agricultural point of view." From Downing's Treatise on the Theory and Practice of Landscape Gardening, *1841.*

quantities of manure he bought from the stables of the Delaware and Hudson Canal Company across the river.

It is not known who designed Ellerslie's elaborate drive-laced pleasure gardens. Kelly may well have engaged the services of Andrew Jackson Downing to help with the design and plantings. Already famous as the master and popularizer of the beautiful and the picturesque romantic landscape, Downing praised Kelly's Ellerslie as "one of our finest examples of high keeping and good management, both from an ornamental and an agricultural point of view," in his immensely influential *Treatise on the Theory and Practice of Landscape Gardening, adapted to North America with a View to the Improvement of Country Houses.*

For the "high keeping and good management," however, Kelly relied ultimately on no one but himself. Using the careful systems that had made him so successful as a businessman, Kelly divided the work into segments and kept accounts for each — pleasure grounds, gardens, wooded plantations and wild preserves, crops, cows and dairy. The farmers in charge of each segment were required to give him a written report every week. And, virtually every day, he toured the property himself, inspecting the work and devising new projects. If he had guests who expressed an interest, he took them along.

Moreover, Kelly identified with the community from the very first. He was always ready to help employees raise the level of their expertise, and he contributed to the improvement of local roads. He supported churches, especially the Baptist, the sect to which he belonged. He helped maintain the Ellerslie School, which Mary Garrettson had commissioned Alexander Jackson Davis to build for the children of the neighborhood. He made a charming picnic grounds, fitted up with swings and seats and tables, for children brought up from New York for the day by steamboat, as well as for local families.

Often he himself would give them a tour of his farm operation.

However, in its grandeur, Kelly's Ellerslie created a new division in the social order — between the Livingston descendants, who were above engaging in trade, and men who were honed in the business world. This split between the old landed gentry and the new would last well into the twentieth century, when basically the old families petered out.

Ties to Rondout

Along with the economic lift, the many new jobs Ankony and Ellerslie offered, the phenomenal growth of Rondout strengthened the hamlet. The number of steamboats landing across the river doubled from four to eight. The exploitation of the region's extraordinary diversity of natural resources exploded and, as the products were heavy and most efficiently carried by boat, shipbuilding grew. Rondout had been sending bluestone far and wide since the 1830s; by the 1850s it had become the world's largest supplier. Almost every day in warm weather, up to two hundred wagons loaded with thousands of dollars of cut stone rumbled to Rondout's docks from the town of Hurley and other nearby communities. Limestone suitable for making high-quality cement was discovered at Rosendale during the digging of the Delaware and Hudson Canal. Cement-making began there around 1838. Shortly afterwards, mining limestone for cement began at Rondout itself. The old art of brick making, another labor-intensive industry, flourished, too. The demand for these products in New York City was insatiable, not only for the construction of the Croton Aqueduct, with its immense New York City receiving reservoir in what would become Central Park and its high-walled distribution reservoir at 42nd Street and Fifth Avenue, but for housing and workplaces for the city's surging population.

By 1840, Rondout boasted 200 dwellings, over half of them housing more than one household. Among the commercial establishments were six hotels, twenty-five stores, innumerable taverns, a tobacco factory, a gristmill, four boatyards, two dry docks, the offices of the Delaware and Hudson Canal Company, three freighting companies, each of which was capable of handling 180 teams at its docks in a single day, and one Catholic church. The buildings had been put up so fast, upland resident Nathaniel Booth commented, they "looked as if they had been dumped from above and had stuck fast wherever they struck." By the 1850s Rondout's population, bursting with Irish and German immigrants, exceeded that of inland Kingston.

Growth on the east bank of the river was nowhere near so robust. In part, its slow development was caused by the long-festering protest mounted by leaseholders frustrated to the boiling point by the great landowners' onerous rent laws. Gaining strength in the early 1830s when a handful of "anti-renters" burned Morgan Lewis's Staatsburg mansion to the ground, the Rent Wars, as they are called, began in earnest in 1838. Inspired by the movement towards popular democracy that elected Andrew Jackson president of the United States in 1828 and 1832 and Martin Van Buren in 1836, it gained energy from crop failures in 1835 and 1837, followed by the national depression that lasted from 1837 until 1843. An unlikely coalition of farmers, artisans, mechanics and disaffected day laborers, the anti-renters waged a series of colorful, unconventional, but fierce guerrilla actions. They often dressed up either in eighteenth-century costumes or as Indians and used tin horns to signal each other as a reminder of earlier farmers' rebellions. Finally, in 1846, they brought the quasi-medieval tenant system to an end. At the same time they were able to change New York State's method of procuring judges from appointment to election, thus wresting control of the courts from the self-anointed oligarchs. The Rent Wars passed over Kipsbergen lightly, because so high a percentage of the hamlet's population were shippers rather than farmers and industrial workers, and because they were not leaseholders but had always owned their land. In fact, Kipsbergen would find itself well-positioned as a transportation hub to take advantage of the opening up of wider landownership throughout the area. A vibrant, if opportunistic, era lay ahead for the waterfront hamlet.

5

The Hudson River Railroad

Rail transportation came to Kipsbergen in 1851. It would be the most defining change the settlements on the east bank of the river would experience for the next hundred years. Unlike Fulton's steamboat, it was not the first scheduled rail service in the world, or even in New York State. But it was still so new and extraordinary an invention that few people believed it would succeed. The perils and discomforts — soot, red-hot cinders, ice-heaved rail, exploding boilers, confined space and backbreaking seats — made it especially vulnerable, for it must compete with the established flotilla of luxurious passenger steamboats that plied the river day and night, as well as the cheap and efficient freight barges.

The skeptics were, of course, wrong. The Hudson River Railroad would transform freighting as well as passenger travel. It was much faster. Winter ice did not close it down. In New York State it was interactive with water transportation, for it followed the river and the Erie Canal — the famous sea-level route to Buffalo — and then proceeded on to Chicago. Villages and towns graced with station stops received an incomparable economic boost. Kipsbergen was chosen to be one of them. For once it had an edge over Rondout, which, having no railroad at all, was forced to transport its passengers and freight across the river to take advantage of the range and efficiencies rail offered. In fact, the purpose of the station stop at Kipsbergen was to exploit the proximity of Kingston, the Delaware and Hudson Canal and the developing Catskill resort area on the west side of the river, as well as the neighboring towns on the east side of the river.

The idea of a railroad from New York City to Albany was hatched in 1846. Moneyed men invested in steamboats and barges were at first wary, but were soon won over by the fear that if they did not finance it, a Harlem River line to the east would get underway first. By the spring of 1847, a multimillion-dollar subscription was raised. "Who can realize that in three years our village will be connected with the city of New York and the thriving cities and fruitful valleys of the Far West by a communication not broken by wind or weather," exclaimed the town's infant weekly, the *Rhinebeck Gazette and Dutchess County Advertiser* — "a Family Journal Devoted to Literature, Education, Politics, Agriculture, Trade, The Arts, Science, Foreign and Home News, Morality, Amusements Etc." By the end of 1849, the rails were through to Poughkeepsie, where the line connected with the steamer to Albany.

There were two major practical reasons that the railroad did not thrust through to Kipsbergen immediately, and a third reason that was social. The first was that there was a great deal of rock to cut through, an expensive labor-intensive job. The second was that the steamboat connection worked reasonably well. The third was that Charles Handy Russell, the member of the New York City–based board of directors most interested in Kipsbergen, was off on his honeymoon in Europe. A widower of fifty-four years, he had just married nineteen-year-old Caroline Howland from an equally wealthy city family. It would be a happy union, perhaps because of their similar backgrounds — their ancestors came from very old New England families.

It was not until October 1, 1851, that the Hudson River Railroad made its first stop at the Kipsbergen station, which was then located at Slate Dock. At first no attempt was made to coordinate the ferry and railroad schedules. In fact, the ferry *Wallabout*, which had replaced the old steam-propelled *Knickerbocker*, left from Kingston Point and capriciously landed at either Slate Dock or Long Dock at the whim of the captain and the passengers. Of the 37.5¢ ticket between Rondout and Kipsbergen, only 12.5¢ was for the river crossing; 25¢ was for the stagecoach ride over the corduroy road between Kingston and Kingston Point, which, as a local wag put it, was a "Primeval Paradise of frogs and mire, that hourly wakes the floundering teamster's ire." Moreover, passengers were advised to leave two hours before their train's departure for a river crossing that took at most fifteen minutes.

Travelers in Kingston became so angry, they threatened suit against the hundred-year-old ferry monopoly because it no longer performed a public service. Thomas Cornell, who was in the process of building a vast riverboat empire in Rondout, may well have set the high fees, for he had every interest in the ferry terminus's removal from Kingston Point to the Rondout waterfront. It took some time to mastermind the change, but he finally accomplished it.

At the same time, Charles H. Russell was endeavoring to coordinate the railroad and ferry in Kipsbergen. It was easy for him to move the depot directly across from Rondout, even though he had to ignore the pleas of a band of Rhinebeckians who disliked adding nearly a half a mile to their journey from the Flatts, for he was not only a director of the Hudson River Railroad, but also a close friend of its president, James Boorman. Moreover, he had just bought for speculation a 241-acre farm, south of Slate Dock, from the estate of the recently

Rail transportation was so perilous in the early days that few thought the Hudson River Rail Road could compete with the luxurious steamboats. But they were faster, more frequent and were not closed down by ice. Soon, train was the way to go for people with tight schedules. This header from an 1854 schedule of a train from Utica to New York City advertised the railroad as the "Shortest & Most Expeditious Route without change of cars or conductors." Collection of the author.

deceased Jacob Shatzell. Among its attributes was a crumbling dock that could be made into a combined railroad station and ferry slip. (Shatzell, one of the procession of New York City folk who put down roots in the community, had bought 101 acres in 1806. In the forty-odd years he farmed there, he added over a hundred acres to it.) The site was boggy and needed filling, but that could be quickly accomplished with rocks blasted from the cliffs when the track was laid.

Russell was not so successful with the ferry. He built a new ferryboat called the *Rhine*; she was almost eighty-six feet long and twenty-one feet wide. Then he bought out the ferry monopoly and made Cornell its manager. (It was undoubtedly a help to him that James Boorman was the executor for the estate of the deceased ferry owner, Peter Radcliff Kip.) Together they resorted to such

prankish stratagems as making important personages walk to the depot from Slate Dock, and forcing passengers arriving on late trains and bound for Rondout to spend the night on moored barges because the ferry failed to show up and the boatman was too drunk to row them across the river. Their final thrust was to stage a splendid viewing of the Shatzell dock site for prominent Kingston and Rhinebeck men. At last, opposition to the direct ferry crossing and the sure connection with the railroad vanished. The first train with coordinated ferry and railroad service went through on December 1, 1852. The system would remain in place until the Rhinecliff-Kingston Bridge opened over a hundred years later.

When the *Rhine* began her scheduled runs, Benjamin F. Schultz, a hamlet man who had been the captain of the *Knickerbocker*, took command of her. It was an important position, for captains acted as freight agents, ticket collectors and hosts to passengers, whom they regaled with river yarns and the latest news of the neighborhood. At the same time, they were responsible for the pilot who steered the boat and the engineer who looked after the engine. Schultz filled every one of the requirements perfectly. Crossing the river with him became an immensely popular segment of the united railroad and ferry experience.

Riding the railroad caught on swiftly, even though not every trip approached perfection. In January 1853, Nathaniel Booth of Kingston noted that he took a seat in an elegant Hudson River Railroad car that left New York at five o'clock in the afternoon, hoping for a relaxing homeward journey. Instead, the train inched along rails covered with snow and ice. When it did reach speed, it was hard to stop, because the wheels slipped on the rail. A second locomotive was added below Poughkeepsie. That helped, but still the train did not arrive at Kipsbergen until half past ten. Luckily, Booth found a sleigh to take him across the river. After a two-mile walk up the hill, he finally got home, cold, wet and hungry. Not expected at so late an hour, there was no fire to cheer him and nothing to eat. All he could do was creep to his room and shiver through the remainder of the night.

The following June, however, he was more fortunate. He left New York at one o'clock in the afternoon and reached Kipsbergen two hours and forty minutes later, utterly astonished at the ease and speed of the trip. Since it was summertime, the ferry was right on hand to transport him across the river.

Rhinecliff Is Born

With everything running so smoothly, at least in clement weather, Russell set himself to the task of turning Shatzell's farm into a development he hoped

would supplant the settlement centered on Long and Slate docks. In a *Gazette* article written forty years later, Russell's daughter described the farm as it was when her father bought it:

At this date the old dock had disappeared and scarcely a trace remained to locate the spot. A large willow tree stood at the high water mark where the dock had been and where the track of the railroad now is.

Most of the road that had led to this dock was [in] an inclosure of marshy ground, too wet for cultivation, and used for pasturage. A large two-story frame house stood about one hundred yards north of this inclosure and about the same distance east of the high bluff at the river. … A large barn stood to the northeast of the house. The bluff at the river had a row of locust trees, and the grounds surrounding the house and barn was an apple orchard, extending from the Hutton Place on the north, for some distance south of the present road to the station.

The old north and south road [Orchard Street] ran directly south, where the turn to the station is at present, and the house and barn were reached by a private lane. A large frame building, formerly a cider press house, stood near the turn of the road to the right of the lane. During the summer of this year the construction of this section of the railroad was commenced, also the building of the dock.

[Pieces of newspaper missing.] The following summer, 1851, they … completed and a roadway was con [structed] on the line of the old dock … filling in for several feet with ... and stone and blasting out a ... rock adjacent to the railroad, ... valuable spring of never failing [water] was covered over to the depth of several feet near the present turn of the road into Ellerslie. ... There were no other ... houses on the promenade at this time. It was a good sized farm of about 150 acres [*sic*] with good farm buildings.

Russell hired builder and architect George Veitch, a recent Scots immigrant with expertise in church design, to divide the farm into house lots with a small commercial district on the road leading to the depot and ferry. This Veitch did, by platting a conventional right-angled subdivision that paid absolutely no attention to the waterfront cliffs or the precipitous eastern slopes. Russell did not care. He was busy trying to find a name for the development in anticipation of a real-estate boom. His first idea was Shatzellville, after the deceased farmer. Veitch told him such a name would never attract buyers. He then put forth Boormanville, honoring his friend. That was no better. Finally, Veitch suggested Rhinecliff. Russell liked its romantic sound. The *Gazette* protested that its Rhinebeck readers thought the name silly. (Possibly they didn't like Kipsbergen's appropriation of the "Rhine" syllable.) William Kelly dryly remarked that East Rondout would be more appropriate, but Rhinecliff it became. A few old-timers, however, still refer to the southern section of the hamlet as Boormanville — probably a very old joke.

To enable the Lark *to run all winter, the ferry company bought a used boat called* Norwich, *thickened her hull and turned her into an efficient ice-breaker renamed* Ice King. *Photograph late 1850s, courtesy of the Hudson River Maritime Museum.*

The rush to buy Rhinecliff real estate did not immediately materialize. However, both the ferry and the train prospered. If the ferry had a problem, it was winter ice. At first the Rhine tried to keep its path open by running back and forth across the river all night, but blocks of broken ice too often smashed its paddlewheels. Although quickly repaired in the Rondout shops, the desperate Cornell hired men to saw a channel through the ice. Even that did not suffice. Finally, the company bought a boat from Cornell's towing fleet to do battle. Its hull was strengthened until, in some years, the Ice King, as it was now known, was able to clear the route throughout the entire winter. In hard winters, however, the ferries were locked out well into March. The choice then was to walk, skate, ride a horse or, as Booth did, take a sleigh.

In 1853 the railroad snatched the mail delivery contract from the Post Road stagecoaches and gave it to William Tremper at Slate Dock. Slowly, however, the energy of the hamlet moved southward. In 1854 the railroad company built a proper ferry house at Shatzell's dock where passengers could

The Rhinecliff Hotel in the 1890s. Hand-painted postcard, courtesy of Richard Kopystanski.

buy train or ferry tickets or a combination of both. Across the road, the fine Rhinecliff Hotel for drummers (as traveling salesmen were then called) and tourists opened in 1855 with John L. Green as its first proprietor. Green also became a postmaster. For three years Green and Tremper competed. In the end, Green won out.

Long Dock and, especially, Slate Dock, which constructed a corral to house livestock awaiting shipment, steadily improved their freight services. They both did well. Sloops and traditional passenger steamboats used Long Dock. Two steam barges, the *Robert L. Stevens* and the *Enterprise*, each sailed once a week from Slate Dock carrying hogs, calves, lambs and live chickens, as well as fruits, vegetables and grains to New York City or Albany. Passengers also used them. Their accommodation was in a towed vessel, called a safety barge because it was separated from the engine. Boiler explosions, caused by holding down the safety valve during do-or-die races between rival steamboats, had made accommodation in the same boat as the boiler too scary for many travelers.

Rondout

Rondout continued to be a boomtown and remained Rhinecliff residents' destination for serious shopping and entertainment. The deepened and widened Delaware and Hudson Canal could now handle barges carrying four times the weight. Lashed to side-wheelers, they could continue on to New York without transferring cargo. Rondout's labor-

intensive industries brought immigrants pouring in. Some of them already had relatives working in Rondout, while others simply heard their countrymen had jobs there and supposed they, too, might find one. Italians, American blacks and four congregations of Jews were the main groups added to the Irish and German old-timers. Later, Poles would come as well.

Socially, Rondout divided into closely layered factions according to language, religion, ethnic traditions and income. The well-to-do lived up on the hill; the vastly more numerous laborers lived by the waterfront, around the industries, and even directly over the mines of the sprawling cement company. There was no public water supply aside from a stream running through the noxious place and a few stagnant pools. Slops and garbage filled the dirt streets. Cholera epidemics were frequent. The air was filled with cement particles and the smoke belching from steam engines. Fist fights, brawls, drunkenness and wife beating were commonplace, for the groups were united only by their helplessness before the companies in whose houses their huge families lived as tenants and in whose stores they bought their daily needs at inflated prices. When four hundred canal workers struck for a raise of wages from seventy-five cents to a dollar for a ten-hour day, they got the raise, but their satisfaction was brief. The following year the company decreased pay to eighty-seven and a half cents, even though the profit on their stock was eleven and a half percent. Limiting the hours of the workday was not even discussed. The men were ordered to go back on the job or be fired, and back they went.

Still, Rondout did not lack for cultural attractions that benefited everybody, if only indirectly. Stores steadily improved, for those who could afford to buy. The Mansion House was remodeled with one hundred sleeping compartments, elegant furnishings and its own gasworks for light. A library, a YMCA and a lyceum — mainly attended by the growing middle and the established upper classes — were built. Reform societies took hold. The temperance crusade was popular, although essentially unsuccessful, as was the women's rights movement, even though the noted touring suffragist Antoinette Brown came to give a lecture. There were also singing clubs, baseball games, firehouse dinners and immense Fourth of July celebrations. Those privileged few who could afford the fare traveled to

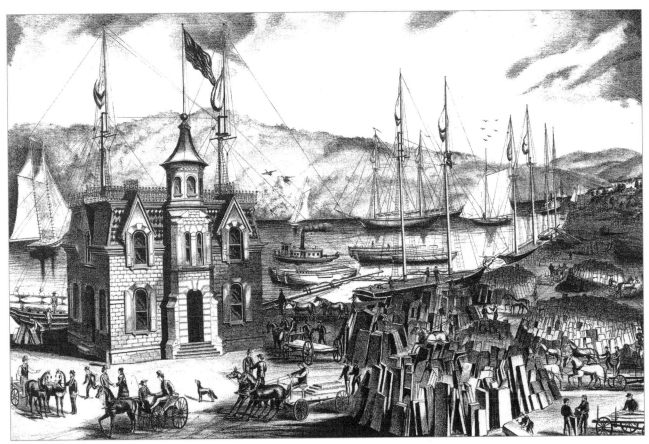

Rondout's speedy growth was tied to its natural resources and its industry. That it had no train connecting it to New York City did not matter; water transportation was what it needed for its weighty natural products. This illustration from the 1875 Atlas of Ulster County *depicts bluestone awaiting shipment as far as the eye can see, for Rondout had become the bluestone capital of the world. Note the boats of every size and type filling the creek. Courtesy of the Hudson River Maritime Museum.*

New York City to view the Crystal Palace. Built far uptown along Sixth Avenue between 40th and 42nd streets (where Bryant Park now is) to rival London's Great Exhibition of the Works of Industry of All Nations, which had drawn tourists from around the world two years previously, it celebrated a new era in which it was envisioned that science and technology would replace war. At the same time, visitors to the city could attend thrilling performances at the Hippodrome or join the stampede to get tickets to the concerts of Jenny Lind. Although it is doubtful that many laborers did more than sing, play ball and celebrate Independence Day, in so tight a setting the wider cultural ambiance was necessarily part of their background. Nathaniel Booth, who said the essence of his education was "to swear well then fight," but was now a bluestone investor, gave an apt description of the spirited caldron of humanity Rondout had become when he wrote, "Our Village is all life and commotion … the whole county is like a nest of hornets stirred up with a crooked stick."

In contrast, the pace of Rhinecliff's growth, though steady, was more sedate. Residents became accustomed to the new name, although they and the close-by estates still regarded the hamlet's boundaries as those of the original Kipsbergen. The year-round passenger and freight business, by water and rail, continued to grow, and the population slowly increased. Some new residents were railroad builders who remained after construction was finished. Others married into the community, while some were former summer visitors. Still others had no previous connection with the hamlet, but simply liked its looks and feel. The number of newcomers was never so great, however, that they could not be easily absorbed into the existing community.

That community remained firmly fixed as a transportation hub. Unlike Rondout or inland Rhinebeck, there was no industry in Rhinecliff. So great was dock-bound traffic that a carriage taxi service was set up to take passengers to and from the village. In 1860 the ferry company built a new boat for the run. State-of-the-art, she was ninety-two feet six inches long, but only fourteen feet nine inches wide. She was nimble and fast, her powerful engine having been built by the famous Allaire Works — the successor to the shop Robert Fulton had set up in New Jersey. She was appropriately called the *Lark*.

Travel between Rhinecliff and Rondout was so brisk that a nimble state-of-the-art steam ferry was built for the run. She was appropriately called the Lark. *This imagined drawing shows her at rest at her Rondout berth. Postcard 1908, courtesy of Sherman-Mann Ephemera Collection of Catskill and Rhinebeck, N.Y.*

The only unpleasant part of replacing the *Rhine* was that the ferry company's Kingston directors decided that an entirely new crew should be hired to run the *Lark*. The popular Benjamin Schultz was sent to man one of Cornell's tugboats and was replaced by James Morrow from across the river. A jovial sixty-year-old Irishman, Morrow soon made his mark and ill feelings subsided. Moreover, the machinery of the *Rhine* was still in such good condition that her hull was completely rebuilt and she was brought back into service as the *Oriole*, a backup for the *Lark* when she was occasionally in dry dock.

New Estates

The estates were gradually changing their character as the Beekman/Livingston properties changed hands. The new configuration was based on financial acumen as opposed to the privileges assured by almost two centuries of the now-defunct rent laws. When he married in 1852, Thomas Suckley, whose father, an émigré from Sheffield, England, had made his initial fortune in the hardware business, bought fifty-two acres on Wildercliff's waterfront from Mary R. Garrettson, daughter of Catherine Livingston and

Freeborn Garrettson. She was glad to have him as a neighbor simply because they shared the socially equalizing Methodist faith. The Suckleys built a comfortable house in a conservative Italianate style and planted around it a garden and an orchard of apples, pears, cherries and peaches. At first, they called the place The Cedars, in honor of the trees that had grown up in an abandoned sheepfold. Later they would change its name to Wilderstein. A more fashionable, faux–German word meaning "savages' stone," Wilderstein picturesquely referred to the Native American image at the river's edge that was said to mark the transfer of the land to the original Dutch proprietors. Suckley and his family lived quietly in this comparatively modest countryseat, supported by an allowance from his older brother, Rutsen, who managed their father's estate brilliantly. (Rutsen lived at St. Mark's Place in New York City with their equally bright, unmarried sister Mary. He accumulated an impressive amount of Rhinebeck real estate, including the site of present-day Ferncliff Forest and the large farm, now called The Meadows, along the River Road.)

John B. James, an Albany man and a relation of Ankony's Henry James Kip, acquired Linwood

- EAST · ELEVATION ·

When Thomas Suckley married, the charming dwarf Mary Garrettson, daughter of Freeborn and Catherine Garrettson, was more than happy to sell him fifty-two acres overlooking the river, for the families were united by their Methodist faith. There the Suckleys built a conservative Italianate house, called Wilderstein, a faux German word for the ancient petroglyph on the property. Drawing of the east elevation by architect James Warren Ritch, 1852, courtesy of Wilderstein Preservation.

through his father-in-law, Dr. Federal Beekman Vanderburgh, a prominent New York City homeopathic physician who had bought the property from Tillotson's son. Vanderburgh brokered Russell's purchase of the Shatzell farm, and perhaps also Kip's purchase of Ankony. After residing at Linwood for ten years, James sold it to his brother Augustus. In *A Small Boy and Others*, published in 1913, their nephew, the great novelist Henry James, recalled the happy summers he had spent at Linwood with his aunt and uncle:

> Didn't Linwood bristle with great views and other glories, with gardens and graperies and black ponies, to say nothing of gardeners and grooms who were notoriously and quotedly droll. … Our Aunt Elizabeth, who had been Miss Bay of Albany, who floats back to me through the Rhinebeck picture, aquiline but easy, with an effect of handsome high-browed high-nosed looseness, of dressing-gowns or streaming shawls and of claws of bright, benevolent steel, that kept nipping for our charmed advantage: roses, and grapes and peaches and currant clusters, together with turns of phrase and scraps of remark that fell as by quite the flash of shears.

Elizabeth Schermerhorn Jones was not of the same stripe. She did not blend in. A rich, dominating *grande dame* New Yorker, it is said that she was the origin of the phrase, "keeping up with the Joneses." In 1853 she hired George Veitch to build the mammoth mansion in the Norman style on eighty acres between Linwood and Wilderstein. She called it Wyndclyffe. Her niece, the novelist Edith Wharton, who visited her there as a child, remembered hating everything about the "expensive but dour speci-

men of Hudson River Gothic. … [F]rom the first," she wrote, "I was obscurely conscious of a queer resemblance between the granitic exterior of Aunt Elizabeth and her grimly comfortable house …" All this was generally true, but small details of the architecture, such as the brickwork around the main entrance, the side porch and the chimney pots, were delightfully fanciful — not that it mattered to Miss Jones. Wyndclyffe was just one of her many imposing residences.

The grandest new estate was Ferncliff, situated just north of Ankony. Brought into being by William Backhouse Astor Jr., whose multimillionaire grandfather, John Jacob Astor, had recently left him most of his fortune, Ferncliff was, in reality, an escape from the fantasy-laden social life in New York, Newport

Wyndclyffe, south of Wilderstein, was designed by George Veitch, a noted British church architect, for Elizabeth Schermerhorn Jones, the New York City grande dame of "keeping up with the Joneses" fame. Jones's niece, the novelist Edith Wharton, remembered everything about the place as being grim, but the ornamental detailing at least is delightful. Postcard circa 1890s, courtesy of Sherman-Mann Ephemera Collection of Catskill and Rhinebeck, N.Y.

and Europe that his wife, Caroline Schermerhorn Astor, had devised. (It was she who would create high society's "Four Hundred," the number of dancers her Fifth Avenue ballroom would comfortably hold and, so she boasted, the only people worthy of being known.) Starting out as an unproductive farm of some one hundred acres, Ferncliff grew as Astor added on neighboring farms, usually demolishing their homesteads (although he did save a Dutch stone house that, much altered, still stands today). Ultimately, the estate would possess over a mile and a half of riverfront. In true Astor fashion, no expense was spared in the construction or furnishing of the house, even though Caroline seldom visited it. In contrast, William spent as much time there as he possibly could, for it reminded him of happy summers with his parents and siblings at nearby Rokeby. (Rokeby had become the Astors' possession when John Jacob Astor bought it for William Astor Sr., who married Margaret Beekman Livingston's granddaughter, the daughter of the original owner, John Armstrong.) William Jr. would make much of Ferncliff's land into

a model farm, but more, it would seem, because it was the thing for a man of fortune to do, rather than because of any talent for farming.

Of all the estates, Ellerslie was the most closely tied to the hamlet, thanks to Kelly's long tenure and caring nature. Residents liked the fact that, although Kelly had been soundly against the Hudson River Railroad because it cut off his land from the water, he recognized it was a great benefit to all and, acknowledging the writing on the wall, became a large stockholder in the venture. When, in 1855, a significant majority elected Kelly to the State Senate in what was supposed to be a tight race, local residents were enormously proud. The Senate was then a divided body rife with partisanship, but Kelly gained the reputation of being an attentive and open-minded legislator and became its leader. Residents were also pleased when he became the chairman of the Executive and Finance Committees of State Agricultural College, a member of Rochester University's Board of Trustees, a trustee of Vassar Female College and of the Hudson River Insane

Ferncliff was built by William B. Astor Jr. in part as an escape from his socialite wife, Caroline Schermerhorn Astor, who seldom came there. It was she who commissioned the New York City ballroom to accommodate 400 guests — the only people worth knowing, she said. William B. increased 100 poor acres significantly and made a fine gentlemen's farm of the property. He had grown up happily at Rokeby, the next estate to the north, which his grandfather had bought for his mother. Photograph circa 1890s, courtesy of Tom Daley.

Asylum in Poughkeepsie, and that he participated energetically in Rhinebeck institutions.

Typically, the now well-established *Gazette* took a poke at the new countryseats. With the opening of the railroad, it observed, they had lost their primitive character and turned from properly pedigreed "places" into estates. (Old families still refer to their property as "The Place.") Nevertheless, despite the new owners' high social standing, their riches and their sophistication, an intimacy born of proximity and interdependence was forged between them and the hamlet men and women who worked for or performed needed services. More in each other's presence in those slower days of horse, wagon, carriage and foot transportation than they would be today, they got to know each other's ways.

The Rhinebeck Flatts

The Village of Rhinebeck had also been transformed in the recent decades, especially by the outcome of the Rent Wars, which terminated the lease system, and by the railroad. In fact, the Flatts outstripped Rhinecliff in almost every way. It was on the Post Road, the large estates did not hem it in, and its land was easily divided into neat lots. Moreover, it had

all the mill sites and, therefore, the industry. There were inns and taverns, hardware, dry goods and grocery stores, churches and a pharmacy. Artisans of all kinds plied their trades. Rhinebeck was where professional men, such as lawyers, doctors, bankers and investors, chose to live. It was also where the services were. The National Bank of Rhinebeck (now the M & T Bank) was established in 1853 with Kelly on the Board of Trustees. (He, in fact, would save it in the financial panic of 1857 by delivering $14,000 worth of Delaware and Hudson stock to its agent, the Mechanics Bank of New York City; his respected name was probably as persuasive as the stock.) The Rhinebeck Savings Bank followed in 1860. The Starr Library, envisioned and funded by Schuyler descendent Mary R. Miller, opened in 1857; Kelly was its president until his failing health took him abroad in 1871. Many considered the volunteer fire company, outfitted with the latest hose apparatus, fondly named Pocahontas, Rhinebeck's most important institution. (Old "Pokie" has recently retired from participating in antique firefighting rallies but, lovingly cared for by the firemen, she is still fit.) Industry flourished on the outskirts of the village where there were a paper mill, three woolen mills, four sawmills, five gristmills and a tannery,

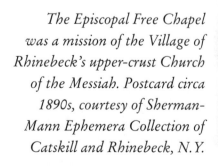

The Episcopal Free Chapel was a mission of the Village of Rhinebeck's upper-crust Church of the Messiah. Postcard circa 1890s, courtesy of Sherman-Mann Ephemera Collection of Catskill and Rhinebeck, N.Y.

The Episcopal Sunday School was built before the church on the south side of William Street. The ground was found to be wet well into the summer, so it was almost immediately moved across the street to higher ground — a perfect example of building in Rhinecliff without attention to the terrain. Photograph by Ian Giddy, 2008.

all powered by the Landsman Kill. Amongst them were two stills. Productive farms studded the surrounding countryside. Virtually all the significant money made locally in professional services, industry, and farming, and even much made in shipping, went to Rhinebeck men. Binding the burgeoning inland community together was its excellent weekly newspaper, the *Gazette*.

It might be thought that Rhinebeck's great activity would attract Rhinecliff residents to it, but it did not. Solidly middle class, with an inclination towards gentility, the village of Rhinebeck had little in common with Rhinecliff. Rhinecliff was still its transportation hub, but whatever convenience that provided was easy to use with little personal interchange. In addition, Rhinecliffers could find what they needed to buy more easily and in greater variety in Rondout than in Rhinebeck. The coverage given Rhinecliff by the *Gazette* was indicative of the relationship between the hamlet and the inland town. Although the weekly was attentive to train, ferry and passenger steamboat schedules, and to freighting and market prices for commodities, the only news it contained about the hamlet tended to be sensational, cautionary or tongue-in-cheek. For instance, one of its few news stories about Rhinecliff was a fracas among the Kips, Coles and Saulpaughs that began when Peter Cole

sank his fishing net too close to Saulpaugh's, and ended with Saulpaugh's death.

In fact, reading the *Gazette*'s pages, it is almost impossible to think of Rhinebeck and Rhinecliff as parts of the same town. Rhinecliff had its own infrastructure, as well as the depot and the docks. Mail was received and dispatched — and still is — at its own post office. Its children went to Rhinecliff's schools — Flat Rock, located at the junction of the road to the village and the road to Red Hook, to serve the original Kip houses, and Ellerslie, built by Kelly on the southern edge of his property. In 1859, Mary Garrettson gave land for a Methodist church in Rhinecliff and paid for its construction. A large, slate-roofed neo-Gothic stone building, the church fronts on Orchard Street, which was then the main road leading into Rhinecliff's business district. It would become a mainstay of the community. The town responded with the Episcopal Free Chapel of the Messiah, a mission of its upper-crust Church of the Messiah, whose church had been designed by George Veitch in 1853. Its congregation was far smaller and less active. It began with a Sunday school, located on the south corner of William and Kelly streets. Three months later a small, but handsome, wooden gothic-style church was built on a lot donated by Charles H. Russell overlooking the river. The cornerstone ceremony, an elegant affair, was led by the bishop of the diocese, assisted by ministers

The Riverside Methodist Church was also built in 1859. Its congregation would be far more numerous and active than that of the Episcopal mission church. Postcard circa 1890s, courtesy of Sherman-Mann Ephemera Collection of Catskill and Rhinebeck, N.Y.

from New York, Poughkeepsie, Kingston, Red Hook and Rhinebeck. Soon a communion service was presented to it by the Church of the Incarnation in New York City. (Its rector, Henry E. Montgomery, was married to a descendant of Margaret Beekman Livingston.) Miss Jones of Wyndclyffe gave the congregation its prayer books, and the Church of the Messiah donated the lectern and the large prayer book used by the clergy. But it did not have its own minister; its services, every two weeks, were conducted by the Church of the Messiah's rector.

What Rhinecliff needed was a bank. It did not have one and, even with William Kelly in its midst, it seemed likely it never would.

The Great Divide

The year 1861 brought the Civil War, the nation's supreme watershed. It signaled the persistent divide between the country's northern and southern regions and their conflicting designs on the developing West. Neither the nation, nor the state, nor the village and town of Rhinebeck, not even the hamlet of Rhinecliff, would be the same when it was finally over.

6

The Civil War and
Its Aftermath

Between the years 1861 and 1865, the Civil War was the primary focus of every city, town and village in the nation. It took a while for Rhinebeck to gear up, but, in 1862, after the second battle of Bull Run, the town put forth a strong recruiting effort. Many, but not enough, men signed up to meet the state allotment, so the town voted seventy to one to tax residents with over $800 annual income to provide a fund of $15,000 to pay each volunteer a $200 bounty. Frederick Cotting, a descendant of the first settlers who was then living in Jacob Kip's homestead, paid $159; Thomas Suckley paid $1,510; and Mary R. Miller, a Schuyler, paid over a third of the purse, $5,430. Enlistments suddenly became brisk; $200 was an attractive sum to a seasonally employed day laborer.

At first the enlisting station for Dutchess and Columbia counties was in Rondout, where the recruits joined the 20th Regiment of the state militia, the Ulster Guards. Sent to Baltimore, Maryland, they made the first leg of the trip in a barge lashed to a Cornell steamboat's side. They built a camp on Baltimore's outskirts, then hunkered down for eight months' drilling. Their initial duty was to defend the railroad to Washington, D.C., a tricky assignment because Baltimore's sympathies were sharply divided between the Union and the Confederacy, and the federal capital was a hot-bed of rebels and spies.

Then Rhinebeck volunteers, mustered in for three years' duty, grouped in Hudson, Columbia County's seat, forming Company C of New York State's 128th Regiment. Stores in Hudson closed on the day of their departure for the South. The cheering populace lined the long main street. The Stockport brass band played martial tunes. With the Hudson Volunteer Firemen as its honor guard, the regiment, clad in smart new uniforms and with four days' rations in their knapsacks, paraded down to the waterfront to the waiting steamboat *Oregon*. According to the *Gazette*, as the boat passed Rhinecliff's thronged waterfront, its high-spirited soldiers carelessly fired their muskets in salute, nearly hitting a baby and causing grown women to faint.

Tired of being dispatched "detached in fragments," Dutchess County formed its own volunteer regiment, the 150th. Rhinebeck men were a part of Company K. Its camp, named Camp Kelly for William Kelly, who had been heading up the recruitment effort, was near Poughkeepsie. After a modicum of training, it also was sent to Baltimore. In June 1863, its men defended the city from marauding Confederate soldiers on their way to Gettysburg, Pennsylvania. They followed the Confederates and, at that awful battlefield, were baptized into war's horrors. Assigned to the Army of the Potomac's 12th Corps under the command of General Henry W. Slocum, the 150th fought through the night of July 2 to regain Culp's Hill. With scant rest, it relieved an exhausted regiment on yet another firing line. Early that afternoon the Confederates launched an artillery barrage, followed by Pickett's terrifying charge. That failed, and, on July 4, under heavy rain, what was left of the Confederate Army began its retreat into Virginia. The Union may have ultimately won the battle,

but the price was high on both sides. The South suffered at least 27,900 casualties; the North over 23,000 casualties. The hearts and minds of Union as well as Confederate survivors were permanently etched with images of the carnage-strewn fields.

In September the 150th boarded a freight train for Tennessee, where it guarded the railroad between Nashville and Chattanooga. After the Battle of Chattanooga, the regiment went into winter quarters among the quirky "bushwhackers" in the eastern section of the state, where they were driven to forage food and fuel for survival. At the end of April 1864, they joined General William Tecumseh Sherman's assault on Georgia. After a brief truce at the Chattahoochee River, during which the opposing armies bathed, picked berries and traded coffee for tobacco, the regiment continued on to Atlanta where they took part in the six weeks' siege. The city fell in September. Sherman torched what was left of it, then drove on to the sea, foraging, plundering and burning throughout the countryside. The 150th was assigned to tear up railroad tracks, a vital job that destroyed the South's scant lines of transport. To ensure that the rails would not be reused, the men made pyres of the stringers, added the rails and, when red hot, twisted them into loops around trees. These they jubilantly dubbed "Sherman's neckties." With no way to move troops and supplies quickly, the South slowly strangled.

From Georgia, Sherman moved up into the Carolinas, relentlessly continuing his scorched-earth policy. When Columbia, South Carolina, was looted and burned, one of the 150th's veterans, weary of the rampant destruction, wrote home that its boys were not among the marauders, claiming that they were a mile or two to the west of the city and, therefore, could not have participated in the mayhem. The 150th's last battle was fought outside Goldsboro, North Carolina, at the junction of the Confederacy's last remaining "lifeline" railroads. According to another exhausted soldier, it was "the longest and, in some respects, the hardest we were ever in."

Confederate General Robert E. Lee finally surrendered his spent, but still proud, army to General Ulysses S. Grant at Appomattox, Virginia, on April 9, 1865. Five days later John Wilkes Booth shot President Abraham Lincoln as he was taking needed respite at Ford's Theater in Washington. Lincoln died the next day. The North was traumatized. "Flags fluttering so victoriously in the sunshine, slowly and sadly disappeared, only to reappear dismally hung with sable steamers," reported Rhinebeck's thunderstruck *Gazette*. Business was suspended. Services were held at the Dutch Reformed and other churches. The funeral train, with the body of the president next to the tender and six forward cars filled with escorts, slowly retraced the route it had followed when Lincoln first left Springfield, Illinois, to take office in Washington. It reached Rhinecliff at 8:40 PM on April 25. Local mourners, augmented by two hundred men, women and children brought over from Rondout on the ferry *Lark*, lined the tracks. As the train slowly rolled by, the *Lark* sounded her horn to signal guns across the river to begin their salute. Church bells rang. Rondout's German Band played a dirge. (A legend persists that a local mortician repaired the president's wound in anticipation of the Albany viewing, but it is highly doubtful that is true.) Despite the late hour, the solemn gathering, united by its loss, did not disperse until the train was long gone.

The 150th Regiment was still in North Carolina at that time; the Confederate general there did not capitulate until April 26. At last, on April 29, the 150th was ordered to Washington, D.C., to be mustered out. It joined the enormous celebratory review on Pennsylvania Avenue that took place on May 23 and 24. On June 8 the 150th finally departed for home, sailing up the Hudson aboard the steamboat *Mary Benton* to Poughkeepsie, where the men

were greeted by cheering crowds, congratulatory speeches, singing children, huge bouquets of flowers and a fine dinner. Some soldiers were embraced by their families at that event; others boarded the train for Rhinecliff as soon as the festivities were over.

Casualties suffered by the 150th were relatively low. Two officers and twenty-eight enlisted men had been killed in action. Another twenty-one enlisted men had died of wounds, and three officers and seventy-eight enlisted men had died of disease and other causes.

Rhinecliff's Postwar Surge

It would be too much to say that Rhinebeck, Rhinecliff and Rondout returned to normalcy immediately after the Civil War. In the war's grinding last years, inflation had gripped the national economy. The price charged to ferry across the river rose from ten cents to twelve cents in May 1864, and to twenty-five cents that December. Still, buoyed by pent-up demand for commodities of all kinds, Rhinecliff, like the rest of the North, entered into an era of marked expansion. New houses, hotels and business structures were built. Depot, Slate and even Long Dock shipped more goods than ever before. With ever more day liners and night boats, passengers returned to river travel in droves. Each new steamboat vied with its predecessor in size, speed and creature comforts. Wine, liquor and food were of the highest quality and impeccably served. The décor was that of the best hotels. Some staterooms even boasted showers with hot and cold running water.

A Roman Catholic church, Mount St. Joseph's, had begun construction in 1864 on a block of land, high above the depot, donated by a Tivoli man. It was designed by George Veitch, who gave it a simple but elegant interior. When it opened its doors on November 11, 1865, the ceremony was filled with clerical hierarchy. It was a signal event, especially for the steady stream of Irish and German immigrants who were settling in the hamlet. The services and rites for which communicants had had to travel to Kingston were now performed close to home. The new church also provided local Catholics with a consecrated cemetery in which to bury their loved ones. From its beginning St. Joseph's had a very broad reach, for it was the mother church for Catholics in northwestern Dutchess County. Mass is still held on Sunday mornings for a sizeable number of communicants. The image the church projects from below is that of a great white hen brooding protectively over its people.

What was remarkable about the three Christian sects that were now established in Rhinecliff was how well they cooperated to strengthen the community. Shortly after St. Joseph's consecration, its parishioners put on a great picnic at which the Esopus String Band and the Butts' Band from Poughkeepsie played. Its newspaper notice emphasized that it would be a nonsectarian affair and invited "the public respectfully to attend." They did. Not long afterwards, the Episcopal church put on a raspberry and cream social to raise the money to move its Sunday school building from the low, insalubrious land on the south side of William Street to higher ground on the north side. (It is now the elongated octagon residence on the north corner of

So many Roman Catholics — mainly Irish, but with a sturdy mixture of Germans and Italians — settled in Rhinecliff because of jobs offered by the railroad, that a church for them became imperative. George Veitch designed it and, in November 1865, Mount St. Joseph's was consecrated. It would be the "Mother Church" of the Roman Catholic churches along the east side of the river. Postcard circa 1880s, courtesy of Sherman-Mann Ephemera Collection of Catskill and Rhinebeck, N.Y.

Generations of Rhinecliff immigrants can be traced through the grave stones in St. Joseph's cemetery. Some stones are engraved with the county in Ireland where the deceased was born. Photograph by Cynthia Hewitt Philip, 2006.

William and Kelly streets.) The event started at noon and went on into the evening. The entrance fee was five cents. Again, all sects attended and thoroughly enjoyed themselves. Among the many fundraisers and entertainments offered by the Methodists year after year were their extraordinarily popular fall fairs and their turkey dinners.

In 1867, F.W. Beers published a map of the Rhinecliff subdivision. In several ways the road system depicted is unlike today's. A major difference is that Orchard Street was the entrance to the hamlet from the north, because the connection between the Rhinecliff Road and Kelly Street was interrupted by the Hutton farm. Those whose destination was the commercial area and ferry reached it by making a sharp jog west along Shatzell Avenue. If they were traveling farther south, they could either branch off Shatzell Avenue at Kelly Street or continue along Orchard Street until it joined Kelly Street at Valley Way. Along this stretch the narrow road was cut into the steep hillside on the east side and shored up on the west side by a twelve-foot stone wall. Several roads were never built. The continuation of Shatzell Avenue straight up to the about-to-be-built Roman Catholic church was impossible because of the ultrasteep grade. Instead, a set of 101 white-painted wooden steps spaced by several landings joined the church with the commercial area. The stairs would become a destination for spooning couples as well as the setting for jokes about lurchings to midnight mass. Vanderburg Street dead-ends before it reaches James Street for the same reason. None of the streets shown as crossing Grinnell Street were built, because of the danger of falling off the high cliff that drops abruptly down to the railroad tracks and the river. Nor would there be an extension of William Street to Orchard Street be built; while not impossibly steep, there simply was no need for it.

Sixty structures are marked in the subdivision. Fifty-one are dwellings. Nine are public buildings — four for the railroad and ferry operations, three churches and two hotels. Among the buildings on the list of businesses are the Rhinecliff Hotel, Wm. Crandall, proprietor, and the store of I. F. Russell, merchant, postmaster and justice of the peace, on the corner of Charles and Hutton Streets. Two schools are identified — a private boarding school affiliated with the Roman Catholic Church, and the Episcopal Sunday school. The Union Hotel, P. O'Neil, proprietor, was on the north side of Shatzell Avenue by the stairs leading up to the Catholic church. O'Brien's General Store on the northeast corner of Shatzell Street and Kelly Street is not among the businesses listed, but O'Brien's name is alongside a symbol for his building, so the store was probably under construction. Also not listed are J.N. McElroy's hostelry and saloon and T. Kelley's lumberyard, on the north side of Shatzell Avenue, and T. Dyer's store on the south side.

Among the homes is that of ferry captain Benjamin F. Schultz on the corner of Hutton Street and Dutchess Terrace, together with two lots he owned across Hutton Street. One of Charles H. Russell's dwellings, the largest in the hamlet, is to the east, fronting on Charles Street; it was probably built to boost the development, for he spent the summer season at his "cottage," Oaklawn, in Newport, Rhode Island. (Had Russell wished to stay in the area, he would have been welcome at the Aspinwalls or the Delanos in Barrytown, for they were all among the New York City elite and their families had known each other for generations. A founder and the president of the New York's Bank of Commerce, Russell also must have known Astor. Through his Hudson River Railroad connection, he was acquainted with Kelly as well.) The handsome dwelling of I. F. Russell (no relation to Charles H. Russell) on Orchard Street has a wide-open view across the river to Rondout. Along Kelly

Street is a row of houses, in part where the Morton Memorial Library and Community House now is. Farther south are the twin Simon and Matthew Pells dwellings, built circa 1827. A number of houses are scattered about the southern end of the hamlet, including another large one belonging to Charles H. Russell high on the hill above where Valley Way and Kelly Street meet.

The Beers map is charming and enormously informative about who had moved to the new Rhinecliff and where — assuming the map is generally accurate. However, because it is a grid, with no indication of the swales and cliffs, its uses are limited. The lack of topography, for instance, might have led a prospective buyer to believe that all the lots could be built upon, but a quick look at the terrain would have made it clear they could not be. Nonetheless, it is a valuable historical artifact. The naming of the streets is particularly interesting. Shatzell Avenue obviously memorializes the deceased farmer, just as Charles Street and Russell Avenue salute Charles H. Russell. William Street takes its name from Charles's brother who in the beginning was a partner, but soon fell ill and dropped out. Grinnell was a preeminent New York City importer and Russell's close friend. Howland was the surname of Russell's new bride. Jones must have been either Elizabeth or her nephew, owners of Wyndclyffe. Vanderburgh Street is named after Dr. Federal Vanderburgh, who negotiated the Russells' purchase of the Shatzell farm. The origin

George Veitch laid out Charles Handy Russell's subdivision as a grid that paid no attention whatsoever to the up-and-down topography. Yet it was he who suggested the name Rhinecliff. The road system in this 1867 Beers map often reflects more hope than reality, but the notations telling who bought lots and who ran businesses more than makes up for this deficiency. Courtesy of the Morton Memorial Library.

of Orchard Street's name is obvious — apple and pear trees proliferated throughout the hamlet, but the land east of northern Orchard Street was an ideal location for growing fruit for the market.

The map proved a fine advertisement. A good deal of buying and selling of lots took place, most of it south of Shatzell Avenue. There was a slight downturn in 1871 when, during an especially hard winter, coal at the dock rose to $7.50 a ton. Several stores and houses, as well as vacant lots, were for sale. An eighty-acre farm on the southern border, with a dwelling house and barn, two sheds, a fine young orchard and fields highly recommended for growing hay or grain, looked in vain for a buyer; most likely it was the Russell property. An almost new, well-built cottage with a beautiful view and located only three minutes from the train station — the former residence of ferry captain James Morrow on the corner of Corning and Dutchess Terrace — was offered by Kelly himself. The architect George Veitch had built a number of river-view summer cottages that were for rent or for sale.

Equally serious for the people of the hamlet as the decline in the real estate market was the deteriorating health of William Kelly. Having sailed that year to England to seek medical advice, he died there in 1872; his body was brought home and buried with great pomp in New York City. The quality of his life was perhaps best expressed by the president of the State Agricultural Society: "Perhaps no man in our day has accomplished so much in so quiet and noiseless a manner as William B. Kelly." Typically, Kelly's will was witnessed not by lawyers or business friends, but by his coachman, his gardener and his head farmer. Childless, he left the property in the care of his widow. She would continue the sale of cattle that he had begun when he became ill, but she did not sell the property. Ellerslie would exist in a kind of limbo for the next fifteen years.

Rhinecliff Embraced in a Web of Rail

In 1869 the directors of the faltering Hudson River Railroad were made ecstatic by news that tycoon Cornelius Vanderbilt was buying its stock for $100 a share so that he could fold that crucial segment of track into his New York Central Railroad. The line would run all the way to Chicago, the new center of the nation's agricultural wealth. Through connecting lines, it would soon be possible to leave the depot in Rhinecliff and travel by rail throughout the country wherever tracks were laid, for the east coast and the west were united by rail when the famous golden spike was pounded into place at Promontory, Utah, in May of that year.

Reinforcing the hamlet's time-honored role as a transportation hub, Slate Dock was extended ninety feet on the land side and fifty feet into the river to accommodate increased demand for shipping both by rail and water. Night boats left from Depot Dock for New York City every evening but Saturday. In the summertime the steamer *Sunnyside* made Saturday excursions from Catskill to New York, arriving at Rhinecliff at 7:15 AM and returning there at 7:30 PM. Cornell was building his Rondout & Oswego Railroad to serve the rapidly growing Catskill tourist trade and switched her berth to his side of the river.

When Rhinecliffers learned that prominent men up on the Flatts were planning a new railroad that would start at Slate Dock, swoop up through Dutchess into Columbia County, then turn back and tie into the Connecticut & Western tracks to go on to Hartford, the capital of that state, they were elated. The first attempt to raise $100,000 in town bonds to pay for the grand project was quashed as a work of "fraud, misrepresentation and deceit of a most scandalous nature" by a group of naysayers led by none other than William B. Astor Jr. Possibly it was a ruse, for surveying began almost immediately on Astor's

Ferncliff. Ultimately, the profit-driven Astor would get a private station stop, a telegraph line and who knows what else out of it.

Track laying with hundreds of immigrant laborers commenced in October 1872. To celebrate the Fourth of July the following year, the new line, called the Rhinebeck & Connecticut Railroad, ran an excursion train between Elizaville and Rhinebeck. The cars were tastefully trimmed with evergreens and bunting to disguise the fact that they were only flatbeds mounted with benches. But everyone was euphoric.

Then, calamity fell. Construction was all but halted by a national depression, largely brought on by failed nationwide railroad speculation. The local fallout was so severe that the *Gazette* urged residents to lock their windows and doors against robbers, and shopkeepers were reduced to begging their customers to buy simply to keep money in circulation. Thomas Cornell came to the rescue by persuading the Delaware & Hudson Canal Company, of which he was a principal, to buy Rhinebeck & Connecticut bonds to keep the work going. It also helped that, as a result of the depression, the cost of rails

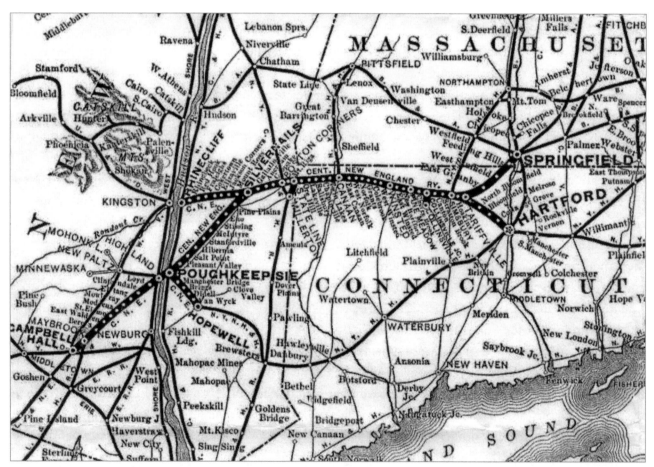

The expanding railroad system made living in the country ever more attractive for second-home buyers. It also made getting product to market faster and easier. In 1888 the Poughkeepsie railroad bridge provided a direct link from the area to the nationwide system whose terminus was on the west side of the river. Map circa 1900 published by the Connecticut and New England Railroad, collection of the author.

fell thirty dollars a ton. Track laying was resumed. Despite numerous accidents caused by haste — the heavy blasting hurled a huge boulder through the venerable Heermance house at the head of Long Dock Road, and a pile driver slid into the river at Slate Dock — through-service went into full motion in mid-April 1875. The round-trip fare to Hartford was five dollars, with more affordable rates promised to the hordes planning an excursion to the popular Rhinebeck Fair in September. At the same time, the company leased trackage rights from the Poughkeepsie & Eastern Railroad Company, soon to become the Poughkeepsie, Hartford & Boston Railroad, significantly increasing its reach.

Compared to the Hudson River/New York Central Railroad, the Rhinebeck & Connecticut was not a fast train, for its primary purpose was to haul medium-weight freight. In fact, its nickname was the Hucklebush, because passengers could reach out the car windows to pick berries as it slowly rolled along — or so it was said. It is true, however, that the conductor and engineer once brought their train to a complete halt to catch turtles sunning on rocks; they took them home for turtle soup. Still, the train ran on schedule most of the time. It carried Pennsylvania coal east into New England and points along the way, and on the return trip carried dairy products, fruit, vegetables, hogs, sheep, cows and hay to Slate Dock in Rhinecliff, where steam barges waited to take them to New York City markets. Farmers found the train far cheaper and less time-consuming than carting their agricultural products themselves to the river landings. The price was only $1.40 a ton from Ancram to the barge *Enterprise*, a round-trip by wagon of around forty miles that often con-

sumed ten to fifteen hours and a good feed of grain for the horses. On just one November day, two hundred porkers shipped by train were dispatched to the city from Slate Dock.

In addition, the Rhinebeck & Connecticut stimulated small industry along its line, bringing in needed supplies and carrying out product. The industries of Rhinebeck and the tin and tobacco factories at Red Hook are examples of businesses that benefitted. The chocolate factory in Annandale would eventually move to the Red Hook station stop to be near its Borden evaporated milk plant. Moreover, local people used the train to visit friends and relatives up and down the line. Summer tourists, too, enjoyed day-tripping through the countryside with its varied flora and fauna and bustling little villages.

Needless to say, the R. & C., as it was called, would have tremendous impact on Rhinecliff, stimulating commercial expansion, providing good local jobs and forging yet one more link to the wider world. Even the *Gazette* finally admitted that the hamlet was growing rapidly. Several new buildings had been put up. Several more were under construction, including a blacksmith and a wagon-making shop, the bedrock of land transportation and an

The proud crew of Engine 19 bound for Connecticut poses at the Slate Dock depot circa 1890. Courtesy of the Lee Beaujon collection.

indicator of how busy a distribution center the hamlet was becoming. As with the building of the Hudson River Railroad, many of the men who built the R. & C. settled in Rhinecliff, further increasing and diversifying its population.

The railroad was good for inland Rhinebeck, too. When work first began, the *Gazette* quipped: "Our friend Cramer is laying out his farm in corner lots. The Legislature will be applied to for a charter for the city of 'Hog Bridge.' The principal streets will be paved, and lighted with gas. Charley will be Mayor, and the town bonds will be used to build a ship canal from the Hog Bridge to the State line." Charley was right. Hog Bridge depot was the first station stop and was heavily used, not only for commercial purposes, but also for passenger service. Although the steep hill down to the dock on the westward run presented no great problem, it made sense to make up most of the trains on the eastward run at Rhinebeck level, and for loaded freight cars to be shunted up there one by one. The centerpiece of the Hog Bridge complex was a coal distribution business. A cooperage, a varnish factory and a generating plant for the Dutchess Light, Heat & Power Company would eventually be built there. Inland Rhinebeck was especially gratified that the name of the operation contained the name Rhinebeck, rather than Rhinecliff.

Rondout and Kingston also benefited by the access the new line provided to a much greater region. The R. & C. distributed not only thousands upon thousands of tons of coal, but a significant amount of Rondout's cement and brick production. The trains also brought increasing numbers of tourists to their area. A steam yacht was added to the ferries to take summer vacationers and fall hunters across the river, where trains and stagecoaches sped them to their boardinghouses, fine hotels and private camps in the mountains. Soon the *Gazette* was urging the ferry to extend its evening runs in summertime. "The last ferry leaves Rhinecliff at 7:22 and after that passengers have to risk their lives in a crowded rowboat," it pointed out. "Why can't the *Lark* make a later trip? It would accommodate large numbers and would pay the ferry company."

Still the River Prevails

As always, the river continued to be a vital source of Rhinecliffers' livelihoods. For one thing, it was a great free fishing ground. Commercial fishermen made a living by supplying New York City's increasingly varied ethnic populations with the food they were accustomed to in their homelands. James Traver, who was known to land as many as 127 herring in a single hoist, could either sell them at the dock or salt or pickle them for future shipment to the city's fast-growing Scandinavian and German populations. George Pratt went into the eel business, knowing that these immigrants also devoured eels by the barrelful. Shad roe and shad filets were in such high demand in upscale city restaurants that during the spawning season a buying agent, staked out at the depot, would send off a ton in one day. Pricey caviar was made from sturgeon roe. The fish itself was so large that its flesh was not only a cheap food, but also was used to fertilize fields. Wild ducks, resting during their migrations, were also plentiful and in demand, both for home tables and for sale. So many Rhinecliff fishermen and hunters studded the waters that the *Gazette* satirically suggested that a free hospital be established especially for them. Ice for shipping these commodities as well as dairy products, fruit and vegetables, became such a necessity that the Knickerbockers Ice Company, which usually built on the west side of the river, put up a storage house at Long Dock. Harvesting ice became a crucial source of winter income, even though the wages paid by the company were low and the cold, backbreaking, dangerous workday was from twelve to fourteen hours long.

The river continued as the hamlet's playground, too. Residents swam from the docks and picnicked on the bluffs. If William B. Astor Jr.'s fine yacht *Atalanta* and a steamboat were passing, residents enjoyed the ritual of their exchanging salutes. As soon as the river froze, everyone who had skates strapped them to their boots, and those who didn't improvised contraptions from scraps of wood and discarded metal to propel themselves over the ice. When the ice got thick enough, sleighs drawn by horses replaced the ferry. Should the ice give way and plunge a horse into the icy water, the trick was to pull the loop of rope tied around the horse's neck, causing it to fill its inner cavities with air. It would then bob to the surface where, it was hoped, strong men would be on hand to grasp its harness and pull it out. Such events were regarded as just another form of entertainment.

The streets of Rondout tell what a thriving place it was. Photograph 1890s, courtesy of the Hudson River Maritime Museum.

Rhinecliff, all agreed, was a good place to live, summer, winter, spring and fall. There were, of course, spats and outright fights, which the *Gazette* liked to call "riots." Mrs. Laughney was arrested, the *Gazette* reported, for throwing "a melee of dishes and other household utensils" at William Cole, who had not paid his rent. The affair was soon amicably settled and, as the paper admitted, "the white winged angel of peace again hovered over the classic shores of the Hudson." Sometimes actual crimes were committed, however. The Rhinecliff Hotel was robbed of goods worth $300; the perpetrator turned out to be a former employee and a counterfeiter. Thieves came from Rondout in a small sailboat and robbed Slate Dock of valuable business papers and $500. Gypsies passing through stole a colt. A scam at the depot involved switching baggage checks on passengers' luggage to luggage filled with trash.

On a more serious note, fatal train accidents were a common occurrence. A woman was pushed off the depot platform and struck by an oncoming train; her crushed body was taken to the hotel, where she died. John Shay, a laborer, fell under the wheels of a freight train as he was leaving the Rhinecliff Hotel and was killed; he was buried in a pauper's grave. McElroy, the hotel's owner, was accused of selling him a glass too many, but when the case went to trial, McElroy was exonerated. Nevertheless, Shay's body was disinterred and buried with full rites in the Catholic cemetery. John Sowers, who kept the hotel at Slate Dock with his wife Anna, was killed when he took his customary walk to the waterfront one hazy morning and, after waiting for an incoming train to pass, fell under the speeding wheels of an outgoing train; the noise of the first train had simply drowned out the noise of the second. Anna was left with a fourteen-year-old son and four daughters, the youngest no more than a toddler. But, together, they kept the hotel going until 1891, when all the girls were married and living in Kingston and the son, who had taken a job in his youth as a deckhand, had become a policeman in Brooklyn.

7

Stability versus Change

The year of the centennial of the Declaration of Independence was a time of national glory. It was also a time of national upheaval. The glory was in the great Centennial Fair at Philadelphia and the sense of inventive achievement and national cohesiveness it celebrated. Americans from across the continent flocked to the fair, brought by the country's ever-expanding railroad system. The fair drew exhibitors and visitors from around the globe, too. The most popular casual attractions were the early American kitchen and the Japanese bazaar with its tearoom and astonishing array of oriental wares for sale. But the heart of the fair was the fourteen-acre Machinery Hall. Its centerpiece was the mammoth 1,400-horsepower Corliss engine that silently and without vibration ran the American inventions that filled the hall — sewing, spinning and weaving machines, metal, stone and woodworking tools, printing presses, refrigeration compressors and the Otis elevator, to name only a few. What amazed visitors most was that this immense engine with its fifty-six-ton flywheel was started up by a slip of a girl and operated by just one man, who spent most of his time seated and legs crossed, casually reading a magazine. The London *Times* exclaimed: "The American invents as the Greeks sculpted and the Italians painted: it is genius." Among the engine's long-term effects was that it spurred urbanization, for industry was no longer dependent on water-propelled wheels.

The well-to-do in Rhinecliff, and those with railroad passes or those who had diligently saved for the journey to Philadelphia, returned with tales no newspaper account could rival. At home, however, the town's behavior was bizarre. Neither the Town of Rhinebeck nor the village put its official imprimatur on any special celebration of the nation's centennial. Nor did they join Red Hook and Tivoli in their events. Unfortunately, the year 1876 is entirely missing from archives of the extraordinarily extensive run of the *Gazette*, so it is impossible to piece together an explanation of why this should have been so. However, from what can be gleaned from scraps of information that have turned up, on February 22 the ladies of the Methodist church in the village marked Washington's Birthday with an evening entertainment that featured large portraits of Washington, General Schuyler and Chancellor Livingston, and period artifacts such as a curious dumbwaiter used by General Montgomery. Members of the congregation also impersonated the Washingtons, General Lafayette and lesser notables of the revolutionary period. The event seems mainly to have been a cheerful escape from the doldrums of winter. In late May a group of citizens posted a notice with thirty-four signatures encouraging interested citizens to meet at the Starr Institute to promote recognition of the centennial of the signing of the Declaration of Independence. The meeting was "a

fizzle"; only two men attended, neither of whom had signed the call. An extant *Gazette* clipping sarcastically remarked: "Our patriotic citizens have concluded not to celebrate until the next centennial year. What's the use to be in a hurry."

The churches filled in the gap, but mainly with fundraisers for their own projects. On the Fourth of July, the Dutch Reformed church staged an evening concert at Town Hall to benefit its Sabbath School Room. Not to be outdone, St. Joseph's parish put on a picnic with dancing in its Grove to help pay for a recent repair to the church building. Attended by over a thousand people, "it was a perfect success, as all pic-nics are which are held at that place," according to a *Gazette* snippet. The only reading of the Declaration, apparently, was at the Wey's Corners Lutheran church during an afternoon gathering at the parsonage with music and prayers, followed by a collation prepared by the church ladies and, in the evening, fireworks. Essentially, each church was using the event to beat its own tom-tom. Credit has to be given to Rhinebeck's fire company for taking its prize Pocahontas hose all the way to Hudson, the seat of Columbia County, to participate in that city's grand festivities. Still, it is a mystery why Rhinebeck did nothing to put on a fitting community celebration of July 4, 1776.

The Mary Powell, *probably the most famous day liner on the river, was launched in 1861 and would continue in service until just before the United States entered World War I. A Rondout boat, she soon stopped landing on the east side of the river. Photograph circa 1880s, courtesy of the Hudson River Maritime Museum.*

One marginally plausible explanation is that political animosities stirred up by the forthcoming presidential election were running so high that it was felt wise to hold back. The contest, the most stubbornly fought until modern times, was rigged almost every step of the way. President Ulysses S. Grant, whose laissez-faire attitudes had launched fortune hunters both inside and outside the government, would have accepted a third term with pleasure, but he was in disrepute for his cronyism. Rutherford B. Hayes, an Ohioan of unblemished reputation, took his place as the Republican standard-bearer and ran on a ticket of party reform. Samuel B. Tilden, a rich and politically savvy New Yorker, was the Democrats' nominee. Both candidates were hard-money conservatives, pledged to maintain the national currency's tie to gold. Although western farmers and miners, who strongly espoused a more fluid currency based on silver, threatened to erode Democrat solidarity by mounting the Greenback Party, Tilden won the popular vote by a margin of 250,000. However, he needed one more Electoral College vote to prevail. The votes in Florida, South Carolina, Louisiana and Oregon were contested. An electoral commission was appointed to break the impasse. Both parties bribed, intimidated and even used violence and fraud to control the recently enfranchised African Americans in the southern states. The commission decided along party lines not to recount the vote and put those states in the Hayes column, declaring him the winner on March 2, 1877, two days before the scheduled inauguration. It was the Republicans' promise to end carpetbag rule in the South and to give those states desperately needed federal aid for education and internal improvements that tipped the balance. Unfortunately, the eventual result turned out to be unfettered white supremacy in the South that lasted almost a century.

Moreover, the country was in the throes of yet another financial panic, caused by reckless railroad schemes. The same creative energy that had made the Centennial Fair such a success sprang from a freewheeling national economy dominated by robber barons who grew so rich that their lust was for power over their competitors, rather than for mere profits. A general strike by railway employees failed, but encouraged the formation of other national wage-earner organizations, such as the Knights of Labor. These, in turn, fomented more strikes, which, despite the Republican platform of reform, were punished by increasingly tough legislation. The era was dubbed by Mark Twain as "The Gilded Age."

The Hamlet Continues to Grow

Rhinecliff weathered the turmoil with its usual equanimity. In part, this was because its job base was diversified, but also because burgeoning New York City desperately needed the commodities it delivered. The New York Central Railroad upgraded its services. It bought Yonkers's discarded corrugated iron station house to replace the Rhinecliff depot that the *Gazette* had likened to a rookery. "Although not at all adequate to the demands or desserts of the traveling public," the newspaper hoped the second-hand station would be "something of an improvement." The railroad added a second livestock corral to its freight yard and bought a car to be used exclusively for funerals. It even put paid advertisements on its tickets. The Rhinebeck & Connecticut also expanded. To increase its service, it purchased one hundred new freight cars — fifty for the terminus at Boston Corners, fifty for the river terminus. It moved its engineering office from Red Hook to Slate Dock and engaged R. L. Otis of Kingston to build a roundhouse at Slate Dock for reversing the direction of its engines and cars. Using a million-and-a-half bricks, it was a mini-boom for Rondout shippers. The Delaware & Hudson Canal Company installed

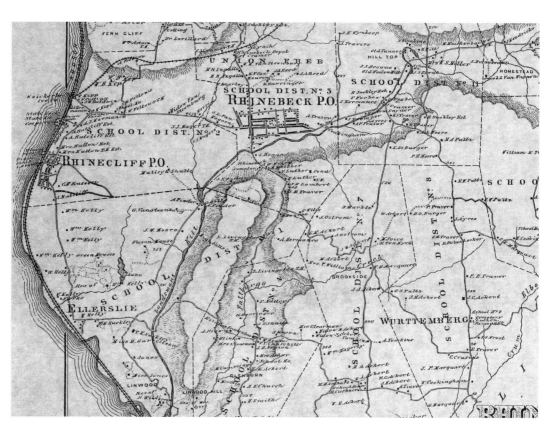

This useful map from Gray's 1875 Atlas shows the town's school districts, post offices and railroads, as well as its major landowners. Courtesy of the Dutchess County Historical Society.

two hoisting engines there to expedite unloading coal from barges to the Rhinebeck & Connecticut freight cars. In addition, the *Olcott*, a transfer boat, was used to carry railroad cars between the Ulster & Delaware and the Rhinebeck & Connecticut railroads. The future of the Rhinebeck & Connecticut looked so promising that it entered into negotiations with the New York Central to establish a direct connection between the two lines to accommodate both passengers and freight.

This increase of activity at Depot and Slate Docks spelled a precipitous decline for Long Dock. Clearly, its commercial life was nearing its end. The Knickerbocker Ice Company was enlarging its icehouse and giving it a tin roof to protect it from being set on fire by sparks spewed forth by the locomotives. During the spring, fishermen launched their boats for the shad run from the wharf. The catch was so important that three men — Pells, Talmadge and Hester — ventured down to Dobbs Ferry to follow

the run upriver. Otherwise Long Dock's uses were recreational. Hook-and-line anglers vied with seine fishermen for bass there. In winter, skaters gathered at a cove on the south side beyond reach of the ice cutters. People bound for the opposite shore by foot or sleigh departed from the dock.

At the same time, the Rhinecliff Road east of its junction with Long Dock Road was building up one house at a time. In addition, the Heermance brothers established a construction materials yard there, selling lumber, lime, brick, cement and also flour. Their major contract was to ship 90,000 barrels of cement made in East Kingston for use in the construction of the new state house in Indianapolis. The *Gazette* offered the name Heermanceville for this section of the hamlet, and old-timers still call it that to this day.

The small businesses along Shatzell Avenue leading to Depot Dock continued to prosper. The three-story brick Nathan building on the northwest corner of Shatzell Avenue and Charles Street was under construction. Thomas Hackett, the hamlet's favorite meat vendor, had already leased its first floor. Once opened, business was so good that he added milk to his offerings and was soon selling two hundred quarts a day in the neighborhood. Moreover, he carried the *Gazette*; his was the first business in the hamlet to do so. In fact, Hackett's enterprises were so successful that he added a little office to his establishment. In 1885 he would become the postmaster. A. D. Butler did well, too. He sold fresh bread, ice cream and cake; the workmanship of the pretty confections exhibited in his showcase was absolutely magnificent, the paper reported. "Boney" Ostrom made a good living painting the handsomest carriages in town, and Mr. V. C. Kihlmire continued as the local tinsmith. The Dedrick Brothers sold a variety of refreshments, including tobacco, cigars, oysters and confectionery at their Ferry House, to which a hairdressing and shaving salon was attached. Frank Culver, Rhinecliff's photograph artist, erected an easily disassembled building to replace his tent. The ferries busily crisscrossed the river, carrying tourists and businessmen to and from the train, as well as hamlet dwellers who shopped in Rondout or attended such sensations as the exhibition of an immense whale that had mistakenly cruised up the river and into the creek.

Summer tourists — those staying in the hamlet as well as those transferring to the Catskills or going to inland Rhinebeck — were welcomed as a stimulus to the economy and to ordinary daily life, although some residents liked to complain that "city vacationers put on more airs than a country trotting horse at a county fair." William Cole bought Frank Carr's steam yawl, painted it up and leased it to boating pleasure parties for twenty-five cents an hour. The three Butler brothers built a fifty-five-foot steam yacht for excursions to West Point. The Cottings offered a smaller steam yacht called the *Midget*. Business was so good in the hamlet that the stage line between Rhinebeck and Rhinecliff ran year-round, although much of the time the Rhinecliff Road was either deep in dust and full of cradle holes or blanketed with snow. Among the most exciting events was the telegraph cable crossing the river into Slate Dock, speeding national and even international communication immeasurably. In connection with the necessary excavations for the cable, twenty-five skulls and other large bones were exhumed near the R. & C. tracks. The *Gazette* was firm that an ancient Native American burial ground had been uncovered, and undoubtedly it was.

As they had always done — and would always do — hamlet dwellers built, refurbished and added outbuildings to their properties whenever they had

George Veitch was the architect for the Orchard Street school, built in 1878 for the rapidly expanding student population of the central hamlet. It boasted one very large room on both floors, but each could be divided into two by strong glass-paned doors. The steep, short pathway cut between Kelly Street and Orchard Street that students scrambled up is still often used as a shortcut. The school was converted into condominium apartments in the 1980s, but its exterior remains essentially the same. Photograph 1930s, courtesy of the Rokeby Collection.

the cash and time to do so. The Butlers put a picket fence around their house, then added a sidewalk along the road. George Veitch designed a house for a Mrs. Funda and a forty-foot-square barn with basement for Miss Mary E. Radcliff; the stones for the foundation and cellar walls came from the quarry up by the Flat Rock Schoolhouse. Having designed St. Joseph's Church, Veitch was probably also hired to plan its new pastoral residence.

Most important, Veitch was the architect for the fine, brick schoolhouse that replaced the wooden school on land owned by Charles H. Russell where Orchard Street and Valley Way meet. Thirty by thirty feet, with a classroom on each of its two stories, it became the centerpiece of the hamlet schools. Residents made an uproar claiming it was taking too long to build because an outsider had been given the contract, but as soon as the children were at their desks, they became delighted supporters. The Orchard Street School, as it was called, would serve the hamlet well for the next seventy-five years; it closed in 1956, when the Rhinebeck district consolidated all its schools in a new building in the village.

The one-room Ellerslie schoolhouse was funded by Mary Garrettson for neighboring children. The architect was the famous Alexander Jackson Davis. Located in District No. 1, it was the hamlet's first school. Today it is a residence. Photograph by Alison J. Michaels, 2008.

The building exists today as a residential condominium, but the inscription over the door, "School District No 1, 1878" and the names of the architect and the town supervisor, are still easily deciphered.

The Ellerslie School was also replaced, for the original building designed by the famous Alexander Jackson Davis had been destroyed by fire. The new board-and-batten structure, also thought to have been designed by Davis, was larger and more convenient than its predecessor, although a sole teacher still conducted all classes in one room. John Bird was the mason, and Civil War veteran Charles Champlin — both locals — did the "wood butchering," as the *Gazette* facetiously termed his carpentry. (That school would serve the community until the Ellerslie property was taken over by the Archdiocese of New York in the early 1940s. Remodeled as a residence, it stands at the south end of the hamlet where Morton Road intersects with Mill Road.) The Flat Rock School apparently was rebuilt, but it is uncertain as to when that happened.

Hamlet dwellers pursued their usual daily rounds. Isaac F. Russell was punctual in opening his post office before daybreak. Henry H. Pearson, formerly the baggage man and telegraph operator, was promoted to ticket agent. Temperance meetings were surprisingly well-attended. Bad boys stole balcony chairs, store signs, front gates and a sleigh that they dumped on an innocent's front stoop. Robert Simmons stabbed Charles Cole, who shot two pigeons owned by Joe Barber. The barman at the Rhinecliff Hotel smashed the fingers of two Poughkeepsie attackers with a mallet, sending them scurrying in pain to Rondout to get their wounds dressed.

The hamlet experienced its share of natural disasters and personal tragedies. During a drought, wells went dry and people were forced to drink river water. Epidemics of whooping cough, diphtheria and scarlet fever claimed children's lives. Women died in childbirth. Residents of all ages continued to be killed and maimed by New York Central and Rhinebeck & Connecticut trains. Everyone agreed that Rhinecliff needed a physician in the community, but none was forthcoming even though 600 people now lived in the hamlet. They also desperately needed a hook-and-ladder and bucket company, for it was widely acknowledged that in a big fire nearly every house in Rhinecliff would burn to the ground because the streets were narrow, circuitous and too often dead-ended. Moreover, a fire company would lower insurance rates. Inexplicably, however, the hamlet would have to wait over three more decades to get one.

But even in dire times, there was much merrymaking. The Daniel Learys provided an evening of classical music for friends at their home on the Ellerslie estate. According to the *Gazette,* the Isaac Shultzes offered so many good things to eat at their elegant party for young people that the table groaned under the immense weight. When, at the end of August in 1881, the aging wooden ferry *Lark* was replaced by the iron-hulled side-wheeler *Transport* with twice the carrying capacity, an immense crowd came out to welcome her. And when a flock of five hundred gulls flew towards Rondout before a gale, old-timers exclaimed that they had never seen such a fine sight.

Ties between the hamlet and the inland town improved. Virtually everyone went to the Rhinebeck Fair held at the Springbrook Driving Park on the northern outskirts of the village, and many also attended the Dutchess County Fair the following week at Washington Hollow outside Poughkeepsie. Rhinecliffers' attendance at the Knights of Pythias annual ball and the performance of a New Orleans minstrel troupe at the village

The iron-hulled side-wheeler Transport *replaced the aged wooden* Lark. *That she had twice the carrying capacity was a measure of the hamlet's growth. She ferried passengers, produce, wagons and eventually cars across the river until the beginning of World War II. Photograph 1930s, courtesy of the Rokeby Collection.*

hall was substantial. The *Gazette* gradually became less caustic. In fact, it graced hamlet news with the heading, "Doings in Our Sister Village."

Even political campaigns provided a binder. In 1880, when Republican "dark horse" candidate James Garfield of Ohio ran against the equally "dark horse" Pennsylvania Democrat Winfield Scott Hancock for the presidency of the United States, the *Gazette* reported that Rhinecliff was "the liveliest place of its size along the river on the political question." Rivalry between the parties ran high. Residents of both parties lavishly festooned their houses with emblems and mottos. The hamlet's Republican mass meeting was the largest ever assembled. William B. Astor Jr. was its chairman. Followers, including the Rondout Club, marched through the streets to martial music and roaring cannon, while swinging an 80-by-40-inch banner from an immensely tall pole topped by a broom to signify a clean sweep of all elective offices. The Rhinecliff Hotel and the Dedrick brothers' saloon were decorated with Chinese lanterns. Martin Heermance addressed the crowd, and the glee club sang. Immediately afterwards, Astor presented the boys' gun squad with fine uniforms and named them the Astor Gun Squad.

To swell the already large contingent of Democrats at their party rally, 700 came to the hamlet from the west side of the Hudson, many of them brought from afar to the ferry by Cornell's Oswego & Western Railroad, while two trainloads came from Red Hook and the Madalin section of Tivoli. The Democrats' pole was almost as tall as the Republicans' and was ornamented with red, white and blue ribbons and a gilded ball. William Kelly's widow and brother financed its gun squad. Both parties' squads proselytized near or far almost every evening.

The huge crowds that went to the polls were unusually decorous. Garfield won by a plurality of only 10,000 out of 9,000,000 votes cast. However,

having taken the populous states of New York and Indiana, his electoral vote edge was much more impressive, 214 to 155. The Republican Party celebrated with a fine spread at the Rhinecliff Hotel. The 160 guests consumed oyster stew, oyster pie, and scalloped and fried oysters, finishing off the feast with cake, pie, candies, oranges, tea and coffee. They then serenaded Heermance, who presented the men with a box of first-class cigars. (Women, of course, could not vote.) Afterwards the guests went on to the village where they made the streets echo with their cannon, and a prominent restaurateur gave them more refreshments. A good deal of that excitement also had to do with William Bergh Kip's election as town supervisor. His was an easily anticipated victory, as the inland town was solidly conservative.

Another tie that bound the inland town and the riverside hamlet more closely was the personal transportation machine called a cycle or a high-wheeler. With an enormous wheel in the front and a tiny wheel in the back, it was, at first, an object of rollicking satire. "A man should receive a large salary for imitating a monkey, dancing after the sweet tones of a hand-organ, which he certainly has to do to keep the affair in motion," the *Gazette* quipped. But improvements came one after another in the form of equally sized wheels (bicycles), pneumatic rubber tires and safety brakes. The horizons it opened to man, woman and child, at infinitely lower cost than the feed and attention required by a horse, are hard to imagine. Its popularity with women was especially high, because it not only gave them freedoms almost overnight that fifty years of concerted women's rights activities had been unable to do, but also because bicycling changed forever the way they dressed. Expected mockery was expressed in a ditty that went:

Sing a song of Bloomers, out for a ride
With four and twenty bad boys, running
    at her side.

While the maid was coasting, the boys
    began to sing:
"Get onto her shape", you know, and all
    that sort of thing.

But "that sort of thing" stopped few women riders who could afford to buy a bicycle or could borrow one.

The Estates Endure on Shifting Sands

Nevertheless, inland Rhinebeck lost none of its nostalgia for the Livingston-dominated past. In a manifestation of the class snobbery typical of that age, Edward M. Smith in his 1881 *History of Rhinebeck* — a valuable, though not a wholly accurate source today — used his convoluted description of the long-deceased Catherine Livingston Garrettson, whose devout Methodist faith made her an egalitarian, to highlight the impenetrable social division between "elite" and "ordinary" people.

> Of course, by her birth and position, Mrs. Garrettson was excluded from the mass of people, and it did not fall to their lot to know to what extent the unfortunate and suffering engaged her sympathies. The working man and woman, who are self-supporting, never in need or distress, have no points of contact with the higher grades of society, and of necessity know little of them. *They* come *down* only to visit the sick, feed the hungry and clothe the naked; and to the working people, who are neither sick, hungry or naked, they are of no *earthly* account, when they are not customers.

What these words signified in this time of transition was that gentility was becoming the warp and woof of social interaction in inland Rhinebeck. Rhinecliff had its own version of it, although it was far less infected by its germ than the village. Still, Rhinecliff did not quite know how to fit into the unvarnished go-getism, the prudish morals and the gentrification that marked this phase of the "gilded age."

This disorientation was apparent among the great estate owners as well as lesser householders. Especially in the southern reaches of the waterfront, newly rich outsiders replaced "owners of breeding." Augustus James's Linwood had been sold at auction during the Panic of 1877 for a mere $25,000. The buyer soon went bankrupt. He sold it to a New York City man named Dunning, who partially tore it down, then sold it for $29,000 to New York City brewer, Jacob Ruppert. Ruppert was distinctly not "of the manor born," but at least the fine property

In 1883, Jacob Ruppert, a prosperous New York City brewer, bought Linwood, which had gone through several owners who were bankrupted by the Panic of 1877. The last one had begun tearing down the original house. Ruppert finished demolishing it and built this rambling Queen Anne mansion in its stead. Postcard late 1870s, courtesy of Sherman-Mann Ephemera Collection of Catskill and Rhinebeck, N.Y.

William B. Astor Jr. never stopped upgrading his property. This gatehouse on River Road was designed by Louis A. Ehlers, a prominent landscapist who also laid out a major cattle- and horse-breeding enterprise on Astor's northern acres. Note the fine gates and the greenhouses just inside the property. Photograph 1980s, courtesy of Tom Daley.

had found an owner with staying power. The first thing Ruppert did was finish demolishing the over-eighty-year-old house and replace it with a rambling wooden Queen Anne mansion that, from photographs, seems more suited to the popular New Jersey shore than the banks of the noble Hudson.

Elizabeth Jones had died in 1876 and left Wyndclyffe to her nephew, Edward Jones. When he died in 1886, it was sold to another New York City brewer, Andrew Finck, whose local distinction was that he piped cold beer down to the waterfront tennis court. Ellerslie's steady deterioration was accelerated by the financial panics. The only exception to the trend, perhaps, was Wildercliff. Miss Mary Garrettson, who inherited it from her mother, died in 1879. Thomas Suckley, whose daughter and wife also died that year, bought it for his cousins; their daughter was slightly younger than his dear Kittie and did much to cheer his last lonely days when his only living child, Robert, was away at school and college.

The northern section fared slightly better. William Bergh Kip, who all along had been active in town businesses and philanthropies, was town supervisor until his death in 1888. Then, his widow continued the farming operation at Ankony with the excellent help of a headman whom her husband had trained. When she died, the next generation was old enough to carry on.

William B. Astor Jr. was, of course, in a class by himself; if economic swings touched him, he did not feel them. He increased Ferncliff to five hundred acres and, in 1877, built a gatehouse designed by Louis A. Ehlers, a prominent landscapist who also helped him lay out a major cattle and horse-breeding enterprise on his northern acres. They became so close that Astor gave Ehlers a contiguous spread of land, on which Ehlers built a house.

In short, the estates endured, but upon shifting sands. An entirely new era was at hand, impelled as before by invention, financial panic and chance, and aided by the usual human foibles. Change started slowly, but soon gained momentum. One of the main differences from the past was that the national arena within which Rhinecliff interacted would become international. Even self-contained Rhinecliff could not avoid being carried into global affairs.

8

Levi Parsons Morton, Vice President of the United States

When William B. Kelly's widow died in 1885, Ellerslie was in an advanced state of decay. The house was crumbling; the roofs of the barns were falling in; the once immaculately maintained woods were filled with boot-clinging brush; unpruned shrubberies sprawled; and the lake was clogged with slimy weeds and frogs. Then, fortune struck. It was bought at auction at, some said, half its value, by the international financier and former United States Minister to France, Levi P. Morton. He not only put everything right, but carried on Kelly's caring outreach to the community. His multiple philanthropies would bolster the hamlet immediately and for years to come. In fact, they continue to do so today.

Morton was a self-made multimillionaire. His, however, was not a Horatio Alger story. Quite the contrary, he was one of those hardy New England boys whose progenitors were among the first settlers of the Plymouth Colony. Unlike the possessors of vast Hudson Valley fiefdoms such as the Beekmans and Livingstons, their heritage was in making their own way from generation to generation. Morton was born in 1824 in Shoreham, Vermont, a village four miles from

Lake Champlain where his father was the minister of a struggling Congregational parish. His mother had been a schoolteacher. (Levi was named for her brother, the first protestant missionary to Syria.) Together, Morton's parents provided him with two Mayflower ancestors and at least eighty kin who had arrived in America before 1650; descendants still lived in the old homesteads. He was taught to be upright, conservative and caring, and would be just that until he died on his ninety-sixth birthday.

Morton received a decent common-school education from the series of New England towns to which his father was called, but he was only fourteen years old when he took his first job away from home. It was at a general store in Enfield, New Hampshire, where he not only tended shop but, in his spare time, was required to act as a hired hand for the owner in whose house he boarded. After two years, he quit. Then fortune struck, as it would again and again. He got a job in a general store near Concord, New Hampshire, and although he was still a teenager, his employer sent him to Hanover to open a branch store. There he boarded with Dartmouth College's Latin professor — who happened to be Daniel Webster's brother-in-law — and received the intellectual stimulation that his abbreviated formal education had not provided. The store failed, but when the principal creditor, the head of the largest importing house in Boston, came to Hanover to see what he could salvage, he found Morton's record-keeping so meticulous that he not only engaged him to continue managing the store, but became his mentor. From that point on, Morton's career path was on such a dizzying upward spiral that his grandfather could only gasp to his mother, "I hear Levi is prospering in this world's goods, I fear lest it be at the cost of his soul."

Morton went on to New York City, that Mecca of all ambitious New England boys, where, nose still to the grindstone, he became a partner in another trading company. In 1856 he married Lucy Kimball, also from an old New England family, whom he had first met when she was a schoolgirl in Hanover. Ideally suited, their sole abiding sorrow was the death of their daughter as a baby; she was an only child.

For the next five years Morton dealt successfully in Southern cotton. He left no record of his

Levi P. Morton, who had been Minister to France and would become Vice President of the United States, Governor of New York and gentleman farmer, sold his "cottage" in Newport and bought Ellerslie just as the eldest of his brood of five energetic girls was about to become an eligible young lady. Photograph late 1870s, courtesy of the Morton Memorial Library.

feelings about trading in slave-produced goods, but his family were early abolitionists and Morton was, through thick and through thin, an ardent, lifelong supporter of the Republican Party starting with Abraham Lincoln. Southern creditors who could not pay their bills bankrupted his company, whereupon he made a radical career change. He went into international banking. It was a brave move; paper "greenbacks," issued to pay for the war, were worth only thirty-five cents to the dollar. However, Junius S. Morgan, a colleague from Morton's Boston days and, not incidentally, also a descendant of an early Plymouth Colony family (and, yes, the father of J. P. Morgan), had a bank in London and sent him clients. Morton's reputation for fair dealing was so strong that others flocked to him. To his great credit, one of the first payments he made with his profits was to reimburse the men who had suffered losses from his bankruptcy. He also bought a fine "cottage" called Fairlawn in Newport, Rhode Island, where he and his wife entertained delightfully, if comparatively simply. Among their guests was President Ulysses S. Grant, Morton's friend and hero to whose election campaign he had liberally contributed.

In 1871, tragedy struck. Lucy Morton died. Morton dulled his grief by plunging single-mindedly into business. His most important work was the peaceful arbitration of the United States' claims (the historic Alabama Claims) against the British for breaking neutrality during the Civil War by sending warships to the Confederacy. These warships had destroyed an estimated 100,000 tons of Union shipping, for which the United States received a $15,550,000 award. The settlement, of which Morton got a percentage, placed him in the limelight of international finance.

Somehow, Morton found time during the negotiations to court and marry Anna Street, a charming young woman in her mid-twenties who had been born in Poughkeepsie. Her family had Livingston antecedents and was part of New York's Knickerbocker society. She would give him the special joy of five daughters; sadly, their only son died in infancy.

Having reached the pinnacle in business, Morton decided to round out his life with a political career, as was considered fitting in that era for an affluent, well-connected man. Although it is hard to believe he was unaware of the rampant wheeling and dealing involved, he seems to have entered the arena with the innocence of a lamb. In addition, he was naturally reticent, never having given a public speech and having no desire to do so. Still, he performed splendidly as the Republican Party's national financial chairman, which made him sufficiently confident to run for the congressional seat in New York City's Eleventh District, then New York City's "silk stocking" district, where he owned a house on the corner of 5th Avenue and 42nd Street. His opponent cast him as "a tool of Wall Street," and he lost. Two years later, he ran again and won.

A congressional reporter described Morton as "six feet tall, straight-limbed, and erect ... a close listener, a silent critic, a genial answerer; neither intrusive nor obtrusive." Morton spoke concisely, but persuasively, in favor of the gold standard and the protective tariff. Moreover, his splendid home was noted for its warm hospitality and its urbanity. All this did Morton little good politically, however, for New York State's Conkling machine, to which he was inextricably bound, was undergoing a wracking transition. Besides, the party cared only for his money. In 1880, Morton had a fluttering hope of becoming his friend James Garfield's choice for vice president; instead it went to Conkling's nominee, Chester A. Arthur. Morton then agreed to head fundraising for the campaign, expecting to become secretary of the treasury. Garfield won, but Morton was not even considered for the position. Instead, he was appointed minister to France, an honor open only to men who had the fortune to pay their way.

In France, Morton's innate civility made him many friends within the government and the diplomatic community. However, the demands on his talents were mild. He began his mission by changing the quarters of the ministry from an obscure second-floor location on *avenue Kléber* in Passy (now the *place des États-Unis*) to the more distinguished 35, *rue Galilée* just around the corner. The main focus of his tenure was France's gift of the Statue of Liberty to the United States. Among his many duties in this connection was hammering the first rivet; it went into her left toe.

When Democrat Grover Cleveland was elected president, Morton returned home. In 1885 he appealed to the New York State Legislature to appoint him United States Senator. (The 17th Amendment giving the selection of senators to the voting populace would not be passed until 1913.) It did not. In 1887 he tried again, but was forced to withdraw his name in the interests of party unity.

Ellerslie

During this unsettled time, Morton's wife persuaded him to sell their Newport mansion and to buy Ellerslie. With a brood of young girls, perhaps she thought a quiet, rural setting along the Hudson River more appropriate than the dazzling social life of Newport, the country's most fashionable seaside resort. At the same time, Anna may have been trying to divert her husband's energies from fruitless political striving. Moreover, not only was Rhinecliff near her childhood home and her Livingston connections, but the Mortons must have known of Rhinecliff through Charles H. Russell, who owned a summer "cottage" at Newport, and the Mortons would have at least rubbed shoulders with his family. If not there, then they almost certainly would have in New York. In addition, the Delanos and the Aspinwalls of nearby Barrytown also had very

early Plymouth antecedents. The Mortons would have been acquainted with the Astors, too. How much this charmed circle of highly successful New York businessmen would see of each other upriver is not clear, but it was undoubtedly pleasant for the Mortons that they were in the neighborhood. Whatever the case, in 1885 Morton bought Ellerslie and set out to add scientific farmer to his myriad accomplishments.

The Ellerslie Morton bought was the over 900 acres that Kelly had assembled piece by piece during his ownership. Finding the old house unsalvageable, Morton took what seemed to him the only reasonable course and had it torn down. As architect for his new mansion, he chose America's high-fashion designer, Richard Morris Hunt. Hunt had already built a ballroom for Morton's place at Newport and a stable for his New York City house, and the two had become close friends. (Mrs. Hunt was Charles H. Russell's sister-in-law, a perfect example of how tightly knit New York society was.) The new mansion, probably on instructions from Morton — Hunt was adept at giving clients what they wanted — was unlike any other in Hunt's extensive oeuvre. It bore no resemblance whatever to the Renaissance palaces he built for the Vanderbilts on Fifth Avenue, or the neo-classical "cottages" he designed for them at Newport. Nor was it similar to the medieval fort genre he was employing in Hyde Park at this same time for New York financier Archibald Rogers. Its style was Tudoresque, mildly reminiscent of Hunt's much earlier stick-style houses or his casino at Newport. The first floor was constructed of solid granite blocks; the second and third stories were stuccoed and timbered. Ample verandas surrounded three sides. A very large, but not grandiose dwelling, it fitted well into the landscape.

Photographs of the interiors show them to have been handsome and comfortable, well-suited to family life. The great hall was twenty-five feet wide,

Morton tore down the decaying house and hired his friend, society architect Richard Morris Hunt, to build this Tudoresque mansion. Despite its grand appearance, it was a comfortable family home. The flag on the roof signified that the vice president of the United States was in residence. Postcard circa 1890, collection of the author.

its ceiling ribbed by black oak beams; its high wainscoting was also of oak. Among the rooms on the first floor were a drawing room, a dining room, a salon, a library where Morton worked, and two clerk's offices. Fireplaces abounded. Upstairs were the family rooms, although in reality the family had the run of the entire place. By the fall of 1887, slaters were putting on the roof and painters were giving the Tudor elements their first coat of paint.

To be near at hand during construction, Morton rented a charming house, called Bois Doré, along the Landsman Kill in the village. It was there that Morton received the glorious news that he had been nominated to be the running mate of the Republican presidential candidate, Benjamin Harrison of Indiana. The story is that it took ninety-nine of the hundred delegates — and perhaps also Morton himself — by surprise. The whole of Rhinebeck waited breathlessly for Chicago to telegraph the news. When it came, their enthusiasm knew no bounds. They lighted a bonfire and shot off fireworks on the green in front of the hotel. A large delegation of both political persuasions marched to Bois Doré to congratulate Morton on being the first Rhinebeckian to become a candidate on the national ticket. His reply was brief, "At this midnight hour I will not attempt, or will you expect any extended remarks. I simply wish to thank you for the compliment of your presence."

Harrison and Morton as a ticket were either complementary or a mismatch, depending on the point of view, for the candidates had been put together only for regional balance and electoral votes, of which New York offered a hefty thirty-six. Both Morton and Harrison were devout Christians in an election where adherence to religious values played a crucial role. Both enjoyed unblemished careers. However, Harrison was a compelling public speaker, but cold in private. In contrast, Morton was impressive in small groups, but still could not — and did not — give rousing speeches. As was typical of the times, the press peppered their campaign with cutting, witty cartoons and doggerel. Those featuring Morton ribbed him as a skinny bride of Wall Street, as a fixer praying over a "Bar'l o' $", for buying votes, and also as a Puritan who owned Washington's Shoreham Hotel (named after Morton's birthplace), at whose bar congressmen refreshed themselves liberally while cutting deals. The dominant issue was the tariff, then the federal government's main source of revenue. Democrats favored free trade; Republicans favored protectionism.

The Rhinebeck Hotel was continually filled with politicians during the campaign, adding a flurry of excitement to the town. However, Morton and his family awaited election results at their new mansion via a special telegraph wire run in for the purpose. Richard Morris Hunt and his wife kept them company. It was a cliffhanger. Despite the Republicans' huge war chest and their scurrilous stories that incumbent President Cleveland beat his young wife and got drunk on the presidential yacht, the Democrats won the popular vote by 96,000. But, as the Republican Party had intended when it joined the two of them together on the ticket, Harrison and Morton took New York and Indiana, and they won the electoral vote 233 to 168. Levi P. Morton was well pleased.

Rhinecliff, and Rhinebeck, too, were ecstatic to have such a great political celebrity in their midst. The *Gazette* followed with relish the entire family's comings and goings, as well as their grand restoration of the estate. It published detailed accounts of the immense new cow barns and the dairy complex that contained the powerhouse for the new invention — electricity. (To run the powerhouse Morton brought John Heywood down from Troy; his descendants are still a vital part of the hamlet.) The paper spoke of the fine carriage house and of the icehouse, the smokehouse, the dollhouse and, especially, the elegant new greenhouses fabricated by the Lord and Burnham Company of Irvington-on-Hudson, still famous today, that replaced Kelly's greenhouses that had so hopelessly deteriorated. There is no record of who did the landscaping, other than that the gardens were under the capable hands of Alexander McLellan, who "produced such flowers as never before had been seen" and that the formal Italian garden by the lake required the constant care of fourteen Italian gardeners. It is clear, however, that the lake, the splendid trees and most of the crushed bluestone drives were the remains of William B. Kelly's Ellerslie.

Across the road, Robert Suckley, who had just inherited Wilderstein, close to half a million dollars, and a good deal of Rhinebeck real estate from his father, had hired Arnout Cannon, a prominent Poughkeepsie architect, to transform the family's modest Italianate villa into a Queen Anne extravaganza. Its stunning five-story tower was a confection of glittering windows and geometric paneling, topped by a candlesnuffer roof, and crowned with a lightning rod disguised as a compass rising out of a bed of sunflowers. Of the outbuildings, only the old icehouse and a small barn were preserved, but scattered around the fifty-two acres were Lord and Burnham greenhouses with a neo-colonial potting shed, and a brand new boathouse for his sailboats and iceboats and a sleek launch. Most satisfying of all was a dramatically sited brick carriage house and stables whose three ventilators were hidden within an immense onion-shaped dome, an octagonal tower decorated with metal flowers, and a cupola embellished with metal cattails. How Henry W. Otis of Kingston and R. Alex Decker of Rhinebeck finished the immense, complicated Queen Anne structure in less than six months seems a miracle. Seen against the background of the river and the mountains beyond, the effect was — and is — fanciful and ingenious, and at the same time, majestic.

Ellerslie gardens and greenhouses. Postcard circa 1900, courtesy of Harry Heywood.

View of Morton's mansion from the lake. Behind the trees on the first level down was an Italian garden that was said to require the attention of twenty-six Italian gardeners. Photograph circa 1900, courtesy of the Morton Memorial Library.

When Thomas Suckley died, his remaining child, Robert, inherited a half a million dollars and a great deal of real estate. The first thing Robert did was to transform the simple Italianate Wilderstein into a Queen Anne confection. This is the third painting scheme. Almost immediately, Mrs. Suckley decided that she did not like it and commanded that the house be returned to somber brown with a touch of very dark red. Photograph 1905, courtesy of Wilderstein Preservation.

Bessie and Robert Suckley on the side porch with three of their soon-to-be six children. Bessie's mother is enthroned above. Her sister Janet is on the left. Photograph 1890, courtesy of Wilderstein Preservation.

The interiors of Suckley's transformed house were designed and installed by Joseph Burr Tiffany, a cousin of the more prominent Louis Comfort Tiffany. In the fashion that had roots in the Centennial Fair, each room expressed a particular époque: the hall, staircase and dining room were in the English Jacobean style, the library in the Flemish medieval style, the drawing room in Louis XVI and the parlor in American colonial. In the midst of his work, Tiffany was asked to install fittings for electric light, to be supplied by a powerhouse Suckley himself was designing on his land on the Landsman Kill. Despite the famous blizzard of 1888, the complex interiors were finished within the allotted year, aided by the fact that much of the woodwork was available off the shelf in New York City, where skilled European craftsmen kept the purveyors well stocked.

To help him with the landscaping and gardens, Suckley hired the aging, but still active Calvert Vaux, former partner of Andrew Jackson Downing who had so tragically drowned in a steamboat accident many years before. In those earlier days, Vaux had also teamed up with the equally famous Frederick Law Olmsted, with whom he had won the competition for the design of Central Park in Manhattan.

Rhinecliff, too, was enjoying its greatest burst of construction, fostered by its prospering shipping and its railroads. The steamer *Ansonia* carried her biggest load in years — 300 barrels of apples, 50 bales of hay, 15 barrels of nuts, and many small lots. Cole's cooperage could not keep up with orders for barrels; he planned to enlarge his shop and build a large shed. Elijah Bathrick fabricated virtually anything he turned his hand to, from shoes to clocks, houses, bicycles, wagons, sleighs and boats. Frederick M. Dedrick built a new hotel in the

Queen Anne style back of the depot. James Kearns, a stonemason, improved the Orchard Street School grounds by taking stone from its lot for a new wall at Jacob Ruppert's Linwood and for Archibald Roger's fortress-style house in Hyde Park. Not all the schoolchildren agreed that this was an improvement, however, for climbing on the stones was one of their favorite free-time activities. The Brice Building across from O'Brien's was added to the Shatzell Avenue business district. Catering to drummers, it offered a well-kept bar and a livery with horses and wagons for hire.

More houses were built during this decade than any other in Rhinecliff's history. Although now more populous, Rhinecliff did not change its community ways, however. Families reveled in the Saturday night clambakes in the locust grove at Slate Dock put on by the employees of the Rhinebeck & Connecticut Railroad. They faithfully attended the church of their choice and participated in their community outreach programs. They patronized the fundraisers of each other's churches. Many took advantage of the steamer *Mary Powell*'s one-dollar

Workers at the rock quarry at the junction of Rhinecliff and River Roads. Photograph early 1900s, courtesy of Richard Kopystanski.

round-trip excursion to New York City, even though it departed at five o'clock in the morning from Rondout.

Everyone had an opinion about the case of Mrs. Mary Brandow and her mother, Mrs. Burns, who were arrested for "disorderly conduct" — perhaps extreme drunkenness, but probably prostitution, also. Justice Coon of Rhinecliff found them guilty and sentenced Mrs. Brandow to six months in the Albany jail, and her mother to thirty days in the county jail. Such behavior, he said, could not be tolerated by the respectable and law-abiding people of Rhinecliff. Typically, there was a good deal of commiseration with Jerome Harris, whose garden had been ravaged by James Ryan's cow, but many switched sides when Harris sued Ryan for damages of twenty-five dollars. Everyone was horrified when some miserable malefactor tried to poison the Dedricks' cocker spaniel puppy.

A peaceful moment around the turn of the century. Shatzell Avenue turns into the northern section of Orchard Street, passing the Union Hotel. Photograph 1910, courtesy of Richard Kopystanski.

At the Orchard Street School, girls won all the badges of honor for attendance, recitation and examinations. Pupils and teachers alike were thrilled when visited by Morton's daughters. Professor C.V. Coon, the school's principal, bought a beautiful new Cortland carriage; with his pretty pony, according to the *Gazette*, he had "one of the finest turnouts in town." Everybody enjoyed the fine display the estate owners' carriages made at the depot; sometimes they were all there at the same time. And Rhinecliffers were visibly impressed when Astor's new yacht, *Nourmahal*, or his friend William K. Vanderbilt's *Alva* was riding at anchor in the river.

In 1891 the *Gazette* changed its tune towards Rhinecliff, instituting a special department for the hamlet's news. The change was announced on its editorial page, where it stated, "By employing an able and active correspondent, we hope to be able to present our Rhinecliff readers all the happenings in their village, and outside of its literary and other features, to make the paper well worth its price for Rhinecliff news alone." Single copies would be for sale on Saturday mornings, its day of publication, or by mail for $1.50 a year.

Tribulations at Ellerslie

With so much local hustle and bustle to keep them busy, Rhinecliffers did not notice that Levi P. Morton's stint as vice president was far from a complete success. Soon after the election, he had foolishly written President-elect Harrison offering to help him with his cabinet appointments. Harrison fired off a handwritten retort telling Morton that cabinet selection was the responsibility of the president alone. This interchange marked the tenor of their relationship throughout their term, although Morton never stopped trying to become more intimate by inviting Harrison and his family to make use of his house in New York City. He even arranged for a steam yacht to carry them up the river to visit Ellerslie, but the president could never find the time to accept either offer.

Nor was Morton's domestic life serene. Although Anna had earned a reputation as an intelligent and delightful Washington hostess, she was not physically or mentally strong. As the hot weather came in the spring of 1889, she collapsed. She left Washington for Europe with their teenaged daughter Edith in search of a cure at the Carlsbad and St. Moritz spas. Anna wrote from Europe that she was escaping from their home because of her weak nerves. "O what will you do without me?" she wailed to Levi. "Who will take care of the children?" Edith warned her father that a gentleman was pleasing her mother with strawberries and flowers. However, when they finally returned to Ellerslie, they were greeted with welcome banners stretched across the driveway, wreaths and garlands decorating the verandas and, inside the flower-filled mansion, one of the girls playing "Home, Sweet Home" on the piano.

In the 1892 election President Harrison summarily cast off Morton for Whitelaw Reid, Morton's erstwhile friend. It could not have been much solace for Morton that the Cleveland ticket won by a wide margin, or that the panic of 1893, the worst so far in the nation's history, would bedevil the incoming administration. Over 15,000 commercial businesses and 491 banks failed; almost a third of all railroad mileage went into the hands of receivers. Free from political responsibilities, the entire Morton family traveled abroad, but Morton stayed in touch with his farm operation. When his great dairy barn burned down in 1893, he immediately rebuilt it, increasing its size and adding state-of-the-art improvements. Employing a Newport architect and Rhinebeck builders, Morton oversaw the construction of the 297-foot-long and 50-foot-high new edifice. Up to

100 men worked on it: 70 carpenters, 10 masons and 20 laborers. At the same time, the rebuilding of the destroyed incubators and brooder house required another gang of workmen. Giving steady employment to so many in the midst of a growing depression was viewed as one more example of Morton's commitment to the community.

Soon after Morton returned to the United States, New York Republicans chose him as their candidate for governor. Winning easily, he at last hit his political stride by perfecting the art of treading the tightrope between acceding to the wishes of the party bosses and running the state in his own conscientious fashion. Both he and the people of Rhinecliff were delighted with his residency in Albany, for it made it easy for him to stop off at Ellerslie when shuttling back and forth between the state capital and New York City. Anna Morton was once more able to perform the role of gracious hostess as the governor's wife. She also entertained frequently at Ellerslie, putting on charming house parties to draw beaux from afar for her girls.

In 1896, Morton declined to run for a second term. A group of gold-standard Republicans had tempted him to believe that, if he ran for president, he could rescue the country from its financial woes. Although he never actually stepped forward, he assiduously kept scrapbooks of the campaign waged in his behalf. In the end, the Midwest won out again. William McKinley, an Ohio man, took the Republican nomination. After a hard-fought battle against the spellbinding populist orator William Jennings Bryan, who championed silver-backed money, McKinley was elected president. Morton never again ran for public office.

The Fabulous Kingston Point Amusement Park

The Delaware & Hudson Canal closed down in 1898. It had been losing commerce to the Erie Railroad since 1858, but it was the opening of the Poughkeepsie Railroad Bridge in 1888 that spelled its doom. Few in Rhinecliff missed the canal, although it would clearly affect traffic on the R. & C. Many in the hamlet even thought its loss was more than made up for by the opening that same year of Kingston Point Amusement Park. Samuel Decker Coykendall, heir to the Cornell empire, was the magician who brought the park into fruition. He bought the original ferry-landing site in 1893 and built a long steamboat pier to accommodate day liners. He then engaged Downing Vaux, son of Calvert Vaux, to design a wondrous pleasure park with brick paths, exotic plants, lagoons with beaches for boating, a merry-go-round, a bandstand and, best of all, a Ferris wheel and thousands of electric lights, undoubtedly inspired by the 1893 Chicago World's Fair.

Alcoholic beverages were dispensed only at the Oriental Hotel, just outside park limits, for the park aimed to be the ideal destination for a family outing. That it was. Almost immediately it was the favorite day-excursion for New Yorkers of all classes, who came up on the huge day liners in the morning and returned in the evening gratified by a full day of pleasure. The four-decked side-wheeler *Washington Irving*, built for the trade, carried 6,000 passengers, for instance. The Ulster & Delaware Railroad brought in tourists from the Catskill hotels and rooming houses. A trolley connected the Point with the ferry from Rhinecliff, which carried east bankers, eager as any to join the fun, as well as New York Central and Rhinebeck & Connecticut riders. Kingstonians, who had no other public park, used it freely, for there was no admission charge. In 1903 the amusement park attracted more than one million visitors. Few of them, however, crossed to the other side of the river except those that lived there or were passing through.

Literally millions of pleasure-seekers cruised up the Hudson from New York City with their families to enjoy a glorious day at Kingston Point Park, built in 1898 on the site of the old ferry landing. Note the Ferris wheel, a new invention. Rhinecliff can barely be seen behind the little sailboat. Postcard 1908, courtesy of the Hudson River Maritime Museum.

The Spanish-American War

The United States was still working out of its long and deep financial panic when it declared war against Spain in 1898. The catalyst was the sinking of the American warship *Maine*, purportedly by the Spanish, in the harbor at Havana, Cuba, an island that had long been viewed as the key to the United States' control of the Caribbean.

"Remember the Maine" became the national war cry. Despite Democrats' general opposition to what they regarded as unwonted imperialism, Rhinecliffers joined the multitudes and the three bands assembled at its railway station to witness the departure of the Fourteenth Separate Company that had been ferried over from Kingston. The company's destination was Hempstead Plains, Long Island, where troops would receive minimal training before being sent to liberate the Cubans from Spanish control. The war spread to the Spanish-controlled Philippines, where the United States' "steel navy" — brought into on-the-ready status by Theodore Roosevelt, who had left the job of assistant naval secretary to take part in the war — quickly demolished Spain's outmoded squadron at Manila Bay. Meanwhile, in Cuba, the untested American army — even Roosevelt's famous Rough Riders displayed more spirit than expertise — easily crushed the Spanish. That the horses of the merry-go-round at Kingston Point Park were renamed for war heroes gives some indication of how excited the American people were made by the victory.

No Rhinecliff men are recorded as fighting in this two-pronged war. And, although the United States government accepted Jack Astor's offer of his double-decked steel yacht *Nourmahal* for use as a gunboat, it did not see battle. Nor did the fully equipped six-gun Mountain Battery he financed to fight in the Philippines engage in more than a skirmish. A young elite corps, comprising ninety-nine men and three officers drawn from the world over, the Mountain Battery was known mainly for its smart, valet-immaculate uniforms, state-of-the-art equipment and the men's perfect physiques. About twenty-three years of age, their ideal height was 5'9", their weight 158 pounds. When the corps passed through St. Louis on its way to San Francisco, a reporter remarked that it "looked like a lot of college athletes togged up in soldier clothes and out for a lark." However, during its sole, brief battle in Manila, three of them were killed and seven wounded; there were also two deaths from disease. The company then sailed to New York City where they were given a huge parade followed by festivities at the fashionable 71st Regiment Armory on Park Avenue.

The Spanish-American War may have been over quickly, but its repercussions were profound. The United States had entered into the world arena in a way that would affect even its smallest hamlets for years to come.

9

The Progressive Era

The turn of a century, although based on a man-made system of counting the passage of time, always seems to produce a special sense of destiny. The twentieth century was no exception. Six months after President William McKinley's inauguration in 1901, he was assassinated by an anarchist while visiting the Pan-American Exposition in Buffalo. Theodore Roosevelt, who had been enjoying governing New York State with ebullient vigor when he was reluctantly persuaded to be McKinley's running mate, was suddenly elevated to the presidency.

It is safe to say that nobody has relished being chief executive of the nation more than forty-two-year-old, freewheeling Teddy. Determined to bring the country up to date, he immediately set out to curb the excesses of the post-Civil War "Gilded Age." He enforced the existing antitrust law and strengthened it. To mitigate the friction between restless labor and grasping industrial magnates, he established the Department of Commerce and Labor. Elected president in his own right by a landslide in 1904 (even Rhinecliff, with its strong Democratic Party, delivered 138 votes for "the cowboy") he got Congress to pass a Pure Food and Drug Act, as well as a Meat Inspection Act. To energize the conservation of natural resources, he set up a commission to inventory them, laying the groundwork for the National Park system.

This progressive domestic agenda responded to the temper of the times. In Rhinecliff it was exemplified by Holiday Farm, whose purpose was to give tenement children recently released from New York City hospitals a chance to recuperate in a friendly, fresh-air setting. Mary, Levi P. Morton's youngest daughter, was its moving force. Her father owned the old Hutton house north of the depot and fitted it up for the purpose with running water, plumbing, a decent kitchen and, eventually, central heat. That spring the farm received twelve little patients recommended by doctors attached to the city's Ruptured and Crippled, Bellevue and Presbyterian hospitals. The children were to stay there for three weeks to six months, depending on their needs. Over the summer the numbers rose to thirty patients from three to twelve years of age. The first annual report declared the charity a resounding success — except for a bout of whooping cough. "Kindness worked wonders on only too often hardened little natures," it said in the words of benefactors of those times.

Hamlet residents pitched in enthusiastically as the numbers of patients steadily increased. The Rhinecliff Needlework Guild made garments for the convalescents, and the Methodist church raised money to take the children to the Dutchess County Fair. Henry H. Pearson was the only hamlet representative on the Holiday Farm board, which was otherwise composed solely of family, estate owners or New York friends. Pearson was well-known to the gentry as the stationmaster, as well as a fine gardener who embellished the depot with potted palms and flowers. At the waterfront house he rented nearby (once the Episcopal parsonage), he cultivated splendid roses and dahlias. He took the Holiday Farm children on excursions to Kingston Point Park. In 1908, despite another financial panic, the hamlet raised enough money from a concert, a fair and donations to spend $490 on a heating plant, $775 on storm doors and windows, and $1,000 to keep Holiday Farm open during November, December and part of January. By 1910 the charity functioned all twelve months; that year, 196 children passed through its care. Its message, that serious illnesses and accidents need not leave a child handicapped for life, had received heartfelt applause.

Levi P. Morton's youngest daughter, Mary, founded Holiday House as a place where New York tenement children recently released from hospitals could recuperate in a caring country setting. An immediate success, it continues today as the Astor Home for Children. Its greatly expanded quarters are now located in the village where the Landsman Kill crosses Route 9. Postcard 1910, courtesy of Sherman-Mann Ephemera Collection of Catskill and Rhinebeck, N.Y.

The Mortons' second act of philanthropy had an even more direct and long-lasting impact on the hamlet. In fact, few gifts have succeeded so completely as the $50,000 Levi P. Morton gave to build the Rhinecliff Memorial Library on the south edge of the hamlet's business district. A tribute to their daughter Lena, who had died suddenly on a trip to Europe, the Mortons spared nothing to make the structure fine. Designed by Hoppin, Koen and Huntington, well-known New York City architects, it was state-of-the-art with its own gas and electricity generating plants. The focus of community activity from its opening in January 1908, it offered a library that was charted by the New York State Regents, as well as classes in sewing, cooking, carpentry and gymnastics. Lectures, card parties, banquets and dances were held in its capacious hall. Women's and men's clubs vied with each other to put on the most imaginative entertainments. Residents of all affiliations and income levels were drawn to its programs.

The governance of the center was held firmly in the Mortons' hands. The presidency was to remain within the family so far as possible, and only one place on the board was accorded to "a representative citizen of Rhinecliff so far as was desirable." (Henry H.

No gift to a community was more wisely given than Levi P. Morton's present of the Rhinecliff Memorial Library in memory of his recently deceased daughter, Lena. Dedicated in 1908, it provided programs for hamlet residents of all ages and interests until the Great Depression forced it to cut back. Today it is enjoying a spirited renaissance. Postcard 1910, courtesy of Harry Heywood.

Pearson was again the chosen man.) But through the years it would more than fulfill its mission to "emanate influences that will be helpful to the home and civic life of the community." As had been wished at its splendid dedication, it spread "happiness and health and strength and smiles." Only the most confirmed rowdies were not touched by its activities.

The first executive director was William W. Hughes. In addition to his salary of $900 a year, he was given an apartment in the wing, with heat and light provided. A district nurse had rooms for examinations and for fumigating, probably to destroy lice, a persistent school problem even today. She, too, was given an apartment. Morton's daughter, Alice Morton Rutherfurd, supplied $100 for books, doubling the state's $50 contribution. Most important,

Levi P. Morton endowed the community center with $80,000 in securities. The anticipated annual yield of $3,050 from those securities, together with contributions from the board and whatever the hamlet could raise on its own, was expected to cover the cost of operations for a very long time.

That first year the activities culminated with a community Christmas tree and a special program performed on the stage in the large meeting room. Fulsomely covered by the *Gazette*, it began with music by a mixed choir. The lights dimmed as three boys dressed in shepherds' costumes entered and a white star appeared among the red stars overhead. While a beautiful angel mounted the steps to the stage with arms outspread, sweet voices sang "Peace, Good Will, Jesus is born to You, Savior and King."

Men and boys eat up in the Memorial Library's ample kitchen. Photograph 1910, courtesy of the Morton Memorial Library.

The grownups entertained themselves with one banquet after another. This one took place soon after the building was opened. Photograph 1910, courtesy of the Morton Memorial Library.

Pretty crepe-paper winged fairies danced around their angel queen as little children sang carols and a Santa song. The tree and a pageant would remain the highlight of Rhinecliff's Christmas season for years to come.

Open three afternoons a week and every evening except Sunday, the library steadily expanded its offerings. Schoolchildren did their homework, joined in the programs and played games there. As early as 1912, a motion picture projector was bought. Accounts for 1914 show an expenditure of $18.55 for motorboat gasoline and $51.53 for camp expenses. The well-attended annual community banquet that year was a splendid affair. A handsome program listed the menu — oysters, bouillon, roast beef, stewed corn, scalloped salmon, ice cream and cake, fruit, nuts and coffee. There were countless toasts, several inspirational talks and an orchestra. On the back of the program were an architectural drawing of the new railroad station and a message of gratitude to Morton for his magnificent gift of the building and its activities. In 1915, when the town

ran water lines to the hamlet, Mrs. Morton donated $500 for bathing facilities that included, according to the quipping *Gazette*, "showers for thin men and 'French tubs' for fat." That same year Morton took on an interest-free loan so that the basement could be rebuilt into a game room, a men's reading room and one more toilet room; hamlet residents repaid the loan within twelve months. Arbor Day was celebrated there. The women held a fair for which they baked fifty cakes and sewed fancywork. Together with the strawberries and ice cream they sold, they made a substantial $45.

The Hudson-Fulton Celebration

Among the excitements of the first decade of the century was the great Hudson-Fulton celebration of 1909. Memorializing the three-hundredth anniversary of Hendrick Hudson's exploration of the river and the one-hundredth anniversary of Robert Fulton's introduction of the world's first viable steamboat, it was especially electrifying for

Peter Talmadge stands with his wife, Caroline Terpenning, a Mohawk, in front of their store opposite the library. They restored the building and made their living quarters in the north wing. Photograph circa 1910, courtesy of Alan Coon.

Rhinecliffers because, ever since the first settlement by the Kips, the river had been the center of their lives. Taking place between September 25 and October 11, the celebration was a great choreographed extravaganza, the first part of which was played out in New York City and its harbor, the second part upriver at the principal waterfront communities. Organized by the state, the underlying message for the wider world was that New York was the richest and most powerful state in the Union. Its overt message was that the nation's Great White Fleet of warships was second only to Great Britain's.

The opening day featured a parade of warships from the great maritime nations, thirty-one of which, including six submarines and eight torpedo boats, were American. Leading the line, replicas of Hudson's *Half Moon* and Fulton's *Steamboat* or *North River*, by now incorrectly, but universally, referred to as the *Clermont*, appeared like toys in comparison.

In the air, Wilbur Wright performed sensational demonstration flights. Taking off from Governors Island, he first flew around it, a distance of two miles that he covered in seven minutes at heights from forty to one hundred feet. He then encircled the Statue of Liberty, a slightly longer distance. These were the very first flights over water, and the din of exuberant tug, steamboat and fac-

tory whistles celebrating the achievement was deafening. Finally, Wright took off for Grant's Tomb with two American flags streaming from the plane's front rudder. Despite sudden air currents spiraling up from the spaces between lower Manhattan's tall buildings, he soon reached the southern end of the great international war fleet that stretched from 42nd Street to Spuyten Duyvil at the northern end of Manhattan Island. With waving flags and blasting whistles, the ships urged him on. One thousand feet north of Grant's Tomb he turned, having made the ten miles in just over twenty minutes, and returned to Governors Island in thirteen minutes. Within a few years the invention would amply demonstrate its impact on domestic life (it was first used for mail delivery) as well as on modern warfare.

Among the myriad land spectacles were parades of international military might on Fifth Avenue, a

Minnie Talmadge, Peter and Caroline's daughter, showing off a fine Model T touring car. A corner of the Talmadges' spruced-up shop building is on the right. Photograph circa 1915, courtesy of Alan Coon.

Waiting for the train to roll into the depot. The house up the hill is still there, but its tower has been removed. Postcard circa 1910, courtesy of Sherman-Mann Ephemera Collection of Catskill and Rhinebeck, N.Y.

Native American encampment and performances at Columbia University, and an exhibition of American decorative arts from 1625 to 1815 at the Metropolitan Museum of Art. It was the museum's first display of house furnishings as art objects, and the show was popular beyond all expectation; it would become the nucleus of the museum's justly famous American Wing.

On October 1 a second naval parade, which included an array of vessels from private yachts, sailboats, ferries and tugs to revenue cutters, submarines and warships, proceeded up the river to Newburgh, where it was greeted with fanfare. From there, a selection of boats continued north, stopping at major waterfront settlements. All Rhinecliff flocked to Kingston's three days of festivities in which elaborate land floats depicted that city's venerable history, and schoolchildren were awarded prizes for the best essay on "The Life and Work of Robert Fulton." Singing and brass band concerts entertained the crowds in the evening, while blazing electric illuminations transformed the length of Broadway. On the last day, fifteen ships and four submarines arrived, forming an escort for the replicas of Hudson's and Fulton's boats. The *Half Moon* anchored off Kingston Point.

The *Clermont* was docked at Rondout, where hundreds of eager men, women and children filed aboard to inspect her. The land parade in the afternoon of the final day took forty-four minutes to pass in review before Governor Charles E. Hughes. In his public address Hughes stressed Kingston's place in the formation of the United States, the beauty of the Hudson River Valley, and America's cutting-edge inventions, all the while emphasizing traditional farming and the rise in tourism.

The world powers were impressed with the entire celebration. Rhinecliffers were especially pleased that the Honorable Levi P. Morton was a charter member of the event and one of its vice presidents. The entire Suckley family enjoyed watching the great naval parade in the city from the decks of Jack Astor's luxurious yacht, another *Nourmahal*, and joining Astor aboard it again when the flotilla came upriver.

New York Central Railroad Improvements

The New York Central began the upgrading and beautifying of its railroad system by starting the construction of Grand Central Terminal in New York City in 1906. It ended with the four-tracking of the line between New York and Albany eight years later. The work in Rhinecliff would radically alter the configuration of its business district. The old depot by the ferry slip was abandoned as unsafe because of its exposed track, and a handsome new Mission-style station was built to the northeast (that is, on the north side of Hutton Street). Nicely landscaped, its crisp lines and handsome flowerbeds were admired by everyone. Passengers reached the boarding platforms by two flights of stairs descending from an enclosed bridge spanning the tracks. In addition, there was a state-of-the-art elevator for baggage as well as passengers. Over-the-track access to the train platforms and the ferry slip was also provided by a separate metal construction with four very high sets of stairs. Vehicular and pedestrian access to the ferry was via a bridge over the tracks at Hutton Street and a ramp to the landing.

Not every hamlet resident believed management's explanation that the move of the depot northward was made to reduce accidents at the grade crossing. In fact, many old-timers grumbled that new estate owners had pushed for the change in order to avoid the proliferating tangle of saloons and commercial establishments around the old depot. Moreover, access to the main entrance of the station was achieved by a new segment of road joining Rhinecliff Road with Charles Street. This occasioned the removal of the public water pump and the ancient cherry tree under which the

The new station was, and is, very handsome. But the focus in this photograph is on the immense steel beam underpinning the bridge crossing the tracks. The former Holiday House is in the background to the left. Photograph 1913, courtesy of the Museum of Rhinebeck History.

The postcard issued when the station and its viaduct were complete features Kipsbergen/ Rhinecliff as it always was — a transportation hub. Note the variety of wheeled vehicles. In another version of this postcard, the steamboat is replaced by a tiny biplane. Postcard circa 1915, courtesy of Sherman-Mann Ephemera Collection of Catskill and Rhinebeck, N.Y.

The Orchard Street side of the Rhinecliff Memorial playground. Lower down were croquet courts and play equipment for children. Postcard circa 1925, courtesy of Alan Coon.

young had always done their courting. Mrs. Anna O. Shuffle, the current owner of the Rhinecliff Hotel, sued the Town of Rhinebeck for damaging the hotel's value by temporarily closing Shatzell Avenue. However, opening day came and, according to the *Gazette*, "Promptly at noon, Henry H. Pearson, ticket agent at Rhinecliff for many years, opened the window of his new office and sold the first ticket to Poughkeepsie and return to William Coon." John Newman, the Suckleys' former chauffeur, now working as a taxi driver for Rhinebeck's popular Hub Garage, stood at the station door proudly awaiting a fare.

Still, another controversial aspect of the railroad's improvements was that the four-tracking took a wide swath of land along Holiday Farm's waterfront. Fortunately, because of rapid growth, the facility needed more space anyway. The Bois Doré property that Morton had rented while his mansion was under construction was available. The house had recently burned down, but with a significant Astor gift for a brand new building, Holiday Farm moved there. (The institution still exists today as the highly regarded Astor Home for Children, run by the Archdiocese of New York.) In the end, the change worked to benefit the hamlet, for Mary

Morton gave the triangle of land left by the new road as it split off from Orchard Street for a hamlet recreation park, and the grading contractor of the new depot contributed the dirt to level it. With tennis and croquet courts, as well as play equipment for small children, it was a popular place. Even village residents picnicked there.

Ellerslie, Wilderstein and Ferncliff

Because, deep down, Morton exemplified virtues in which they themselves believed, there was never any question that in the hearts of Rhinecliffers Ellerslie ranked first among the estates that surrounded the dense section of the hamlet. The author of an effulgent, but reasonably accurate, article in *Country Life in America* told how he was driven in an English trap from the railroad station along a road lined with oaks and chestnuts to Ellerslie's thousand acres. Catching the estate's magic, he wrote that it possessed "the retirement and individuality of an ordinary farm." Despite the grandeur of the mansion and the splendor of its location, it was the farm operation that continued to be Morton's greatest pride. Morton was not quite so hands-on as Kelly, because of his political commitments, but he

Looking north from the high bluff off Grinnell Street, this fine landscape was, perhaps, the work of Frank Culver, Rhinecliff's resident professional photographer. The turreted house barely visible at the far right is still standing, as is the house in the middle ground. Photograph circa 1910, courtesy of Harry Heywood.

approached running the place with the same generous and resilient spirit.

Ellerslie was nearly medieval in its self-suffi-
ciency. Up to one hundred men and boys, and also
some women, worked there — dairymen, shepherds, farmers, orchardists, stablemen, blacksmiths,
wheelwrights, groundsmen, masons, carpenters,
plumbers, painters and even a trunk repairman. Yet
Morton took trouble to see that each person was
regarded as an individual and that a good working environment was provided for all. Those with
families were provided with houses if they needed
them. Unmarried workers lived in dormitories and
ate their meals in a dining hall. A huge bell atop the
water tower to the north of the mansion told them
when it was starting time, lunchtime and quitting
time. Morton actively encouraged his workers to
better their skills and helped them to get more training should they need it. He hired workers' sons and,
when there was work they could do, their wives
and daughters. The only drawback of working at
Morton's seemed to be the copperhead snakes; one
spring thirty-nine of them were discovered sunning
themselves in a woodland clearing.

Morton's prize herd of Guernsey cows and his
sheep became world renowned. His farm's excellent
milk and butter was in demand in New York City's
fine restaurants and elite clubs. That the farm was
never a paying proposition did not bother him. In
fact, one of his standard jokes was to offer guests
a choice of milk or champagne: they were, he told
them, of equal expense to him. What did matter to
him was that Ellerslie, with its wide acres and its
up-to-date practices, was universally recognized as
being first class.

There is little indication that Morton was on intimate terms with nearby estate owners. Partly it was
a question of age. Morton was approaching ninety.
Wilderstein's Suckley was in his fifties, Ferncliff's
John Jacob Astor IV in his forties and Harry Spies

Kip of Ankony in his twenties. True, Governor
Morton had made Astor a state militia colonel, but
it obviously was no more than an honorary title.
Morton may have admired the Astoria Hotel that
Astor had built on 34th Street and Fifth Avenue
to rival his cousin's neighboring Waldorf Hotel, as
well as Astor's own St. Regis Hotel on 56th Street,
but otherwise they had nothing in common. Jack,
as Astor was called, was patently a lightweight who
without vast wealth would probably have floun-
dered, whereas Morton had earned his way in the
world by buckling down.

It is clear that Suckley would have liked to
have known Morton better, but beyond superficial
exchanges about road maintenance and the like, that
never happened. A poor manager, Suckley had mis-
spent so much of his inheritance that, in 1897, he
had been forced sell his livestock and nascent rac-
ing stable, dismiss his employees and decamp with
his wife and their family of three boys and three
girls to Switzerland, where living was cheaper. He
returned to America yearly, but during his brief vis-
its to Wilderstein he camped out. When the family
returned ten years later, he was still on a descending financial curve. He tried to maintain the farm
and grounds, but did not quite succeed, even though
helped by his brother-in-law, Harry Montgomery,
who was constantly improving Wildercliff. In fact,
Suckley's only strong friend outside his family was
Jack Astor. Temperamentally, they were well suited.
Both were dabblers in minor mechanical inventions;
both had unsatisfactory marriages; and both were
essentially at loose ends, Suckley because he had
frittered away his fortune and Jack Astor because
his was so well managed by others.

A measure of Suckley's financial incapacity
was that whenever he devised a scheme to turn a
profit, it failed. Just after his family returned from
Switzerland, for instance, he tried to lure his acquaintances among "the river people," as the estate own-

ers called themselves, into turning the over-two-hundred-year-old Hendrickus Kip homestead, which he had inherited, into a private country club. His pitch was to use the house for an inn and the surrounding land for riding, golf and other sports. He should have known that the old families had no taste for country clubs — the little club for golf and tennis they had established at Tivoli in 1884 was simple in the extreme — and the new people would have bought property on Long Island if a country club setting was what they had wanted.

Besides, the Panic of 1907 had severely depressed real estate values; many places were for sale, with virtually no buyers in sight. Rhinebeck lawyer Martin Heermance, for example, put together a potential estate comprised of several large Rhinecliff properties, including Suckley's Kip homestead. In a letter to an estate owner in Red Hook whom Heermance hoped would have a friend who might buy it, he described the package. Its centerpiece was the Radcliff homestead. "The house is an old one," he wrote, "heated by [a] hot-air furnace [and] having a bath-room with hot and cold water." High on the bluff, there were fine views of the river and the Catskills from its two piazzas. Moreover, the 664-foot waterfront extended south to Slate Dock, which would give the property access to the river. That property, together with the two smaller properties, would bring the parcel up to around 450 acres. Should a prospective owner wish more, he believed Morton might sell the 120-acre Holiday Farm. Such enticements were in vain.

Suckley's efforts to sell the Kip place on his own also failed. As a last resort Suckley rented the house to a Mrs. Marr who, some said, sublet rooms to "pleasure girls." At any rate it was she who was living there when it caught fire in 1910. As reported in the *Gazette*, Mrs. Marr smelled smoke and telephoned the Rhinebeck Village Fire Department. No driver could be found to take its equipment to the hamlet. Although neighbors extracted most of the furniture, and Astor reportedly drove over from Ferncliff with twelve fire extinguishers in one of his twenty-seven cars, only a shell of the venerable structure was left standing when the blaze went out of its own accord. With so many Kip descendants still living in the hamlet, its demise sent shivers up everyone's spine.

Jack Astor's hapless marriage to Ava Willing was dissolved by divorce in 1909. Two years later he married an eighteen-year-old girl; he was then forty-seven. According to gossips and as her subsequent marital career suggests, she was a fortune hunter. Their return voyage from a European honeymoon was booked aboard the "unsinkable" *Titanic*. Astor was among the over 1,500 passengers who drowned. (Apparently, he asked permission to join his pregnant wife in a lifeboat, but graciously stayed behind when he was refused.) His body, covered with soot and partially crushed, was found trapped in wreckage off Nova Scotia. It was reported there was $2,500 in cash in his pockets. His body was sent first to New York, then by private train to the Astors' heavily policed stop at Ferncliff. To avoid visiting hours, it arrived just in time for the funeral.

The service took place in the village of Rhinebeck at the Episcopal Church of the Messiah where Astor had been a warden for the past sixteen years. It was an impressive affair. The chancel of the church was transformed by palms and flowers brought up from New York along with a decorator. Floral tributes from mourners spilled out into every remaining space; the Prince of Wales sent a splendid wreath, and the employees at Ferncliff "a broken column." The solid-oak coffin with silver handles and a plaque simply inscribed with Astor's name and dates was mantled with lavender orchids. Rector William T. Manning from Trinity Church in New York assisted Messiah's Reverend Dr. Saunders in the traditional Episcopal funeral service, the same as is performed for all members of that sect no matter their social status or income. Trinity's organist and choir led the hymns "Hark, Hark, My Soul" and "Peace, Perfect Peace." As is customary, the family sat in the front pew — Vincent and Alice, Astor's children by Ava Willing, and his young pregnant widow supported by her mother and sister. Behind them were reserved seats for the five parlor cars of mourners who had been brought up from New York on the

Ruins of Heermance Home, Arrow shows hole made by British Cannon Ball, Rhinecliff, N.Y.

The Heermance family owned the Kip homestead in the late nineteenth century. When it burned, it belonged to Robert Suckley, who had tried to make it into a country club house and failed. In the 1930s President Franklin D. Roosevelt would raid the site for stones to build Rhinebeck's new post office, for at his behest its design was based on the original homestead. Postcard circa 1915, courtesy of Harry Heywood.

Astors' special train. Seated behind them were local friends and prominent townspeople. Astor employees and members of the Poughkeepsie Hudson-Fulton Celebration Committee were given reserved seats in the chapel alcove. Somewhere in the crowd was Ava, who had brought Alice from England as soon as she heard of the catastrophe. Shops and businesses in town were closed during the service, enabling ranks of onlookers to cluster around the church entrance. As soon as the ritual was over, the casket was taken back to the funeral train in its glass-sided hearse. Astor was buried alongside his parents in the family mausoleum in Trinity Church's 153rd Street cemetery. In Rhinebeck, both the pomp and the simplicity of the funeral — and its underlying loneliness — were not quickly forgotten.

Following Astor tradition, Vincent inherited the bulk of his father's estate, conservatively estimated to be worth $92 million, after the few bequests had been fulfilled. Not yet twenty-one years old and an indifferent student, Vincent immediately dropped out of Harvard to assume the burdens of running Ferncliff and his fortune. Soon he was racing around with young Arthur Suckley in a Lancia automobile capable of going 120 miles an hour. In May 1914 he married Helen Dinsmore Huntington, whose family estate was in Staatsburg. She was an able young woman of far stronger intellectual bent than Vincent. Their union, which was childless, would last just over twenty years.

The Rhinecliff Volunteer Fire Company

Exasperated by the fact that Rhinebeck's volunteer fire company had made it a practice to forbid its equipment from going beyond its district boundaries, Rhinecliff at last founded its own fire company in 1915 by purchasing a hose cart, 500 feet of hose, ladders and fire extinguishers at a cost of $600. The equipment was housed in a garage on Kelly Street across from the library apartments. The town, then in the process of laying water pipes in the hamlet, put in three street hydrants. In August the company tested the water pressure at a celebratory evening event whose feature was a mock battle against another hose. The pressure proved more than adequate. A huge dinner at the Morton, with dancing afterwards at St. Joseph's, raised $200 for uniforms. In September the volunteers proudly wore them to the firemen's jamboree at Staatsburg. Everyone in the hamlet was delighted when having its own fire company significantly reduced the cost of property insurance. The library committee went so far as to install special water outlets on each floor of its building.

Summoned by the resounding ring of the bent train rail used as an alarm, the first fire the company put out was on a roof in the densely populated section of Charles Street. Shortly afterwards it extinguished a brush fire at Ellerslie, prompting Mrs. Morton to give the company a discarded six-cylinder Stevens-Duryea, which the firemen altered to transport their apparatus; volunteer William Tewkesbury, a former chauffeur for the Mortons, taught the men how to drive it. Levi P. Morton was made an honorary fireman, but his role was more that of a rich uncle who in a pinch could be depended on to fill a gap, rather than that of a chief benefactor. The Rhinecliff Volunteer Fire Company was immediately — and would remain so to the present day — an independent and energetic focus of Rhinecliff's public life.

The United States Enters World War I

In 1912, Democrat Woodrow Wilson was elected president of the United States by a landslide in a hotly contested campaign against the sitting Republican, William Howard Taft, and the politically self-resurrected Theodore Roosevelt, who ran on his newly formed "Bull Moose" ticket. The president of Princeton University, Wilson was an able campaigner who in clear language outlined policies he called the "New Freedom." In his first year as president, he saw the income tax amendment ratified as well as the amendment that took the election of federal senators away from state legislatures and gave it to voters. Continuation of radical change on the domestic front, however, was soon overshadowed by the dilemma caused by the outbreak, in June 1914, of the First World War, in which Germany endeavored to conquer France and what remained of the Ottoman empire, as well as the British empire. Wilson chose the path of neutrality. Up for reelection in 1916, his winning slogan was, "He Kept Us Out of War." However, Germany's unrestricted submarine warfare against United States shipping resulted in so many casualties that Wilson reneged on his campaign promise, announcing, "The world must be kept safe for democracy." On April 6, 1917, America joined in the struggle against Germany.

Over 4,890,000 American men, almost half of them drafted, served in the armed services during the last year and a half of World War I. Around 1,390,000 saw active combat, first in Picardy, and then in the Battle of the Marne. Well over a million Americans fought in the protracted, but ultimately successful, Meuse-Argonne offensive. On the home front, everyone collected twine, tinfoil and walnut shells for the manufacture of munitions, and they participated in the many Liberty Bond drives. Men created a Home Defense unit that drilled in uniform, readying themselves to go overseas should they be called. Women knit sweaters and washcloths, and even children helped roll bandages. The churches held socials to aid European victims of the war.

Of the 179 men from Rhinebeck that went away to war, twenty-four from Rhinecliff are listed on the hamlet monument; among them are two Pindars, three Wheelers, Lester Trowbridge and George VanWagnen. To that number should be added Henry Suckley, who volunteered early on. The leader of a corps of ambulance drivers on the Eastern Front, he was killed outside of Salonica when German pilots bombed his clearly marked vehicle. His older brother Robin, an excellent musician, was drafted and sent abroad as the member of a band. His brother Arthur was chosen for his linguistic abilities to serve refugees in Paris.

On November 11, 1919, an armistice was at last declared. American deaths totaled 112,400. Half of those fatalities were caused by the influenza pandemic that ravaged their camps. Rhinecliff's Guy Pindar was one of them. He, along with Henry Suckley, were Rhinecliff's gold star soldiers.

The End of an Era

Death claimed Anna Livingston Morton in 1918. Although she was eulogized and missed, her passing came as no surprise. It was Levi P. Morton's death two years later, on his ninety-sixth birthday, that shocked the hamlet. A revered father figure, he had seemed immortal. As customary, he celebrated his anniversary with a party for the hamlet children. It was not as lively as it had been in the past, with rides in donkey and pony carts around the grounds. Rather, the children sang his favorite hymns under his bedroom window. That evening he simply closed his eyes and died. Hundreds filed by his coffin in the great main hall paying their profound respects. The funeral took place at the Church of the Messiah on May 19. It was a grand and solemn affair. Six of his most devoted employees carried his coffin. Among the honorary pall bearers were: Charles E. Hughes, governor of New York State during the Hudson-Fulton celebration; Alfred E. Smith, the present governor; Elihu Root, secretary of state in Theodore Roosevelt's administration and a Nobel Peace Prize winner; the mayor of Shoreham, Vermont, Morton's birthplace; Archibald Rogers, New York financier as well as Hyde Park estate owner; and neighbor Robert B. Suckley. The eighty-five children who were at his birthday party attended the funeral in a group. The Dean of the Cathedral of St. John the Divine and the Bishop of New York participated in the service. The cathedral chapel choir and its boy choristers led the hymns. Those who had witnessed the funeral outside the church, together with those who were seated within, followed the cortege to the family plot situated in a lovely corner of the old Rhinebeck cemetery. There Morton was interred next to his daughter, Lena, and Anna, his wife.

In the thirty-five years since he had bought Ellerslie, Morton had become much more than an employer and benefactor to hamlet residents. They had grown deeply fond of him for the honorable, caring person he was. Now that he was gone, they realized they would never again enjoy the presence of a man of his stature. They adjusted, but not without profound regret.

10

The Roaring Twenties

*B*e it known, loyal readers, that from this point on I was able to interview old-timers who remembered these years firsthand. I did not meet one who recalled life in the hamlet with anything but relish, for the small, tight-knit community enfolded them and at the same time gave them immense freedom. This might be explained by nostalgia, or that those who felt trapped by its small size simply got out. But the gleam in the eyes of those that stayed, and their deep, knowing chuckles as memories of their lives in the hamlet popped into their minds persuades me that their delight is the real article. Rhinecliff at this time reminds me of an update of a Bruegel painting or early American Dutch court proceedings — a great hubbub of activity pursued by individual talents and personalities, yet bound together in the common bonds of place and an ability to bounce back. In the fast-moving twentieth century, Rhinecliffers still felt extraordinarily lucky to live in the hamlet. They still do.*

The decade of the 1920s would be dubbed "the Roaring Twenties." Relieved that "The War to End All Wars" was over, Americans made merry. They sang, they danced and those who were so inclined cheerfully substituted speakeasies, bootlegging and homebrew for outlawed saloons. Like most people, Rhinecliffers believed there were only good times ahead. They even took in their stride the amendment to the Constitution giving women the vote, for the hamlet was one of those pockets in America that had always had an active core of women's rights supporters. Traditionally, Rhinecliff had not differentiated strictly between what men did and what it was proper for women to do. Some descendants of the original Dutch settlers, of whom there were an impressive number, may even have recalled the astonishing degree of equality women enjoyed in those bygone days.

As in most semirural areas during the 1920s, residents were beginning to install the technological improvements in their homes that made living a little easier and more comfortable, although they rarely felt any need of possessing the most up-to-date versions. If a house had central heating, a pipe-

less heater fired either by coal or wood usually provided it. Hot air was forced through a single yard-square grate situated in the front hall so that the heat circulated downstairs and up as best it could. A hand pump brought cold water to the kitchen sink; hot water was heated on the cook stove. Only a few houses had indoor plumbing; outhouses and chamber pots were still common. Electricity was available, but not many houses were wired; kerosene lamps were more the rule than the exception. The telephones that existed in individual homes had up to eight parties on the line. Service was personal, for all calls were made through an operator. This was generally considered a convenience, because anyone visiting a friend simply asked to have their calls routed to that house while they were there. Besides, surreptitious listening in was a good way

Orchard Street schoolchildren pose on the rocks behind the schoolhouse with the principal, Charles Hainer, who taught grades 5–8. His wife taught grades 1–6. Photograph 1925, courtesy of William R. Allen.

to catch up on gossip. The *Gazette* found it noteworthy that the Atkins and Heermances had radios installed in their houses in time for Christmas 1926. Automobile ownership slowly increased. The Rhinecliff road was paved. An unintended consequence was that wagon horses had a hard time gaining purchase on the smooth surface of the hill and often stumbled under heavy loads. But most Rhinecliffers liked the progress.

Jobs

The railroads remained the best-paying employers, especially the New York Central. It employed two ticket agents, not necessarily Rhinecliff men. The baggage master bore especially heavy responsibilities. Only he wore a uniform, a fine blue jacket whose nickel-plated buttons were adorned with the train company insignia, and a visored cap emblazoned with the words "Baggage Master." He handled shipped baggage and large parcels that were unloaded by hand onto carts at the platform, then taken to the upper level by elevator; outbound baggage and small freight reversed the process. Very large or heavy items were received and sent from the New York Central's large brick freight house or the R. & C.'s small wooden freight house. The postmaster himself picked up the mail in locked bags.

The tower men's duty was to ensure the safe passage of trains through the Rhinecliff section, which ran from Staatsburg to Tivoli. They followed the trains on the route by means of a special telegraph line and operated the levers and rods that switched cars onto sidings. Four gangs of men maintained the tracks in mint condition. In addition, a special group was entrusted with the task of keeping the right-of-way free of rocks and fixing broken track. As there were no porters, hamlet boys vied with each other to carry travelers' luggage for tips, especially in summer and on weekends. They got a nickel or a

dime or, if they were lucky, more when they accompanied patrons across the river to catch transportation out of Kingston. The R. & C., by then absorbed into the New York, New Haven and Hartford, had shed its passenger service, but hamlet men were still employed as freight handlers and track inspectors. In addition, there was work handling the livestock destined for Kingston slaughterhouses.

Entrepreneurial Rhinecliff

Equally important were the independent entrepreneurs. Many did well. Edna Cornwell had inherited the provision store, originally O'Brien's, on the northeast corner of Shatzell Avenue and Charles Street. Its interior was a delight to behold. A glass counter with a rounded top stood just inside the entrance; it contained whatever items needed protection from flies and casual handling. Beyond that, on the main counter, was a hand-driven coldcut and cheese slicer. Packaged, tinned and bottled groceries filled the shelves. Clerks made up orders while patrons gossiped. Often children were sent to pick up last-minute groceries. They thought nothing of walking a mile to do it, probably because it was a chance to mingle with "downtown" life. Otherwise, Fred Holsapple drove the store's horse-drawn wagon from house to house to take orders in the morning and to deliver filled baskets in the afternoon. Little children's idea of joy was to ride along with him and, as they grew older, to help with the deliveries.

Rosewell Beach's and James Hester's grocery store occupied the south end of the Newman Building across from Cornwell's on Charles Street. (Before he became a grocer, Beach had been the manager of Morton's stock farm; his daughter had married Hester. John and Nellie Newman now owned the Keilly Building, which they had inherited from her parents. Later it would be called the Newman

Ostrom and Cornwell's general store. With the exception of the loft on the far left, which recently burned, and the firehouse, which is set back and can't be seen, this stretch of upper Shatzell Avenue looks much the same today as it did in the early 1900s. The large white building on the northeast corner of Orchard Street, now a private home, is the Union Hotel. Postcard circa 1920, courtesy of Sherman-Mann Ephemera Collection of Catskill and Rhinebeck, N.Y.

Building.) This store did a good business, too, and was also known for tiding customers over when winter layoffs made pocketbooks slim. A peanut roaster, a popcorn machine and a foot-square cookie rack stood by the entrance. The main counter, with shelves of groceries behind it, was to the left. Specialty goods were displayed on a counter at the back of the store. As at Cornwell's, customers could count on a lively interlude while their order was being made up. However, according to the *Gazette*, Hester looked "very smart making deliveries in his new bridal grey truck."

From the north end of the grocery, patrons could enter a space where, by the end of the decade, Harvey Holsapple and Emery Hyatt — friends, but not partners — operated a shared shop where they sold newspapers, tobacco products, penny candy and ice cream. The ice cream was a special draw; patrons came from all over town to buy the hand-packed, overflowing quarts. A small addition behind that shop first housed a pool table, then a barber named Cyrus took over. A careful man, he gave a good haircut, even though his hand clippers yanked patrons' hair. At the end of the day, he pushed aside his barber chair and, after supper on winter evenings, hamlet men gathered there to spin yarns and argue about politics — national and international, as well as local. For sizzling emphasis they shot streams of tobacco juice into the coal-fired potbellied stove.

Fred Goldsmith kept a meat market on the downhill side of the Newman Building. His large cooler on the ground floor was filled with chickens, pork chops and sides of beef. (Beach and Hester sold only whole hams, and Cornwell's only cold cuts and hot dogs.) The Goldsmith family lived above the market. At the foot of Shatzell Avenue was that small hotel and bar that had gone underground in more ways than one during prohibition. Across the street the venerable Rhinecliff Hotel rented rooms to an occasional traveling salesman and to a flock of summer boarders. For the entertainment of patrons, it offered ping-pong, darts, a pool table, shuffleboard, badminton and horseshoes, along with dancing. Many Rhinecliffers made it a habit to "trip the light fantastic" there. And on Friday nights they could buy clam chowder for fifteen cents a bowl.

On the south side of Shatzell, going back up the hill, were two more erstwhile bars. In the ground floor of the four-story apartment building was a millinery shop, run by Miss "Loulou" Ahearn. The Brice Building across Kelly Street and opposite Cornwell's was not as prosperous, for the building was beginning to deteriorate. Prohibition had turned its long mahogany bar into a far less

popular soda fountain; its livery business vanished as ownership of automobiles and trucks increased. The Brices still lived upstairs, but they were aging. Tall, stout Mr. Brice, whose eyesight was fading, spent most of his time sitting outside to catch chance conversations with passersby. One of his most memorable entertainments was witnessing Elmer Harrington skid in a patch of horse manure and do a head-over-heels as he whizzed around the corner on his bicycle.

The main, though not officially sanctioned, hamlet dump, located on Rhinecliff Road just north of its intersection with Orchard Street, should also be included in the catalog of entrepreneurial sites. Boys, mostly, but some older men, too, fished out from the pile of cast-off items any useable parts they could mend, transform or build anew into an object to use themselves or to sell. To describe the dump's riches, it need only be noted that the town disposed of its beat-up old cars at the site. One fine summer's day word spread like lightning that prohibition agents intended to dump a seized truckload of Canadian ale around noontime. Rhinecliffers, and inlanders, too, staked out positions well in advance. After tossing a few bottles into the dump, the sympathizing agents invited the onlookers to take the brew directly off the truck, a truly spirit-raising windfall.

Slate Dock was still used by occasional barges, the fading R. & C. Railroad, two commercial fishermen and a clutch of hobos. Jake Pindar, a short, stocky, bowlegged widower noted for his suspenders and high boots, knew the river bottom better than other people know the palms of their hands. His layout, north of the railroad complex, was a

When Lester C. Trowbridge became postmaster, he ran the post office in the front room on the ground floor and sold Sonoco gasoline from a pump on the sidewalk. The family lived upstairs. Postcard 1920s, courtesy of Alison J. Michaels.

long, narrow landing with a gravel surface running parallel to the river. Even at high tide it was impossible to land his round-bottomed Kingston-built boats, named *Gloria* and *Shirley* after his daughters, so he attached the boats to a stout pole off the dock and drew them in and out with an ingenious system of rope pulleys. His dock had a shed for gear and two bunk beds, as well as a small icehouse for storing the ice he cut in winter to keep his catch cool on its way to New York City during the warmer months. When the shad run was over, he caught bass, sturgeon, eels, bullheads, catfish and carp. It is said that Pindar also operated an active still, more or less out of sight.

Although seldom seen downtown in the hamlet, Pindar was no recluse. He often took along his brother and his nephew, or special friends such as Bert Kip and his son, to help lay the drift nets. But they had to ferret him out at his landing. So did anyone who wanted to buy fish retail from him. He emphatically did not peddle his catch, although he did sell it to others who sold it from house to house. In winter, Pindar spent more time at his federal-period house on Long Dock Road between the old stone houses built by Jacob and Jan Kip. There he knit shad nets and made herring scapping nets* for himself and for sale. Remembered as a man of a few soft-spoken words, Pindar was a marvelous talker when the spirit moved him, however. Still, it was a great surprise when he suddenly married again and took to attending parties at the firehouse. In fact, he would become a fire company commissioner in 1932.

"Joke" Talmadge fished for the commercial market on the south side of the railroad complex, but he could not rival Jake either in the lore of the river or in commitment to fishing.

John Locke, known for his wide-brimmed slouch hat and sweeping mustaches, put up a one-pump gas station just south of Long Dock road. It catered to people going to and from the train or the ferry, as well as to hamlet residents. The building is still there. Although hard to see because of the high fence shielding it from the road, it can be identified by the rustic trellis ornamenting the roofline. The fuel was pumped into a glass container with gallon markers running down its side. Customers indicated the amount they wanted, and when the container was filled to that mark, Locke pulled a chain and gravity rushed the gas into the automobile's tank. Inside the little station he sold candy and ice cream, and to those in the know, the chance to play slot machines. During prohibition, he is said to have run a still out back. His house was across the road on the north side of the Kip homestead ruins. There he grew flowers for sale.

The old Flat Rock School, located where River Road branches off from the Rhinecliff Road, had been handsomely rebuilt in 1915. It had neither electricity nor a furnace, but its large north and

The first Flat Rock School was also established by 1849. This modern picture shows the 1914 version, now converted into a residence. Photograph by Alison J. Michaels, 2008.

---

*These nets, typically used in the Hudson River Valley, had a square frame with four bowed ribs attached to the corners and drawn together in the middle where a pole on a swivel was attached. With it the fisherman scooped huge catches of milling herring out of the water.

west windows provided all the light it needed and the potbellied stove, with a low fence around it to prevent burns, kept it snug in winter. Its impressive modern improvements were separated boys' and girls' toilet rooms. There was no playground, but the rail truck in the abandoned quarry behind the school provided endless opportunities for derring-do, especially for the boys. Today, the school is a private residence.

The south end of the hamlet adjacent to Ellerslie was more rural. There, William Tiffany and Alvin Toof, a carpenter by trade, ran a sawmill. Toof had made small first-class greenhouses for home growers during the violet boom. By the 1920s, however, plant diseases and changes in fashion had shattered the industry. Toof had also replaced the old Flat Rock Schoolhouse with a new, airy one. Using horse teams to haul huge logs into Rhinecliff, the two men thinned or cleared much of the forested places around Rhinebeck. Some of the lumber went to the shipbuilding industry in Rondout, but most was used locally. The screech and groan of the saw cutting through the timber was a sound that, like the foghorns and the whistles of the trains, became part of the fabric of hamlet life.

Summer visitors swelled the population. Creating a lively stir throughout the hamlet, many returned year after year, generating a host of seasonal jobs, especially for women. However, Adair House, high on the hill south of St. Joseph's Church, was the only Rhinecliff boardinghouse bold enough to advertise in the special pamphlet the Rhinebeck Businessmen's Association put out in 1927. Its notice boasted large airy rooms, spacious porches, beautiful lawns, parking for automobiles, electric light and a telephone, as well as mail delivered three times a day. There was dancing and tennis, too. Singled-out attractions within easy walking distance were the hamlet churches and shops, as well as the railroad and ferry. Rates of $16 to $18 a week included meals made with the best ingredients from local markets and farms.

Itinerants, most of whom came by ferry from Kingston, certainly added color to the hamlet. There were wholesale grocers with wagonloads of supplies for the retail establishments, as well as a peddler named Colburn who went from house to house in a converted furniture truck that he had cleverly outfitted as a variety store. Although he did not carry a great deal of any one thing, he offered convenience to housewives and also a few minutes break from their daily routine during which they caught up with the latest gossip. Two separate rag pickers made their rounds almost as frequently. They paid by the pound — weighed on a handheld scale — and ran a generally good-natured battle against the women to prevent them from increasing their rags' weight on the sly, while they, of course, did not neglect stratagems for lightening the scale. From time to time, a knife and scissor sharpener and an umbrella repairman came, carrying their equipment on their backs and hollering out their services to attract customers. A hurdy-gurdy man with his music on wheels and a performing parrot, and an organ-grinder with his music box on a stick and a dressed-up monkey to dance and pass his hat for money, would also suddenly appear. Gypsies also drove through the hamlet when the spirit moved them.

In a different category was the hobo jungle at the south end of Slate Dock near the never-failing spring. The men exchanged odd jobs for food, but kept mainly to themselves. Jake Pindar and "Joke" Talmadge maintained an easygoing relationship with them, each being respectful of the other's way of life. There were also several shanty settlements called "sturgeon towns," where squatters lived along the southern bluff and down by the railroad tracks. Mainly fishermen, they were a shifting population that generally kept to themselves. Only a few brush-covered foundations remain of their shanties.

Work on the Estates

The estates continued to hire seasonal labor for their farms and pleasure grounds. At Ferncliff, for instance, twenty-six men were needed just for the lawns and for the Italian, rose and cutting gardens. Howard Mattison, who had worked at Wilderstein since 1913, went to Ferncliff in 1920 after Robert Suckley died and the family could no longer afford to pay him for his work as their gardener and grounds-man. He was sorry to leave the Suckleys, but he felt lucky to get good, reliable wages at Ferncliff. In the autumn, both men and women were hired to pick apples; women were preferred for the sorting and packing. These seasonal workers got lifts to Ferncliff by buckboard or car, or they walked.

Archie Van Etten tended the farm horses. As it was a year-round job, he lived on the estate with his family in the old Dutch house. From 3:30 to 7:30 in the morning, he prepared the horses for work in the fields, then returned home until 3:30 in the afternoon, when he went back to the stables to wash, curry and feed the horses and maintain their harness until 8:00 in the evening. With the exception of July and August, when all hands were given Saturday afternoon off, he worked six days a week for $70 a month. He received coal, wood and two quarts of milk a day as part of his pay. Running the green-houses and providing the Astors' St. Regis Hotel with eggs and chickens were also year-round occupations. In addition, the Astors needed permanent staff in the house and for such positions as chauffeur, express man and security guard.

Mrs. Jacob Ruppert died in 1924. According to her husband's will, after her death their multiple properties were to be divided among their children. As they had made other lives and were unwilling to take on the burden of maintaining a large property in the then-unfashionable Hudson River Valley, Linwood went to her nephew, J. Ruppert Schalk. (Jacob Ruppert Jr., for instance, was a sporting man who had bought the Highlander baseball team immediately after his father's death. He ordered sharp uniforms with thin blue stripes for the players and renamed them the Yankees. His main contact with the hamlet was that once a year he treated the saloon keepers of Rhinebeck and neighboring towns to a tour of the brewery in the city, a fine dinner and seats at a ballgame.) Schalk was a shy, perennial bachelor. He engaged in various projects on the property, such as raising dogs, cats and ducks. Chickens, however, were his great success. Over time he built poultry raising into an immense, long-lasting operation that gave full-time jobs to local men. His recreational interests were yachting and historical boats. Otherwise his cars and his own predilections allied him more closely with the village. Beyond, say, giving a dozen balls to the local baseball team and a modest, for him, contribution for fire equipment, he did not involve himself in the hamlet.

In short, nobody got rich in Rhinecliff, but the community possessed a lively intimacy. Almost everyone saw everyone else on an almost daily basis and they took each other as they were. Of course, some were better friends than others, but this did not fracture the intrinsic unity of the hamlet. Nor did it leave room for pretension. Its spirit was essentially generous. If a family was down on its luck, someone would step in to give it a boost or even tide it over. Moreover, nearly every resident possessed some kind of skill or craft others might need, from heavy lifting of a rock to fixing a jammed sewing machine. For instance, Oscar Allen — Lyman, Ike and Bill's father — was a railroad man who had come to the hamlet from Southern Illinois via Albany, where he had helped build the Castleton Bridge. (His wife, Hattie, was the daughter of Franklin Dedrick and Lizzie Kip, which is why he ended up in Rhinecliff.) A man of multiple talents, he was sent for whenever a task demanded ingenuity. Once, in the depth of winter, a fancy car down by the hotel refused to start and could not be pushed. Allen took some kerosene-soaked rags, placed them in a tin pan, ignited them and calmly passed the blazing mass under the car's oil box. A tremor of fear that a great explosion was about to occur rippled through the crowd of eager onlookers. Nothing happened. The heat was just strong enough to liquefy the oil. The car took off.

The Rhinecliff Memorial Library

The Rhinecliff Memorial Library and Community House continued as a center for socializing for all ages. In his subdued New England way, Morton would have been pleased to know that under the energetic leadership of the incomparable Miss Harriet Wooley, who had been hired as the executive secretary the year before he died, the center was going from strength to strength as a great unifying force. Miss Wooley was an intelligent, forceful, unmarried young woman of great clarity of purpose who bobbed her hair and wore tweed jackets. Neither tall nor especially good-looking, she made her imprint through her ceaseless energy and lively imagination. She gave a twist to entrenched programs and brought in new ones. For the next twenty years she would be an endless font of invention and encouragement for young and old alike.

Few holidays went by without a celebration. On New Year's Eve the Women's Club held a dance with an orchestra playing for round (ballroom) dancing and Harvey Holsapple calling the figures for square dancing. The festivities ended with a joke tree festooned with inexpensive, but amusing, presents. The Valentine's Day party featured a fortuneteller. Washington's Birthday was marked by a fair and a turkey supper put on by the Methodist church ladies. The St. Patrick's Day minstrel shows with the black-faced Tambo, Bones, Dusty and Goldy making local wisecracks also presented a chorus of girls wearing pretty white dresses accented with broad green ribbons; people flocked from miles around to see it. Over fifty children ran animal cracker relay races at the Easter parties.

Throughout the summer the park offered myriad programs for all ages. Vincent Astor held a magnificent fireworks display on the Fourth of July for friends, for the help on his and neighboring estates, and for the wider community. The last week in July there was a tennis tournament for grown-ups, ending with an evening social in the hamlet's recreation park. The week before Labor Day virtually everybody went to the Dutchess County Agricultural Fair, now held only at the Springbrook Driving Park in the village. This event marked both the highpoint of the summer and a farewell to it.

When school started up again, the Rhinecliff Memorial, never entirely abandoned for the great outdoors during the summer, hummed once more with slide shows, movies and club meetings for every age and interest. Over a hundred guests dressed in colonial costumes attended a dancing party. At the eighth annual Women's Club dinner, the women dressed in gowns color-coordinated with the table linen as they waited on the men. The Men's Club reciprocated with a hearty roast beef dinner. Often, too, the men cooked a supper of oysters following the spir-

ited bowling contests played on a long table made for the purpose in the building's ground floor. Virtually every week there were card parties — euchre, bridge or a game of Go. On the more sober side were edifying lectures; when Mrs. Helen de LaPorte, a town genealogist, was brought in to talk about historic preservation, she scolded Rhinecliff residents for not keeping up the Kerkhoff, their eighteenth-century graveyard. At a Halloween party put on by the Girl Scouts for the Boy Scouts, one youngster came dressed as a farmer, towing along a chained friend who had been transformed into a bear; others were more simply costumed as ghosts. The party did not stop "the gang" from playing pranks, however. On one such inspired occasion, the boys took a surrey and an ancient buggy from Brice's barn and heaped them into H. H. Pearson's yard; Pearson was not amused. At Christmas, the Rhinecliff Memorial sponsored a

A tough and winning Rhinecliff baseball team, the original Cubs. Top: (1) J. Cunningham (2) W. Heywood (3) G. Weber, manager (4) R. Goodrich, captain (5) E. Forsman (6) C. Weber (7) G. Adair, treasurer (8) J. Stienmetz. Bottom: (9) H. Wheeler (10) W. Cutler (11) L. Allen (12) H. Kipp (13) A. Weber, secretary (14) H. Matison. Not present: O. Van Etten, Dorothy Dedrick, scorekeeper. Photograph 1931, courtesy of the Rhinecliff Volunteer Fire Company.

community tree hung with little presents for all the hamlet children. John Secore, a father who was perfection in the role, dressed up as Santa Claus and threw candies down to them from the small window overlooking the stage. With New Year's the round of activities began again.

Both the Girl Scouts and Boy Scouts met at the Rhinecliff Memorial. Miss Wooley herself headed the girls' troop. During the cold weather they fulfilled their requirements for badges — cooking, sewing, crafts, first aid — but when warm weather came, they went on expeditions. One was a daylong trip to Ulster Park across the river. They took the early ferry to Rondout, and the chain ferry across the creek, then hiked to the park where, after a frolic in the river and a hearty picnic, they entertained each other with song and dance. Finally, they had a second glorious swim and packed up, making the last ferry home.

The Boy Scouts were led by math teacher, volunteer fireman and civil engineer, Rudy Zachow, who fascinated the boys because he had a metal plate implanted in his skull, the result of an engineering accident. The scouts made such useful items as tables and birdhouses from wood salvaged from grocery store packing crates. To the day he died, in the summer of 2008, Ray Dedrick was still proud of producing a model sailboat that really sailed. To teach them construction techniques, Zachow oversaw their building a log cabin clubhouse — complete with a large fireplace, windows and two doors — in the woods south of Grinnell Street. They felled the trees and skidded the logs down the hill themselves. Zachow also headed the popular Sea Scouts. Vincent Astor provided two sailboats and uniforms as close to navy regulation as lawful. He also delighted the boys with stem-to-stern tours of his great steam yacht, *Nourmahal*.

Baseball, the favorite sport of men and boys, operated outside the library. Every Sunday in the summertime, the smartly uniformed men's team, the Rhinecliff Cubs, played neighboring towns as far south as Poughkeepsie, on the east side of the river, and Highland, on the west side, either "at home" or "away." Games against inland Rhinebeck and Kingston were particularly intense. Everyone's hero was short, wiry outfielder "Pump" Wheeler. (His given name was Morton, although no one ever called him that.) His specialty was sliding into base headfirst. The field, out on Russell Avenue, had a small covered bleacher section for spectators. There was no spring, so the players commandeered small boys to lug water up the hill in buckets from a well on the corner of Kelly Street; most, but not all of the time, they did so happily, imagining themselves already part of the team. Teenage schoolboys bicycled to play against Rhinebeck and Upper Hook. The name of the Red Hook team was the Swamptown Never Sweats; the Rhinecliff team thought of themselves as the Cubs, which they were not quite, but as they were very good competition, nobody cared. Looking ahead to greater glory, grade-school kids practiced whenever and wherever they could.

Crisis in the Volunteer Fire Company

There were, of course, groups and cliques in Rhinecliff, as there are wherever human beings congregate. Although the differences did not prevent the hamlet from functioning as a community, there were momentary spats. Some of them were soon forgotten; others were repeated so often that they became the fabric of life; others, more serious, but not less personal, rocked the whole hamlet.

The crisis in the volunteer fire company was of the last variety. By 1922 the company had grown to seventy-eight members. Needing a proper firehouse, it bought the unused property on the northwest corner of Shatzell and Orchard streets from the Widow Leary, and had its old icehouse and its feed

The Sanford and Ford pumpers are proudly displayed in front of the new firehouse. Photograph early 1930s, courtesy of William R. Allen.

and building supply store torn down. But, although the firemen were successful fundraisers, construction bids came in too high. Ground was not broken until October 1926. When the building was finally opened, in December 1927, the company was relieved to get the boost of a hundred dollars a year for renting space in the building to the town for elections. (Rhinecliffers still vote and hold meetings in this firehouse.) They also converted the old firehouse into a rentable five-car garage. (The original building exists as a three-car garage, cars being wider these days.)

So far, so good. The trouble began when the firemen decided they needed more formal rules. Meetings were to be held quarterly — January, April, July and October. Any able-bodied man at least twenty-one years of age could become a member. Dues were set at ten cents a month, three months in advance. Members in arrears for dues or fines were prohibited from holding office. Children under age eighteen were not allowed at meetings. Tools were not to be removed without permission, nor could outsiders use the building without permission. Insulting, indecent or improper language, intoxication, or any other conduct unbecoming to a gentleman or a disgrace to the company was pro-

hibited. Finally, members were forbidden to discuss meetings in any public place. Violators of these rules were to be fined or expelled.

Sweeping as they were, the rules did nothing to solve the long-festering tensions that had grown up between new and old volunteers. No sooner had the company moved into their fine building than a battle royal over control of the organization erupted. In the extraordinarily large turnout for elections in January 1928, John LaPolt, an insurgent, won the position of fire commissioner with 116 votes; H. H. Pearson, old and very conservative, got only 76 votes. But LaPolt failed to go to meetings and, in June, together with his brother and three others, insisted on putting his friend Cleary Simmons up for commissioner in another vote. They even went so far as to haul Rudy Zachow, the company's secretary, before a judge to explain why Simmons should not be included on the ballot. The judge ruled in their favor, and Simmons won handily. Not letting up, LaPolt criticized the map Zachow had made of the fire district for insurance purposes, protesting that it ran too far north. Chief Philbrick retaliated by refusing to pay LaPolt's attorney's bill. LaPolt was still not subdued. When the question came up of how to buy the new 500-gallon Sanford pumper with ladders, hose and tools that they desperately needed, he strenuously objected to the $5,000 cost and the contract was not signed. To display their indignation, he and Simmons continued to skip meetings.

When the election for a new chief came around again, both LaPolt and Simmons reluctantly agreed to the nomination of George Van Wagenen. Elected, one of the first things Van Wagenen did was sign a contract for the Sanford. Its cost was the same, but the terms seemed slightly better — $2,000 up front, and an interest-bearing note for the remaining $3,000. Fortunately, Mrs. Helen Morton came to the rescue with a $2,500 contribution. Vincent Astor gave $500. Thereupon, LaPolt and Simmons informed the company that they would attend no more meetings. When the roof of the Suckleys' Heermanceville tenant house burned (it was set off by fireworks), nineteen firemen responded. LaPolt was not among them. The following year he resigned from the company and, at long last, peace was restored.

Rhinecliff Characters

Like most small communities, Rhinecliff possessed its share of "characters." Pete Flynn was an immense Irishman. He had wanted to be one of the mailmen who sorted letters on the railroad, but although he practiced diligently in the tower of the big brick house on Grinnell Street where he lived with his brother, he never got fast enough. Instead he smoked fish, mostly for sale to local customers. He also cut ice from Ellerslie's pond and sold it from house to house. He would note the weight needed — marked on the special card left in a customer's front window — knock off a chunk of ice of that size from the huge block in his truck, then carry it into the house with a huge set of sharp tongs and place it in the icebox. A poet

in his spare time, Pete's sign on his vehicle read, "Winter Fruit for Summer Use." To entertain his friends and customers he would render stanza after stanza of his own and others' compositions. When asked when his works would be available in printed form, he always answered, "publishing pending"; many did indeed appear in the *Gazette*. Perhaps to counteract the cold of his trade, Pete also spent a good deal of time, arguably more than he should have, in the local saloons. This may have been a contributing cause of his constant battles with Miss May O'Brien about their contiguous properties up Grinnell Street. Or maybe she started the fights, for both were what was called "swearing Irish."

Jimmie Cunningham was another tough Irishman. A mason, carpenter and jack-of-all-trades, he was an expansive man, especially when recounting his adventures. Once, after he had built a chimney for a lady on the outskirts of town, she told him that, at the moment, she had no money to pay for it. "Fine," Jimmie said, "when you decide to pay, let me know." Soon after, she called in alarm to tell him that her house was filled with smoke. He replied that he would fix it the minute he got his money. In retaliation for her not paying, he had stopped up the chimney with a glass panel. She paid. At least that was the story he told with great frequency in the hamlet saloons.

George Cave, all agreed, danced to his own drum. In his youth he got an infection in his finger and chopped it off at the middle knuckle to cure it. Somewhat later he whacked a finger off the other hand. He had a small house and barn at the southern end of Kelly Street and, to set himself up in the plowing business, he bought what he thought was a horse. It turned out to be a mule that adamantly refused to be hooked up to a cultivator. Cave was such a heavy drinker that his wife, Eudora, finally left him. One day he ran his little runabout into a buttonwood tree. While recuperating in the hospital, he had a vision that inspired him to woo his wife again. She returned, and he became an attentive, churchgoing husband, a town constable and an excavator. When they moved to another house, so the story goes, he put the stove in his wheelbarrow with bread still baking in the oven.

Knags was an educated man, a pharmacist from Philadelphia, who bought a shanty sight-unseen back in the woods off Russell Avenue where he lived off the land. No one remembers his ever having a job. Occasionally he walked downtown for provisions, such as sugar or flour, which he put in a white gunnysack, and then walked home again. Otherwise he and his mother, who lived with him, ate wild things such as dandelion greens and raccoons. Before his mother died, all anyone ever registered about him were his blue eyes, long white beard and baggy woolen clothes. Afterwards, during chance encounters, he turned out to be a compelling conversationalist.

Self-contained as it was, Rhinecliff could not entirely separate itself from the currents in the wider world. In 1928, when former Governor of New York State Alfred E. Smith, a Roman Catholic, was running against Republican Herbert Hoover for the presidency of the United States, a group of Dutchess County Ku Klux Klansmen, whose wide range of hates included Catholics, protested Smith's candidacy by burning a huge fiery cross on the hill where Orchard Street enters the hamlet. It illuminated the whole sky. Fortunately, it was a one-time assault and, although a few hard-line Rhinecliffers joined in, most were horrified, even traumatized. Old-timers, inlanders as well as Rhinecliffers, do not like to speak of that event.

And then came the Great Depression.

11

The Great Depression

When the Great Depression struck in October 1929, Rhinecliff was able to pretend, at least for a while, that it was a distant event that affected only the rich. At Christmas the store windows were filled with seasonal displays and all the houses were decorated with a wreath, a candle or at least a spray of green. The community tree in front of the Rhinecliff Memorial Library was lighted every evening. Along with the churches, the library put on its usual Christmas party with gifts for children. Vincent Astor paid his employees bonuses. His annual party for them and their families took place on the Saturday before Christmas and was held in the great entrance hall of the tennis house. A mammoth Christmas tree glittered with real candles. Underneath were presents of shirts, leather jackets and tins of candies. The tea sandwiches, ice cream, coffee and milk were plentiful.

Slowly but surely, however, the tentacles of the financial crisis reached down into the hamlet. Although the ferry ran on schedule, fewer passengers used it on a frequent basis, mainly because they did not have money to spend freely but also because Rondout was suffering a dramatic decline. Shopping had been reduced to two or three large stores. The Orpheum movie theater was closed. The lighthouse foghorn sounded through heavy mists and fog, but fewer and fewer ships made Rondout a port of call. The bluestone and cement industries had essentially collapsed, and the brick enterprises were on a rollercoaster ride dependent on the vagaries of the New York City real estate market. The New York Central bought out the Ulster & Delaware Railroad, and its repair shops in Rondout were closed down. Every year Kingston Point Park drew fewer and fewer patrons. In 1922 its fabulous Oriental Hotel had burned and was not rebuilt. In 1931 the park, which had given so much pleasure to millions, folded. According to one former booster, the once bustling Rondout was fast becoming "a picturesque slum."

In Rhinecliff the casualties also mounted. The railroads cut back service. Clients of the self-employed melted away. Men took whatever jobs they could find, and even shared them. When the firehouse needed painting, Rhinecliffers Lyman Allen, Leonard Winkler and Harry Vosburgh happily divided the $45 job. The firehouse remained a core institution in the hamlet, but it was also having a hard time with finances. It could afford to pay George Van Wagenen only $20 a month for cleaning the firehouse and the sidewalks, stoking the furnace, starting the pumper every morning, taking it out when the weather was favorable, and blowing the fire alarm every Saturday morning to make certain it was in working condition and fixing it if it wasn't.

The estates, too, were hit. Helen Morton, now the sole owner of Ellerslie, let it go downhill. She occasionally asked ladies to informal garden par-

Nicknamed the "Galloping Goose," this bus outfitted with flange wheels was one of the last cars to run on the Rhinecliff and Connecticut tracks. Photograph early 1930s, courtesy Martin Wheeler–William Fahey Collection.

ties and to attend Roman Catholic services in the "artistic, private chapel" filled with bouquets of seasonal flowers that she had made in an outbuilding. Otherwise, she was in terror of losing all her money. One of the ways she economized was by tearing down unused workers' houses in order to save on taxes.

The situation at Wilderstein had only worsened. Mrs. Suckley had inherited $12,500 from a rich relative, but it had quickly disappeared. The coach house was rapidly deteriorating; so were the mansion and its furnishings. The family's chief, but unheralded, joy was that Daisy, who was then working part-time as a social secretary for her wealthy aunt, was enjoying rides about the countryside with her cousin, Franklin D. Roosevelt, then president of the United States. It was only after her death in 1991 that a cache of diaries and letters between her and Franklin was found in a little trunk beneath Daisy's bed. Still, no one knows exactly what the relationship was, except that she accompanied him to Vincent Astor's indoor pool where he swam to strengthen his polio-stricken legs, helped him design Top Cottage, his retreat in the hills, and gave him the Scottie, Fala, whom she had personally trained. She accompanied Franklin on his cross-country political and war bond funding train trips as Fala's chap-

erone. Occasionally, Roosevelt came to tea. A marvelously telling description of one such visit details how the family scurried through the house in search of a chair that would not collapse and from which Franklin could enjoy the view. Unquestionably, Daisy and Franklin's close friendship was a very great pleasure to both of them; the letters are full of delightful banter and secret jokes. Geoffrey Ward probably hit on the truth when he titled his edition of those letters *Closest Companion*. Although they had plenty of opportunity, it is highly doubtful they were ever lovers. Lucy Mercer filled that role. Daisy was a conduit between them. It was Daisy who would call Lucy to his side at Warm Springs when he was dying. Interestingly, Edith Morton Eustis was also a strong supporter of that romance. By sheer coincidence, when Eleanor Roosevelt found out about the affair and Lucy realized it must stop, Lucy married Winthrop Rutherfurd, the widower of Alice Morton, and brought up his and Alice's children as well as a daughter of their own.

Wyndclyffe just stood there; it had a new owner, but few knew or cared who it was. Linwood's short-range future seemed assured, however, for Schalk's chicken business continued to grow. The chicks were raised in buildings north of his main gates. (They have since been converted into apartments.)

Margaret "Daisy" Suckley's and Franklin Delano Roosevelt's witty, sentimental and most probably platonic relationship began when she accompanied him to Vincent Astor's indoor swimming pool, where he strove to regain the use of his legs after his devastating bout of polio. She was with him at Warm Springs when he died. But the depth of their great affection was not known until a box of their letters was found under her bed after she died in 1991, almost a hundred years old. Photograph September 1937, courtesy of Wilderstein Preservation.

The adult chickens were housed in a two-story building across the street. (It would become a high-end wallpaper factory, and then it partially burned. Recently its remains have been transformed into a private dwelling.) The slaughtering plant was down by the cove. Chet Holsapple, who worked there, thrust the birds' heads through a tube, stuck a knife down their throats, then sent them on to a machine that defeathered them. Schalk, who was thorough, had the chicken droppings incinerated and bagged for sale as fertilizer in a plant by Linwood's back entrance. However, he was not always in residence. He loved yachting and boats in general, and it was during this period that he organized a team to raise the gunboat *Philadelphia*, which had lain in the waters of Lake Champlain since it was sunk in a battle Benedict Arnold fought against the British in 1776. Human bones, cooking utensils, buttons and buckles were among the myriad relics still in the wreck when they brought her up. As the only raised gunboat built and manned by American forces during the Revolutionary War, she has been declared a National Historic Landmark and, along with the relics, is proudly displayed at the National Museum of American History.

William B. Kip Jr., who had inherited Ankony, could not afford to keep the place after 1929 and reluctantly sold it to what turned out to be a front for Vincent Astor. Tired of it by 1935, Astor sold it to the flamboyant Allan A. Ryan Jr. who established, with famed cattlemen Les and Lee Leachman, the premier Aberdeen Angus herd in the

Allan A. Ryan Jr., outwardly flamboyant but inwardly "cold as any fish that swam in the sea," bought Ankony from Vincent Astor who, acting as his front, had bought it from Depression-strapped William B. Kip Jr. Ryan raised premier Aberdeen Angus breeding stock on the place. This is one of his favorite cars. He is known as Senator Ryan, because he served between 1939 and 1942 in Albany. Photograph 1948, courtesy of the Rhinebeck Historical Society.

country. To open land for grazing, Ryan tore down the very old Bergh house; to be fair to him, few at that time viewed the remaining stone houses in the Hudson Valley as anything but nuisances. (Franklin Roosevelt was one of the exceptions.) Elected to the State Senate in 1938, Ryan would become renowned for his immense political picnics held on the Fourth of July, his birthday. According to the *Gazette*, at one of them an estimated 650 persons consumed "30,000 clams, 700 lbs. of chicken, 100 lbs. of fresh mackerel, 700 ears of sweet corn, 3 bushels of sweet potatoes, 30 watermelons" and untold quantities of beer and soda pop.

Although Ferncliff comprised forty-five properties totaling 2,972 acres, it was not as strong an employer as it once had been, for Vincent Astor's marriage to Helen Dinsmore Huntington was falling apart and they were seldom there. In fact, in 1940 Vincent tried hard to sell the entire property. But, even with a handsome brochure, he did not succeed. Instead, he tore down the mansion, which had become a white elephant, and refurbished the Casino for his living quarters when he was in Rhinebeck.

Hard Times in the Hamlet

In the hamlet even youngsters were called upon to help keep their families afloat. Boys trapped small animals, then cured and sold the skins to raise money for school clothes. To put food on the table, they shot squirrels for stew, and when they were older, they shot deer. They fished for bass and shad and scapped for herring to eat and to sell. Les Atkins paid them five cents a peck to pick dandelions, with which he made wine. They earned tips carrying pedestrians' bags between the railroad and the ferry, and, on holidays, sold sandwiches made by their mothers and sisters to lined-up motorists. Girls scapped for herring, too, and gathered hickory nuts in the woods and picked berries for pies,

some for the home table and some for sale. They worked double time in their mothers' kitchen gardens. As the fruits and vegetables ripened, they helped with canning. They chopped and carried the wood used for cooking and heating. They helped do the laundry that their mothers took in. As a matter of course, virtually all the children put cardboard in their shoes to prevent holes when they had complete soles, and to fill holes as the soles wore out. Many routinely picked up scattered coal from the railroad tracks to heat their houses.

Harry Heywood Sr. was luckier than most, because he still had a secure job at Ellerslie that gave him a house. (It was called the White house, not because it was white, which it was, but because that was the name of the former residents.) Harry had been raised on the place, for it was his father who was brought in to manage the power dynamo. After Harry finished his schooling, he went to New Jersey to learn plumbing and tinsmithing, and married there. However, when one of their seven children was afflicted with severe asthma, the family returned to Ellerslie, hoping the boy's breathing would be eased by country air.

The heart of the farmhouse was a huge kitchen; it was the room where everyone congregated. It had a three-burner kerosene stove and a sink with a pump. There was an icebox, also; the children loved it when the iceman came to fill it, because he would give them each a sliver of ice to suck on. Mary Wieber and her sister, daughters of one of the Heywoods' New Jersey friends, came up from the Bronx as summer boarders; as both families were staunch Catholics, their father knew they would be well looked after. Mary's memories of those times are still vivid. She was especially fascinated by the patterns the stove's burners made on the toast, and she still remembers the fortunes Mrs. Heywood told in tea leaves after supper, and the singing that took place around the player piano in the living room.

Part of the Heywood family, with friends in front of their house on the Morton estate in 1931: Mrs. Mary Hamill Heywood and Clara in the back row; Mary Wieber, and Marion and Joey Heywood in the center row; Harry Heywood and Betty Wieber in the front row. Photograph 1931, courtesy of Harry Heywood.

There were daily household chores — preparing meals, washing dishes, emptying the pan under the ice box in which water from melted ice collected, trimming the wicks of the kerosene lamps and polishing their globes — but she did not mind these chores. She even enjoyed helping with the laundry Mrs. Heywood took in, scrubbing it on corrugated washboards. When the linens they put in the sun to whiten, dried, she liked ironing them, even though the old irons had to be heated on the stove and were heavy. She got accustomed to using the outhouse. Because all the children took weekly baths in the same water, which had to be lugged to the stove to be heated in huge galvanized tubs, then lugged to the bathtub Mr. Heywood had installed in a special room, she was simply thankful to be the first and not, like young Harry, the last to bathe. On weekends and festival days everyone trooped to confession and to mass at St. Joseph's up on the hill.

When September came, Mary and her sister tagged along to the Ellerslie School, for schools in the city started a week later than Rhinebeck's. Tall, long-skirted, high-button-booted Miss Van Steenburgh, the sole teacher in that eight-grade, one-room schoolhouse, rode there on an old-fashioned tricycle from the Mill Road house she had built for herself. Eighty-odd years old, she had taught most of the children's parents and even some of their grandparents. A stern disciplinarian, she was not afraid to tease or strike her charges, for not only were such practices accepted in that day, but the school had become her fiefdom. Children who suffered under her piercing gaze the entire year thought of her as "the wicked witch of the west," but Mary recalls her days there as sheer bliss. In fact, she would have gladly given up all the comforts of her family's apartment in the city to live in Rhinecliff full time. (She eventually got her wish. Later on, she would marry a Rhinecliff man.)

Still, the Heywood household budget was always slim. Harry Jr. began pulling weeds in the crushed bluestone drives at Ellerslie when he was eight years old. Paying him only fifty cents a day, Mrs. Morton impressed on him that her father had begun work for fifty dollars a year. (It seemed to Harry that they got the same bargain.) He also vividly remembers his disappointment when, having carried a dead skunk all the way home from the north end of the hamlet and cured the skin, he got no more than thirty-five cents for his efforts. Nor was the Heywood household exempt from heartache. Joey, the son whose asthma had brought them back to Rhinecliff, was hit by a train and killed. No hamlet dweller still alive has forgotten that dreadful day. Then, seventeen-year-old Clara died after an appendix operation. Apparently, the Poughkeepsie doctor had placed a faulty drain in the wound. The family wished they had brought in local Dr. Cookingham, whom they called when absolutely necessary. A big heavy horse of a man, he was once an army surgeon, but had lost his license — some say because of drunkenness, others for performing abortions. But he had served them well in the past and was not particular about collecting his fees.

"Radio" (Leroy) Brown had a far harder time making ends meet, for Brown supported his wife and seven — soon to be eight — children by fix-ing radios. The problem with that kind of work was that it required electricity. If he could not pay for the electricity, he resorted to whatever odd job he could find. One of them was shoveling snow on the estates; often he was obliged to walk long distances in rough weather to earn a dollar for a long day. Sometimes the family went hungry. One of his son Ken's embedded memories is of eating the last bit of peanut butter on a heel of bread his mother had saved for his father's lunch pail; he has never forgotten the withering look his mother gave him when she realized she would have to send his father off with no midday meal. When Brown finally got a WPA job working on the roads — north Orchard Street was widened and officially renamed Orchard Drive, although no one ever called it that — he felt blessed to receive a steady twelve dollars a week.

During these hard times, the Browns moved from rented house to rented house. Finally they

All hamlet children attended the Orchard Street School in the 1930s. Harry Heywood, who has assumed an altar boy expression, was nowhere as prim as he looks. He is the middle boy in the second row from the right. Ken Brown sits in front of him. Photograph early 1940s, courtesy of Harry Heywood.

found a dilapidated stone dwelling above Slate Dock. (It has since been pulled down, but was possibly the original Sleght house, for it was very old, built of fieldstone and had a dirt cellar.) Its great advantage was that farmers who had lived there had left behind overgrown, but salvageable, blackberry and raspberry bushes, grape vines, fruit trees and a patch for vegetables. That left finding money to buy staples such as meat, margarine, coffee, sugar and, if Rhinebeck's federal allotment for needy families fell short, flour. When they had no money, the family simply did without.

Yet the Browns' life was not devoid of pleasure. They had a special place for picnics, on the flat ledge that overlooked the dock, where they cooked the fish they caught. They picked bouquets of wildflowers and collected the ancient and abundant Native American flints in the fields. There was also an informal hamlet dump just west of their home where the cliff dropped abruptly down to the railroad yard. It was not as popular as the Rhinecliff Road dump, but useful items could still be retrieved from the general litter.

Virtually all the children's entertainment relied on their imaginations and their initiatives. When the snow was slick they managed to find time to slide from Ellerslie down to the hotel. The shorter, but even faster rides were from the Catholic Church to Corning Street and across Charles where a lookout, called a "chickie," was stationed to warn the few oncoming cars. Loaded and lucky, the sledders could go halfway around Dutchess Terrace. Even faster was the ride from Tator Hill (Upper Hutton Street) across the bridge and down the ramp to the landing. These were the routes favored by Ike Allen, who piloted a sixteen-foot bobsled piled up with friends. Those who owned sleds and skates shared them with those who did not. Some had regular skis, held on only by a single leather band; others mimicked them with skis contrived out of barrel staves. A courageous few rode

the ice floes. More walked across the ice, tied together by a rope, to play pirates on the barges decaying along the banks of Rondout Creek. Sometimes, to round off the excursion, they sneaked into the movies. The ploy then was for those not so brazen to send in a false message that the icebreaker was coming to open the channel. The thought of being stranded in Rondout was so appalling that they didn't think twice before scurrying home.

When warm weather came the children flew kites, shot marbles, jump-roped and whizzed down the railroad viaduct on roller skates. They played in the sawdust piles at Toof's sawmill, swung on vines, rode on bending birch trees and camped overnight on the ball field. They swam at Slate Dock, where there was a diving board and strong swimmers could ride the swells made by passing steamboats. The boys and girls seldom had dates; they "walked around" in a group. But when they knew a couple was "sweet" on each other, the rest kept a respectful distance.

The boys were masters at devising pranks. Once, they reassembled an abandoned wagon on top of the library roof. Another time Harry Heywood rescued a surrey from being tossed into the river. He managed to get it home all by himself, dragging it a few paces up the hill, then putting a log against the wheel while he caught his breath before dragging it a few more steps. One day some predatory boys "borrowed" it for a ride. The herdsman at Ellerslie lent Harry a wheel wrench. He loosened the nuts and patiently waited for the miscreants to "borrow" it again. When the wheels flew off, the rig and the yelling boys made a racket that could be heard in Rondout. That was the end of their borrowing.

Sometimes Anthony Kallop, who sold vegetables door-to-door in the village, would load kids into his wagon and take them to town to the movies, charging them five cents each and getting their help in washing the beets and carrots. Throughout the year the youngsters serenaded newlyweds with what they called "skimmingtons" — blowing horns and whistles and banging on pots and pans until the newlyweds rewarded them with treats at the ice cream store.

Never idle, the children had a fine time. Best of all, very little of it cost a penny.

Franklin Delano Roosevelt, President of the United States

The spirits of hamlet Democrats were raised when presidential candidate Franklin Delano Roosevelt came over on the ferry from Kingston to electioneer before the vote in 1932, for they hoped against hope he would be able to put the economy back on track. Over a thousand people greeted Roosevelt at the Rhinecliff dock. A cavalcade led by the Rhinebeck band took him up the hill to the Beekman Arms, where he delivered a neighborly, car-side speech. Nevertheless, in Dutchess County he ran far behind Herbert Hoover. His local credentials — he had grown up in Hyde Park and spent happy boyhood days at Steen Valetje, his uncle's waterfront estate that straddled the Rhinebeck–Red Hook line — as well as the fact that he knew something about farming, could not win over a decisive number of Republicans in Rhinebeck. The national vote, however, was a smashing victory. With promises of a "new deal" for farmers and wage earners, Roosevelt won 42 states and 472 electoral votes over Herbert Hoover's 6 states and 42 electoral votes. The Democrats also took both branches of Congress.

However, it is safe to say that, with the exception of a handful of diehard temperance workers and a few men who had made easy money by

Roswell Cole notes the quality of his internationally prized anemones. Photograph late 1940s, courtesy of Betty Cole.

renting barn space to bootleggers or by distilling liquor themselves, the hamlet was mightily pleased that one of the first moves Roosevelt made as president was to get rid of the prohibition amendment. The immense mirrored bar at the Rhinecliff Hotel was immediately restocked. Across the street, Bob Benson's place reemerged, bestowed with a special luster because Benson wore a black derby hat day and night. Rhinecliffers were equally grateful when the administration instituted civil works programs to alleviate joblessness and implemented food allotment programs to supplement meager diets.

Rhinecliff Slowly Rises

As the decade wore on, a number of bright spots perked up the hamlet. Roswell Cole, the eleventh generation of one of the Cole (originally Kohl) families in the area and the son-in-law of James Hester, began an entirely new business in the early 1930s that he would make into an international concern through hard work and imaginative entrepreneurialism. He bred large, richly hued, greenhouse-grown anemones to replace the violets that not only had fallen out of fashion, but were succumbing to disease. His brother Raymond, who got his training at

the last large violet house in Red Hook, took on the growing side of the enterprise, while Roswell, who remained an employee of the Rhinebeck post office until retirement, handled the breeding of new strains and the distribution of the flowers. They grew the first florist-quality anemones in the world on a farm Roswell bought east of the intersection of Rhinecliff Road and Orchard streets on land that was once part of the Kip homestead and was lately owned by the Suckleys. Through the years the anemones would give near-to-home jobs to Rhinecliff residents, many of them women who did much of the picking. It would provide a good living for the Coles' two sons as well.

A second bright spot, though not so long-lasting, was the exploitation of a vein of molding sand that ran from the north border of the Cole property behind the ruins of the Kip homestead. Used in the manufacture of precision metal fittings, it was a geological phenomenon in high demand. Owned by a family named Pettina, the mine was managed by energetic Charlie Flynn, "a prince of a man" who had been a fireman on the New York, New Haven and Hartford Railroad, formerly the R. & C. The sand mining provided hamlet men with pick-and-shovel jobs until winter froze the ground. They dug the sand, then shoveled it into a Model T truck that motored it across the road, where they reshoveled it onto a conveyor belt that took it via a high trestle across the railroad track to the waterfront. There, men inside the waiting barges or boxcars leveled it. What was left over was heaped into piles according to grade to be ready for loading when an order came in. A tough, sweaty job at anytime, in the intense heat of midsummer it was grueling. Fortunately, the gang was usually made up of friends who urged each other along with jokes and mutual commiseration. One summer when the fishing was poor, even Jake Pindar worked at that job.

A cheering event of another sort was that Alvin Toof was elected town superintendent of highways. Well-liked throughout the heavily Republican town, Toof, a Democrat, was a consummate politician. He organized hamlet boys, whatever their parents' political persuasion, to parade around the polling places bearing great placards proclaiming his virtues. When he won, he treated them to all the ice cream they could eat. As highway superintendent, Toof finally gave Rhinecliff roads the attention they had so long needed. He graded and scraped them, filled the potholes with crushed stone, then oiled and rolled them. He made a garage for the town's road equipment out of an abandoned shed at his lumber mill. Respected for his planning abilities as well as for his expertise with machinery, Toof pleased residents because he always wore a business suit and a natty fedora hat to work.

In addition, as increasing car ownership made the sharp turns around the decaying Brice building dangerous, Toof urged the town to buy the building and tear it down. Fanny Brice Knickerbocker, teacher at the Flat Rock School who now owned the building, wanted $4,000 in cash for it. The cost of tearing it down and realigning the road was estimated at $1,225. When it went to a town-wide vote, the hamlet voted 21–19 against the sale. However, as the two inland districts strongly favored the project, Fanny got her money and the building was demolished in 1938. The empty space quickly became a favorite location for pickup softball after the usual five o'clock evening meal; the best contests pitted married men against bachelors. As the games coincided with the evening mail call, there were always enough players and plenty of spectators. One of the quirks of the game was that if the ball landed on "Skunk" Denu's property on the corner down from the library, he would grab it and keep it. A car was then rushed pell-mell into town to get a new one, and so the game carried on.

Edna Cornwell and Fred Holsapple were married in the mid-1930s. They built a fine house on the former Holiday Farm property north of the railroad station, but Edna found it too modern, so they moved back into her childhood home close to her provision store. Although she enjoyed the reputation of being an ardent moneymaker — it was said of her that "if a buck was to be made, Edna was right there" — she was openhanded with the increasing army of hobos. Whenever they came around asking for food, she always gave it to them — baloney, bread, cheese and coffee. She hired a black hobo named Walter Williams because, she said, he was too old and too slow-moving to be on the road. She made living quarters for him in an unused outbuilding, and he ate his meals with her and Fred. He took care of the gardens and did odd jobs around the store. When she decided to raise laboratory mice, he looked after them.

The Morton Memorial Library and Community House

The Morton Memorial Library and Community House, officially renamed to highlight the Mortons' many contributions, carried on as the Depression deepened. Although Miss Wooley had to take several cuts in pay because income from the endow-

ment was shrinking, she stayed on. Children continued to drop in on the way home from school and, when their homework was done, played games or did projects there. On Friday nights they gathered for dancing. The library received a top rating from the New York State Board of Regents and commendation for its service to the community. Yet the Board of Trustees — still composed mainly of estate owners (even Eleanor Roosevelt was briefly a member) and members of the Morton family — talked about closing the library on Saturday evenings, citing low attendance by adults, who liked to shop that night and then go to the movies in Rhinebeck. The board's final decision was to keep the library open "even for a few children, it being a bad precedent to be closed any evening."

However, Miss Wooley was let go in 1938. The existing correspondence in the Morton Memorial's archives paints the picture of an elderly benefactress putting an employee in her place in a polite, but unmistakable manner, and that employee answering back. "You know, dear Miss Wooley, that no one thinks more of you than I do, and I am sorry that my request [for information about how the endowment had been spent] disturbed you," Mrs. Helen Morton's opening salvo began. "As I told you the other day, I do feel that your interests are spreading to the county work and it would seem wiser to confine them more to Rhinecliff. ... You must realize that neither you nor I shall be here forever," it concluded, "and we must have a record of how the money which my parents gave is being spent."

Miss Wooley replied with a carefully worded offer to resign. Thereupon, Mrs. Morton offered Miss Wooley a three-month vacation. Miss Wooley then agreed to stay as long as it was "mutually satisfactory," adding, "I shall be happy for any and all suggestions you care to make. ... I am sure you know I have been most sincere in acknowledging your confidence in me & your ever ready help in carrying on this work so near & and dear to your heart." And she closed, "Over 100 people were at the play last night. It was very enjoyable." Mrs. Morton was obviously not one of them. Shortly afterwards, in a very brief typed note, Miss Wooley decisively resigned: "Times have changed, with so many radios and cars, making it possible for the people to enjoy the bigger things. However, I like to feel I have been able to bring to the people old and young, some of the finer things of life." Her final suggestions were that the Morton might unite with the Starr Library, which had also experienced declining attendance, and "tap into the Thompson Fund." These suggestions were red flags, for the two libraries were rivals. Mrs. Morton was proud of her family's contributions to Rhinecliff, while the Thompson Fund gave liberally to inland Rhinebeck. (The Thompson Fund, established to aid aging seamstresses in Rhinebeck and Brattleboro, Vermont, is still a major benefactor of the town; the scope of its grants has greatly broadened, while remaining confined solely to those two towns.)

Although Miss Wooley said she wished she might sever her ties of eighteen years by folding up her tent and going silently into the night, she told Mrs. Morton that she would announce her departure at the upcoming annual dinner of the Women's Club (of which she was the founder and president) and that she confidently expected at least eighty men and women would attend; over a hundred did. Mrs. Morton was not one of them. However, she did send a large box of snapdragons and roses from the Ellerslie gardens. She also wrote a letter to Miss Wooley to be read to the gathering by a member of the board. It was sprinkled with double-edged words of praise, such as, "Only in future years will we fully appreciate your fine work, which you have so admirably accomplished." Miss Wooley was still full of ginger. Immediately following the club dinner she engineered a final grand fare-thee-well at the monthly Hospital Auxiliary luncheon. It was

another huge and thoroughly heartwarming event, which Mrs. Morton also did not attend.

It seems clear that there was more to Miss Wooley's departure than the board's desire to reduce expenditures still further, for the minutes of a subsequent meeting record that the investment portfolio had been maintained and that $20,000 had been deposited in savings accounts waiting for the right bonds to show up. Obviously, personal friction was a strong element, for Mrs. Morton spent a good deal of time after Miss Wooley's departure congratulating the board on how much pleasanter running the center was without her presence. In any case the board was so constituted that it would not have needed much persuasion to agree with her rationale that the Roosevelt administration had instituted so many community social services programs for the less fortunate that a "social worker" such as Miss Wooley was no longer needed.

The board decided that the Morton Memorial could easily be run by a local woman whose duties were to serve as a part-time librarian and a part-time "hostess," scheduling the use of the auditorium for organizations such as the Women's Club, Hospital Auxiliary, Young Men's Club and Boy Scouts and Girl Scouts. H. H. Pearson highly recommended his housekeeper, Maude Zegelbrier, and she was duly chosen for the position. Engaged on trial for a week, she did her job so well that she stayed on for thirty-five years. An expert librarian was called in to cull "obsolete" books; in two days she removed 1,800 titles and added 177 new ones, the state footing the bill to the amount of $100. The park, which had not been used for two years because of budgetary constraints, was sold to Roswell Cole for $500; the play equipment was sent to the Orchard Street School.

Hamstrung by reduced hours and a limited budget, Mrs. Zegelbrier was, in her own words, mainly "a hander out of books," an organizer of

Maude Zegelbrier, keeper of the Morton Memorial Library for thirty-five years. Photograph 1969, courtesy of Mildred Young.

space were also very popular. For the gamesters there were Ouija and backgammon boards. Even teens who had no money to spend were encouraged by Marion to join their friends. Like Miss Wooley, Marion was an active, can-do spinster. Like Maude Zegelbrier, she was a local woman. A fine athlete, she would get her half sister Elinor Winkler to take over or simply close up shop to pitch balls to the boys or teach the girls to swim; she herself was known to swim across the river for fun. She also

Christmas festivities and a procurer of movies. (One double feature presented *The Night Cry* with Rin-Tin-Tin and Will Rogers in *Don't Park Here*.) But hours were reduced to twenty a week for eight months. During the summer months, she meticulously cleaned the books and the shelves and limited book borrowing to readers who happened by when she was cleaning. Organizations that had always met at the Morton now often held their gatherings at the firehouse or the hotel.

Shifting and Multiplying Focuses

In part, the new Sugar Bowl, owned and run by Marion Conklin, took up some of the slack. Located east of Cornwell's on Shatzell Avenue (where the Rhinecliff Post Office now is), it became a hangout for teenagers, who liked its soda fountain, penny candy and, most important, its magazines, otherwise hard to get in the hamlet. Its jukebox and dance

Marion Conklin and Marilyn Wheeler in front of Marion's Sugar Bowl. Photograph late 1940s, courtesy of Jeffrey M. Loeber.

put up a basketball net behind her store for anyone who wanted to practice shooting hoops. As one old-timer said, "Every kid was waiting for her for something."

Hamlet residents carried on in many positive ways, finding entertainment in the hamlet, as always, but now also farther afield because more of them owned cars. The boys and girls of the Methodist church put on a minstrel show followed by dancing that raised $104 for the fire company's uniform fund. A large number of Rhinecliffers journeyed to Red Hook to see the breakthrough Disney cartoon movie, *Snow White and the Seven Dwarfs*, the first of its kind, and to the Bardavon in Poughkeepsie to see the romantic Civil War extravaganza, *Gone with the Wind*. Town Justice of the Peace Ben Philbrick, a large stout man who could not quite fit behind the wheel of his Model T touring car, occasionally held trial in the firehouse. Once he postponed opening court for half an hour so that those who had gathered for the proceedings could listen to the popular program "Amos 'n Andy" on the radio he had brought along with him. (On weekends Philbrick was employed by Vincent Astor as a security guard to keep hunters and curiosity seekers off Ferncliff property.)

The World's Fair in Flushing Meadows, Queens, furnished Rhinecliffers with still another grand distraction. To raise money for their causes, churches and organizations held raffles with round-trip tickets to the fair's "World of Tomorrow" wonders as prizes. Other residents banded together to go down for the day or, like the Talmadges, took in the fair while visiting relatives. It was a heady experience. One of the displays featured a television that broadcast pictures of the crowd walking by; those who got close enough could see themselves on the screen. The automotive section was immense. Ford, Chrysler and General Motors vied for the handsomest building. All offered rides. General Motors took streams of viewers on moving chairs through a mock-up countryside that was actually what motoring on the Taconic Parkway turned out to be. The railroad section displayed historic and contemporary trains. The Pennsylvania Railroad's new 140-foot steam passenger locomotive, styled by the renowned industrial designer Raymond Loewy, was a winner. A four-act extravaganza with narrators, singers, a full *corps de ballet* and 125 actors brought the history of the American railroad to life. Kurt Weil, famous for *Three Penny Opera* and *Knickerbocker Holiday*, composed the music. The parachute jump (eventually taken to Coney Island) and Billy Rose's Aquacade, a band of sleek young women swimming and diving in choreographed unison, were the most popular attractions of the amusement park. Food of all kinds was easily available throughout the fair. Smart visitors could get a free lunch by doing the rounds of the brand-name food pavilions that gave away samples of their products and at the international buildings that offered ethnic fare. An ultimate relief to all, the superb landscaping was studded with comfortable sitting areas, fountains and statuary. The only succinct way to describe the effect of the fair on the Depression-weary was that it was mind-blowing.

Back to earth in the hamlet, things were not quite perfect, as in real life they seldom are. Two sad events threw a lasting veil of gloom over its residents. In October, Charlie

Flynn died suddenly of complications from an appendix operation performed by Dr. Cookingham on the dining room table in his brick house on Grinnell Street. (In those days penicillin, "the miracle drug," was not yet available to combat infection.) Only forty-six years old, he was much beloved. In addition to managing the sand lot, he had been town assessor, commissioner of the fire company, manager of St. Joseph's "Fighting Irish" baseball team, and custodian of the church's cemetery. The grief in the hamlet at his passing was profound. Equally devastating, Harry Talmadge Jr. was shot in a freak accident by a friend with whom he was collecting Christmas greens. His friend had put his hand into the sack in which they were carrying a shotgun. The gun was cocked. It went off and killed Harry; he was fourteen years old.

Just as the hamlet was beginning to emerge from the Depression, a different kind of blow struck. The New York, New Haven and Hartford Railroad finally closed its Rhinebeck-Connecticut line and ordered the rails pulled up immediately, for the metal had already been sold to Japan. The sunny side, according to Ray Dedrick, who signed up for the job when he graduated from high school, was that it paid pretty well. In fact, it gave him enough money to buy a new grey convertible. It was the fanciest car in the hamlet. "It took off like a scared cat!" he proudly reminisced. Even more important, it enabled him to commute weekly to a still-better-paying and less muscle-dependent job in the Connecticut River Valley.

Interaction with the Wider Community

Another pleasant consequence of increasing car ownership was that it made interacting with the wider community much easier. For instance, the Dutchess County League of Women Voters often met at the Morton. Neither the inland town nor the village had a suitable public space for such meetings. About fifty members car-pooled to attend a talk urging the right of women to serve on juries. At another meeting a Central Hudson Gas and Electric speaker discussed the relation of the cost of electricity to living costs. At yet another, eighty-five women from Ulster and Dutchess counties heard the wife of the New York State Commissioner of Public Works speak on "Taking an Interest in the Legislature." Inlander Mrs. James Bourne spoke to the Women's Club about Puerto Rico. As a professor at Bard College and a first cousin of the rising foreign affairs expert, John Foster Dulles, Mrs. Bourne was considered quite a catch. Joint meetings of the village and hamlet Needlework Guilds and Hospital Auxiliaries were also held at the Morton. In return, many Rhinecliffers attended the dedication of the new town hall that had been funded by federal Public Works Administration money.

Moreover, Edward B. Tewkesbury, whose father had been Morton's coachman, was elected town supervisor in 1939. Well known and liked throughout the town, he had previously chauffeured John Jacob Astor IV, Frederick W. Vanderbilt and Levi P. Morton, and then gone on to sell automobiles in New York City. When the Depression came, he returned to Rhinecliff and worked as a car salesman in Rhinebeck. At the same time, Alvie Toof was reelected town highway superintendent. Both stood testimony to the high caliber of citizens fostered in the hamlet.

In 1939, President Roosevelt came to lay the cornerstone of the new Rhinebeck Post Office he had been so instrumental in bringing about. The whole hamlet rushed to view the impressive ceremonies. The design of the building was based on Hendrickus Kip's homestead and, at the president's behest, would contain many stones from the ruins, despite the protests of Arthur Suckley, who then owned the site; Suckley legitimately claimed that there were many quarries nearby from which similar stone could be ordered. President Roosevelt, the Crown Prince of Denmark, who plied the trowel for him, the Princess of Denmark, the postmaster general of the United States, and the secretary of state were the celebrities on hand. The dozens of newsreel and metropolitan reporters and photographers that accompanied the entourage fascinated the entire Rhinebeck populace as well. (The famous *Life* magazine photographer Margaret Bourke-White was among them.) Over five thousand attended the ceremonies, which featured a grand parade with two companies of soldiers, five bands, five drum corps, five fire companies, several American Legion units and a smartly turned-out group of equestrians from the local area. Rhinecliffers were especially proud that Town Supervisor Tewkesbury was the star greeter. Shortly afterwards, the hamlet joined in the ceremonies marking the installation of Olin Dows's murals in the post office, but they were a little disappointed. Depicting the history of the town, it was difficult to pick out the long life of Kipsbergen/Rhinecliff in the murals.

It was during this period that Rhinecliff residents began to be called "Dock Rats." Apparently a Rhinecliffer named Weber had two sons who were always hanging out at the dock, and so in jest he called them "Dock Rats." The nickname caught on and, from that day to this, old-time villagers enjoy referring to Rhinecliffers as "Dock Rats." Sometimes Rhinecliffers apply the name to themselves, but usually there is at least a hint of irony in their voices and, tit for tat, they dubbed inland Rhinebeckians "upstreeters." Still, in these last years of the Depression, a more solid relationship between inland Rhinebeck and riverside Rhinecliff had been set in motion. It would gain momentum from the need for civilians to close ranks and pull together during the long years of World War II.

12

World War II

World War II changed Rhinecliff radically, as it did virtually every town and village in the country. At first, it was Europe's war. In the autumn of 1939, Poland and Finland were crushed by the Germans. They were followed by Norway, Netherlands and Belgium in early 1940. The British pulled off their spectacular evacuation of Dunkirk in late May of that year. Then France fell. The Luftwaffe's blitz of Great Britain raged from August to October. At terrible expense, the British held firm.

With two vast oceans dividing the western hemisphere from Germany's sweep through Europe and Japan's marauding in the Far East, Americans felt reasonably safe and the country remained officially neutral. The Depression and the havoc wrought by the Midwest "dust bowl" had made them inward-looking. Nevertheless, Congress approved its first peacetime program of military service.

Bit by bit, the United States was drawn in as the war quickly became global. Stepping up their successful attacks on allied and neutral shipping in the Atlantic, German submarines sank an alarming number of merchant ships, many of them American. The nation retaliated by establishing a patrolled security zone across the Atlantic and by passing the Lend-Lease Act, a device for providing the British with arms that put the German-Italian Axis on notice without exactly eradicating America's neutral status. The Axis then invaded Egypt, Greece, Yugoslavia and Russia in swift succession. At the same time, Japan joined the Axis and continued its conquests in the Far East, making plain it would brook no interference from the United States.

War was obviously in the wings. On December 7, 1941, that "day of infamy," the Japanese launched a surprise attack on the United States fleet, massed at Pearl Harbor. Most of the ships were destroyed or disabled. Over 2,400 soldiers, sailors and civilians were killed. Congress declared war on Japan the next day. On December 11, Germany and Italy declared war on the United States. On December 19, Congress extended the draft to men between twenty and forty-four years of age. The country was in for a very long haul on two widely separated fronts.

Rhinebeck became the center for northern Dutchess County's selective service. Of the town's over 400 men and women who were sworn into the armed forces, 69 were from Rhinecliff. Sent off with great farewell dinners, they trained at bases throughout the country from Maine to Texas, Kansas and Alaska. They came home for furlough when they could — some of them brought back fiancées or brides — then most were dispatched to the European or Pacific theaters of war.

Ray Dedrick, Edwin Heywood and Archie Van Etten, out of patriotism and in anticipation of the chance of improving their skills, signed up even before the declaration of war. Ray, one of the first to be taught to use radar in the Signal Corps, became the noncommissioned officer in charge of Northeastern coastal defense with headquarters at Bath, Maine. Edwin was sent to India, where he rose from first lieutenant to captain in the Air Corps, a service he continued in with marked success after the war ended. Archie was at Mitchell Field, Long Island.

Roger Cole was the first Rhinecliffer to be drafted. He was sent to Fort Benning, Georgia, where he prepared for an assignment in the Infantry Medical Detachment. Landing at Utah Beach in Normandy, he went on to Germany, where he fought at Hurtgen Forest. Surviving that, he was sent to North Africa, where he won more decorations than can be counted, including the Purple Heart. His brother Don trained in Detroit, then went in a mine sweeper unit to the Pacific theater; his favorite saying was, "If the destroyers are there, you know we were there before them." Howard Holsapple was awarded a Certificate of Merit for keeping Signal Corps vehicles in tip-top shape in France and Belgium. Chester Holsapple served on a tanker and fought in the battles of Okinawa and Iwo Jima. Glen Adair went to Trinidad. Pete Wheeler, one of five in that family who served, attended the Naval Service School at the Ford Motor Company in Dearborn, Michigan, then was sent to the Pacific theater; he would reenlist in 1945. Howard Mattison, in the Air Corps, wrote home that he was keeping the aircraft in good working order and was staying happy as long as his feet were on the ground. Gordon "Ike" Allen gave up an offer to train with the Pittsburgh Pirates baseball team because, he said, he would soon be "batting the ball for Uncle Sam." He was sent to the Philippines and then, after the Japanese at last surrendered, to Yokahama as part of the occupying force. His brother Bill was so anxious to get into the Air Corps Cadet program that he volunteered before graduating from high school. Bill became the tail-gunner of a B29 Super Fortress, graduating from training with the silver wings of a "sharpshooter of the sky."

Meanwhile Rhinecliffers put their all into the war effort. They accepted the rationing of gas, sugar, meat, and motor vehicle tires, as well as lowered speed limits, with good grace. They fished as ardently as they had during the Depression, and they shot wild fowl, deer, rabbits and squirrels to amplify

The Rhinecliff Hospital Auxiliary was ready and able when the United States declared war on two fronts. Photograph 1939, courtesy of Alan Coon.

their diets. Those with a piece of arable ground planted a Victory Garden. Qualifying adults gave blood. Even small children collected rubber bands and aluminum foil to be transformed into munitions. At a "junk rally," twenty pounds of metal for every man, woman and child in the village and town were collected. Women made "buddy bags" with treats and necessities. The Victory Knitting Club made wristlets and afghans, and the teenage girls' club rolled bandages for the Red Cross at the Morton Memorial. The library collected books to be sent to servicemen; its slogan was, "Give a book you really want to keep."

Much of this work tied Rhinecliffers more closely than ever before to inland Rhinebeck. They participated in the same surprise air raid drills. For instance, when the Rhinecliff railroad station was "bombed" and "casualties" were heavy, ambulances, first-aid squads, firefighters and demolition trucks rushed to the rescue from throughout the town. Airplane spotters received observation instruction at the American Legion in the village using models made by volunteers. The Legion was also the collection place for used musical records that were sold to buy new ones for USOs.

This is not to say that Rhinecliff's sense of independence was diminished. It merely lost some of its sharp edge and begot some mild rivalry. It made the front page of the *Gazette*, for example, that the Flat Rock School was the first in northern Dutchess County with over 90 percent of its students buying war stamps and bonds systematically. In just five months the Hospital Auxiliary in Rhinecliff made 13,505 compresses, 386 cotton balls, 326 bed pads, 105 towels, 32 abdominal bandages, 35 flannel bandages, 30 screen covers, 18 laboratory sheets, 18 wrappers, 46 crib sheets and 2 dozen baby dresses. During blackouts, the local Civilian Defense Corps, headed by Marion Conklin who, as always, made her duties an adventure, patrolled the streets to make sure every house had its blinds down. She also drove the fire truck when the railroad men, deferred from military service to keep the vital supply line running, were at work. Teenage boys hopped on board with her and manned the hoses. Although Marion had never before driven the pumper, she handled it as if she had done so all her life. The hamlet was also edified when Edward Tewkesbury, the town supervisor, became chairman of the town's Red Cross Fund Drive. Most of all, they were proud of the service flag hung across Charles Street near the post office, with stars for those in the service.

Rhinecliff flag flying over Charles Street honoring hamlet men in the armed forces. Photograph early 1940s, courtesy of Jeffrey M. Loeber.

Daily life followed its accustomed patterns, as in times of profound stress it must. Among the events reported by the *Gazette* as noteworthy was that the Zegelbrier's dog, Bozo, died and was much missed by his young friends at the library, that Harry Heywood and his friend George Wheeler took a long hike, cooking their lunch over a fire in good Boy Scout fashion, that a huge crowd gathered on the riverbank to watch as a civilian plane that had made a forced landing on

Marion Heywood and Marilyn Wheeler hoping the war would be over soon. Note the snow-covered stairs to the St. Joseph's Church in the background. Photograph 1943, courtesy of Jeffrey M. Loeber.

the ice was pushed to Port Ewen for repairs, and that, on Halloween, despite parties for the young intended to divert pranks, the ferry sign was snatched from its standard and deposited at the four corners, several outhouses were overturned and quite a few windows broken. Boys flattened the whitish copper-free wartime pennies under the wheels of passing trains, then filed them down in order to pass them off as dimes. Mrs. Helen Morton's small, but festive, Christmas party for hamlet children took place at the community center because New York's Archbishop Francis Spellman had persuaded her to give the Ellerslie mansion and its property to the Archdiocese of New York, and she had moved into the gardener's cottage. The traditional New Year's Eve joke party was held at the firehouse. There were far fewer marriages and births in the hamlet than before the war. But death continued to stalk unexpected quarry. In 1942 a freak accident killed Alvin Toof at age seventy-two. A falling tree on Mt. Rutsen Road broke his back. His obituary counted the days of his service as highway superintendent: ten years and nine months. He was long missed.

A radical change in the hamlet was the suspension of ferry service to Rondout. Passenger car patronage had dropped precipitously from just over 59,000 in 1941 to less than 27,000 in 1942. Trucks, which numbered 11,300 in 1941, decreased a breathtaking 90 percent. Some attributed the severely reduced use to gas rationing, and others to a lowering of tolls over the Poughkeepsie and Rip Van Winkle bridges. It may well have been a combination of both, but the result was the same — expenses could not be covered, even with a dramatic rise in foot passengers. The superstructure of the valiant, but aged *Transport*, which had been in active service for over fifty years, was dismantled and the boat retired to New York Harbor as a mooring for barges waiting for a tow. The still-fit *Kingston* crossed the river for the last time in December 1942, then was sold to

Texas to work on the Houston Ship Canal. (She made the rough 3,400-mile trip under her own steam, although twice the Coast Guard fired upon her thinking she was part of the German submarine fleet in disguise.) To have no ferry cast a pall over the hamlet far deeper than a nostalgic reaction, for many of its businesses relied on patronage from the commercial and private motor vehicles that came from afar to make the crossing.

The Cardinal Farley Military Academy of Rhinecliff

Once the church had received Ellerslie, the archdiocese began converting it into a military school for teenagers. The Irish Christian Brothers were put in overall charge, with military training handled by retired officers of the United States armed services. The still-handsome fifty-six-room mansion was swiftly transformed into a boarding school with a dining room, library, office and classrooms on the first floor, and living space, including a chapel, for the Brothers on the second floor, a dormitory for cadets on the third floor, and a tailor shop with storage for uniforms in the attic. In the basement were five pool tables, several ping-pong tables, an office and a kitchen.

The academy opened its doors to pupils in September 1942, with seventh and eighth graders in its grammar school and freshman and sophomore grades in its high school. At the dedication ceremonies, Cardinal Spellman placed a crucifix in the mansion's reception hall and praised Mrs. Helen Morton for having offered her resources to Christ's

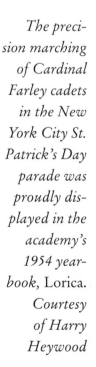

The precision marching of Cardinal Farley cadets in the New York City St. Patrick's Day parade was proudly displayed in the academy's 1954 yearbook, Lorica. *Courtesy of Harry Heywood*

work and for being as close to God as any human being he had known.

The academy grew and strengthened each year. Most of the boys came from the East Coast of the United States, but there were enough from Central and South America to justify a class in English as a second language and to mount an excellent soccer team. For Rhinecliff residents the academy was a pride and joy. They approved its patriotic fervor and its lofty motto, "Act Manfully." They delighted in the cadets who, clad in smart uniforms patterned after those worn at West Point, marched with precision to the beat of their own fine band. Their hearts were gladdened that the grounds, despite the war, were once more in mint condition. They were deeply moved when the cadets sang Memorial Day mass at St. Joseph's and marched with the firefighters and fife and drum corps in the hamlet commemoration service. And they thoroughly enjoyed observing such events as the five-hour "Airborne Task Force" war maneuver in which the 135 cadets divided into two companies and fought each other with fake aerial bombs, demolition charges and Molotov cocktails. Rhinecliffers were especially pleased that Cardinal Farley continued to acknowledge that it was situated in Rhinecliff. Its official name was the Cardinal Farley Military Academy of Rhinecliff.

Rhinecliffers were happy as well with the jobs the academy offered. Although these were far fewer than in Levi P. Morton's heydays, there were enough positions in grounds maintenance and gardening for the few available men, as well as in food preparation, laundry and sewing for women, to make a difference.

Postwar baby-boomers Wanda Loeber and Marilyn Wheeler Loeber, sisters-in-law as well as cousins, take their babies for a stroll. Grandmother Wheeler has joined them with a Wheeler granddaughter. Photograph 1947, courtesy of Jeffrey M. Loeber.

Peace

Peace came in two steps, beginning with V-E Day on May 8, 1945. School was dismissed and businesses, including the post office, closed. Cardinal Farley cadets, ninety-three strong and in full dress uniform, marched through the hamlet to the Good Shepherd Roman Catholic church in town. On May 13 all the churches participated in a day of prayer. V-J Day finally arrived on August 14. A carnival spirit reigned at the hamlet's parade that evening. The air sizzled and banged with the noise of firecrackers that magically appeared from private hoards and of firearms set off in backyards. Celebrations lasted throughout the month, the most prominent being at the large Assumption Day mass at St. Joseph's and at the 100th anniversary of the Dutchess County Fair, attended by Governor Thomas E. Dewey and his family. As the soldiers returned, one by one, everyone rushed to the railroad station to greet them. Happiness was transcendent.

Although the community grieved for the two hamlet servicemen who had been killed — Carl Hoffman and William J. McCue — it felt that they had given their lives for a vital purpose. Within the year Lester Trowbridge, the postmaster, and his

The war memorial at Shatzell Avenue and Kelly Street would become the site of Rhinecliff's moving annual Memorial Day commemoration. Photograph by Alison J. Michaels, 2006.

wife Nellie solicited enough money from fellow Rhinecliffers to erect a memorial at the corner of Shatzell Avenue and Kelly Street where the Brice Building had once stood. A handsome bronze plaque bearing the names of the twenty-four men who served in World War I and the sixty-eight men and one woman — nurse Mary Louise O'Brien — who served in World War II was mounted on a great rock flanked by yew bushes. A flagpole was placed in the center of the triangle. Three fine lampposts mark its angles. The town highway department contributed concrete curbing, bases for the lamps and topsoil for the plantings. Nobly marking the heart of the hamlet, it is to this day the locus of Rhinecliff's stirring and tender Memorial Day commemoration.

The veterans who returned to Rhinecliff to live were in many ways changed men. Older in years and infinitely older in experience, many had survived month upon month on the threshold of death in distant countries with languages and customs utterly strange to them. Most had been stationed, at least for a time, in regions of the United States that seemed to them almost as varied and foreign. Before

Bill Allen left the United States for the Japanese theater, for instance, he was at Fort Dix, New Jersey, for three weeks, then Greensboro, North Carolina, for basic training. His next stop was gunnery school at Harlingen, Texas. After graduation from there, he was shipped to Lincoln, Nebraska, where he was reassigned to Clovis, New Mexico, to learn the new B-29's armament system. That accomplished, he was sent to Harvard, Nebraska, the main training base for heavy bombers. After a ten-day furlough, during which he went home to Rhinecliff, he returned to Harvard to be assigned to a crew that picked up its brand new B-29 in Kearney, Nebraska, then headed to Methafield, California, the jumping-off place for planes going overseas. With a daredevil buzz under San Francisco's Golden Gate Bridge to keep their adrenalin high, the men were at last headed towards the Pacific theater. After brief stopovers in Hawaii and at the island of Quadulan, the bomber finally landed on Tinian in the northern Mariana Islands, the launch site for planes making the 1,500-mile flight to Japan. The great airstrip was hidden in the middle of sugar cane fields, but surrounded by Japanese soldiers who were staked out in caves. It would be the crew's home for the next seven months. They flew thirty-three combat missions, the first on January 29, 1945, against Iwo Jima, softening it up before the American invasion. After that they flew incendiary bomb missions over Tokyo and other major Japanese cities. It seems a miracle that none of the crew was killed or even seriously wounded, for the night skies were filled with deadly anti-aircraft explosives and the flaming fragments of stricken planes, and there was always the chance of running into another American plane in the thick smoke. On one mission an anti-aircraft missile ripped a huge hole in the side of Allen's bomber. As luck would have it, however, a replacement crew was flying the plane that day. Somehow it got back to the base and was repaired, and up it went again and again. On

June 6, 1945, Allen's crew escaped death once more. Their bomber was shot down over Tokyo, but, again, a replacement crew was flying that mission.

Allen was still at Tinian when the atomic bombs to be dropped on Hiroshima and Nagasaki were loaded into the *Enola Gay* and the *Bockscar*, named after Frederick C. Bock, the pilot who flew her. Allen actually saw one of the immense bombs before it was loaded and, not knowing what it was, described it as "like a big Bermuda onion squashed on each side and bulging in the middle." On November 15, 1945, Allen finally received his discharge back at Greensboro, North Carolina. He was then only nineteen years old, thankful to be alive and proud to have received a Distinguished Flying Cross, the Air Corps' highest medal. Best of all, he was free to return to Rhinecliff. (He still keeps in touch with the men in his crew, now scattered all over the country. All but two are still living.)

Not every returned Rhinecliff serviceman elected to stay in the hamlet, but the many that did, energized it. The skills they had acquired during the war, coupled with the steadily growing ownership of cars and the consequent increased mobility, made them able to take advantage of a greater number and variety of work opportunities. Industries, such as Federal [Ball] Bearing and IBM in Poughkeepsie, had grown rapidly during the war. "Ike" Allen went to Federal, where he remained his entire working life. Later, his brother Bill joined him, having decided it would be more promising than the clerking job he had first taken at the Oneida Market in the village.

It was at Federal that Bill met his wife Ruby, an enterprising young woman who had been able to get work there during the war while the men were away. They were married in May 1950 at the Rhinecliff Methodist Church and spent their first winter in its then-vacant parsonage. The heating bill was so horrendous, however, that they soon moved

Bill and Ruby Allen on the way to their wedding reception. Ike Allen was his best man. Ike's wife was the matron of honor. The flower girl was a niece. Photograph May 1950, courtesy of William R. Allen.

into the two-family house across the street, sharing it with Bill's mother and father. Ruby, who had been raised in Clinton Corners and had then lived in Poughkeepsie, was delighted to find Rhinecliffers so welcoming and their clubs and organizations so active. When her first baby was born, she joined the other young mothers pushing prams. Amused to notice that her mother-in-law and two neighbors ran a little contest over who would be the first to hang out her washing on Monday mornings, she surreptitiously entered the game by washing one Sunday night and having the fun of their surprise when her laundry was almost dry before theirs was hung. One of the things Ruby missed most when she later moved inland was hearing the anchor chains of the oil tankers clatter down in the middle of the night as they took their stations off the Rhinecliff dock, their last anchorage before the Port of Albany.

During this time, Bill left Federal Bearing for IBM, drawn by the pay, the remarkable benefits and the challenge of working in a cutting-edge industry. He would remain with the company for the next thirty-five years. Ray Dedrick was also a career IBMer. Other companies in Poughkeepsie at which Rhinecliff people found jobs were the milk equipment manufacturer Delaval Separator, Whitman (later, Western) Publishing, and Luckey Platt, the city's preeminent department store.

Many men went into business for themselves. Alvin Van Etten established a small, but successful home heating oil business. Married to Elinor Winkler, Alvin made a comfortable house from the shell of a small barn across Valley Way from Ray Dedrick and his wife Helen Holsapple, whose family owned the land. Roger and Donald Cole joined their father in running his anemone business. Roger focused his attention on the growing end, and Don on the financing and marketing. Roger and his wife Jean, a

The Rhinecliff-Kingston Bridge that replaced the ferry provided easy, year-round access to Kingston, although it was not as direct a route. Photograph by Alison J. Michaels, 2007.

New Jersey girl with family connections in the hamlet, bought the house Edna and Fred Holsapple had built on the Holiday Farm property. Don married his Detroit sweetheart, Betty Ziegler, whom he had first met on a blind date while training. First they lived in the apartment attached to the greenhouse power plant, and then they built a home on land where the Morton Memorial's outdoor recreation center had once been. In those days the Coles were growing strawberries, potatoes, delphinium, corn and hay, along with the anemones. Betty remembers with fear and trembling, intermixed with pride, the day that Don asked her to drive the tractor while he threw baled hay onto the trailer. Somehow she managed it, although her Detroit upbringing had done nothing to prepare her for such a job. Through the years, Don played an active role in the wider community, becoming chief executive officer of the First National Bank of Rhinebeck. Always in pursuit of a little diversity, he also raised prize-winning Shetland ponies that he showed at fairs as far away

as Cleveland, Ohio. And, he bought a modern iceboat, a Detroit National (perhaps for sentimental reasons, but it was a great boat). He would become an ardent member of the revived Hudson River Ice Yacht Club.

Industry came to Heermanceville at this time in the form of a potato chip factory. It seemed promising, but it operated for only one year before it burned to the ground in a mighty fat-fueled blaze. There was nothing the fire company could do to put it out. Miraculously, no one was injured. Its only lingering contribution was that underneath the building was found an ancient cache of Native American arrowheads.

The Ferry Run Revived

A great sigh of relief coursed through the hamlet when the New York State Bridge Authority, which had assumed operation of the ferry crossing, bought a modern steel boat capable of holding thirty cars

The new potato chip factory located on the Rhinecliff Road was soon demolished by fat-fueled flames. Courtesy of the Rhinecliff Volunteer Fire Company

Ferry service was revived by the purchase of Manhattan's 125th Street boat called the Richmond. *More appropriately renamed the* George Clinton, *it would serve while the Rhinecliff-Kingston Bridge was under construction. Photograph early 1950s, courtesy of the Museum of Rhinebeck History.*

and seating seventy-five passengers. The boat had been retired from Manhattan's 125th Street crossing only because it was no longer large enough for that run. Repainted dark green with jaunty Indian red and ivory trim, its name was changed from *Richmond* to the more appropriate *George Clinton,* the name of the governor of the colonial province when Kip and Cantine received their ferry monopoly back in 1752 and, after independence, also the name of the first governor of New York State. Several hundred jubilant people attended the inaugural ceremonies, first in Kingston, then in Rhinecliff. The largest ferry to have operated on the line, the *George Clinton* had a virtually unobstructed main deck where cars were parked in four rows. In the center of the upper deck was covered seating. The ferry's only shortcoming was that its schedule was cut back. The first round-trip began at Rondout at nine o'clock in the morning, and the last arrived at Rhinecliff at seven o'clock in the evening, making it no good for getting to work

at the new IBM plant in Kingston. Anyone with a job there was forced to drive down to Poughkeepsie, cross the Mid-Hudson Bridge and loop back upriver to Kingston. However, the ferry functioned perfectly as an entertainment for small children. It took just twelve minutes to cross the river, and there was just enough time for ice cream before boarding to catch the boat back home. Many in Rhinecliff clung to the hope that the ferry would continue to run forever. It was, after all, the time-honored way to reach Rondout and Kingston.

Newcomers

Only a few new houses were built in the post-war era. Because of the steep slopes, usable vacant lots were scarce. Moreover, a growing number of houses were for sale, mainly because older owners died or moved to warmer climes. Many properties languished on the market, for even well-built

Ed Tybus presides over his mirrored bar for this semi-formal portrait. Photograph late 1960s, courtesy of Andrea Evans.

dwellings required extensive renovation to meet the desires of the younger generation. Still, a handful of "out of town parties" braved the hamlet's slightly down-at-the-heels appearance, drawn by its extraordinary site and the abundance of its low-priced real estate. Most new residents came from the New York metropolitan area, just as they always had done. They were not so many, nor so different, that they changed the hamlet's character, for they lived in Rhinecliff full time and became woven into the fabric of the community.

Ed Tybus wanted a more rural livelihood than New Jersey offered after he was discharged from the service. He bought the Rhinecliff Hotel from the aging widow Steinmetz and refurbished it. It was, he said, a perfectly miserable place — lead plumbing, sooty kerosene space heaters, doors off hinges. When he opened for his first summer boarders, his flyer proclaimed: "Hotel Rhinecliff nestles along the east bank of the Hudson in the heart of the river valley" with the "ever-enchanting Catskills in the distance. From comfortable wicker chairs one can view the daily activity of commercial and pleasure vessels traveling up and down the river. It would be difficult to find a more interesting and picturesque locale." The flyer went on to tout the refreshingly cool breezes "even in the warmest weather," the two-hour travel distance from New York City via train or state road, the ample home-cooked meals, and the fellowship that reigned at shuffleboard and around the pianos, where singing and dancing broke out spontaneously. It also boasted a fully licensed bar. The cost was moderate, though almost double what the Adair House had charged before wartime inflation — $32 dollars a week American plan for a single person, $30 each for two persons, or $5 a person a day. For outings, the

notice lauded delightful daytrips to area historic sites, the quick ferry to Kingston, the golf courses at Red Hook and Staatsburg, and the picturesque Village of Rhinebeck. What Tybus failed to mention was that the New York Central tracks ran between the west porch of the hotel and the river. The steam engines were changed to diesel in the mid-1950s, but the noise and odor of stopping and starting the locomotives were only marginally improved. Nevertheless, Ed and his wife Ruth Locke, the Art Lockes' daughter, would run it, together with Ed's mother, for over four decades.

Annie Jordan, from New York City, bought the Sugar Bowl building and transformed it into Paddy's Bar and Grill. Paddy, her husband, died relatively young, and over the years Annie became a beloved "knows everything" fixture in the community. During her more than forty-five years as a saloonkeeper, there was a period when her place was known for serving underage drinkers, but that problem was resolved and she survived. Paddy's ended up as a quasi-clubhouse for fire company volunteers — her boys — who, if she were not there,

Annie Jordan, who would become a beloved fixture in the hamlet, bought the building that Marion Conklin and her Sugar Bowl had vacated and transformed it into the popular Paddy's Bar and Grill. Here, she is dancing with Lyman Allen at the fire company's annual dinner dance. They were both fire commissioners at that time. Photograph 1980s, courtesy of the Rhinecliff Fire Company.

simply noted on a sheet tacked up on the wall whatever refreshment they had helped themselves to.

Mabel Harms had been raised in Rhinecliff, but had migrated to New York City where she worked a succession of jobs. Married there, she and her husband bought acreage in Rhinecliff for a vacation home. A "knockout," with her long legs, short shorts and love of dancing, she galvanized Rhinecliff with her energy and enterprise. She claimed she did most of the work building their log house, including the immense fireplace, single-handedly while her husband and his friends were busy hunting, swapping yarns and drinking beer, and it is entirely possible that she did. She also planted and maintained an apple and pear orchard of some eighteen trees. When Mabel and her husband split up, she kept the house. Over the years she supported herself with every kind of job, from feeding horses to looking after elderly people. In her late eighties she was the salad chef at the Kopper Kettle, a village eatery frequented by Rhinebeck politicians. In her nineties she and her husband joined forces once more and drove off to Florida in a big white Cadillac. She took care of him until he died, then moved to South Carolina. She lived on her own

there until she was over a hundred years old. Alert and always in touch with her Rhinecliff friends, she died peacefully in the spring of 2007.

The William Steglitzes — Germans from the Yorkville section of New York City — wishing to bring up their toddler son in the country, had bought a property on the corner of Kelly Street and Russell Avenue in the 1930s. Another IBMer, Steglitz became somewhat of a community asset when he began raising pigeons for sale. But both he and his new neighbor, a Czech, were cranky and insistent men. Both claimed a pie-shaped sliver of land on their shared boundary. (Irregular lots, caused by the up-and-down terrain, were the rule in Rhinecliff.) The Czech grew so exercised over this dispute that he moved away to prevent himself from doing serious harm to Steglitz — at least that is what he was said to have said. In reality, his house turned out to be partly on Steglitz's land.

In the aftermath of the war, Rhinecliff seemed to be a sterling example of the old saying, "The more things change, the more they remain the same." But the hamlet was beloved by all who lived there and even by some who, for one reason or another, left it.

13

An Uneasy Transition

The 1950s were unsettled times at home and abroad. The country was in the midst of a prolonged boom. A key to its prosperity was the swiftly developing highway system that would transform living and working styles throughout the land. City suburbs exploded. Towns grew randomly. Smaller settlements tended to be engulfed or simply to fade away. Rhinecliff, relying on its strong traditions, did none of these things, but it lost some of its spark. Its shops closed, many of its houses were vacant, renters came and went.

Rhinebeck, too, was having a hard time adjusting to the postwar world, but it dominated the hamlet as never before. Despite its extraordinarily beautiful setting, the hamlet was labeled as the poor and, therefore, insignificant part of town. Bridges built between the town and the hamlet during the war became decidedly one-way. The flow was from Rhinecliff to Rhinebeck; only a trickle of inland Rhinebeck residents ever entered the hamlet and, if they did, they rarely journeyed farther than the railroad station. There was little new about this, but at a time when the reach of local political power would grow exponentially, Rhinecliff was finding itself left out of the loop. Nevertheless, Rhinecliff did not lose its spirit. Its people hunkered down, finding a living in the near vicinity so that the hamlet could remain the center of their lives.

The Ellerslie Conflagration

Of all the local events during this period, the most dramatic and, indeed, terrifying, occurred on the evening of Saturday, October 26, 1950. According to the *Gazette*, just after six o'clock, two Cardinal Farley cadets who had intended to play an after dinner game of ping-pong in the attic discovered a small fire there. The Rhinecliff Volunteer Fire Company immediately dispatched its 500-gallon Sanford and its Ford 250-gallon front-end pumper. Mutual aid brought more equipment from Rhinebeck and Hillsdale. But none had the power to throw water high enough to put out the blaze. The fire spread. Three of the mansion's seven chimneys collapsed, throwing bricks far and wide. The slate roof fell in. Fuel tanks and several rounds of small-caliber ammunition exploded. Flames shot so high into the air that

Shortly after dinner on the night of October 26, 1950, two cadets found a fire burning on the top floor of Ellerslie. By ten o'clock all that remained was a stone shell, three forlorn chimneys and a stunned hamlet. Courtesy of William R. Allen

the glow could be seen as far away as Tuxedo Park, over fifty miles to the south and across the river. By ten o'clock all that was left standing was the stone shell of the ground floor and three forlorn chimneys. Miraculously, only two firemen were injured.

Fortunately, the entire cadet corps safely evacuated. Somehow they managed to get out a few cots, desks, religious objects and a canary. The Brothers saved the records of the academy. But an Irish setter was lost and — a great misfortune for posterity — so was Mrs. Mary Heywood's album containing Ellerslie photographs that went back to the late nineteenth century. The following day some four hundred cars loaded with sightseers came to view the ruins, but it was like the mournful wake of an old and valued friend to many in Rhinecliff whose friends and families had worked at Morton's.

Despite what to almost any other institution would have been a disaster, the Cardinal Farley Military Academy hardly missed a beat. The Brothers converted the gym and the Ellerslie schoolhouse into dormitories, and the carriage house into a dining hall. The hayloft in the immense barn was used as a running track. Instead of one dormitory, which had already been planned, the archdiocese sanctioned two. Rising mightier than ever from its ashes, within eighteen months the academy was ready for Cardinal Spellman to dedicate and for the cadets to occupy.

The Korean Conflict

Abroad, the hot war was replaced by the cold war. Russia imposed its communist form of government on country after country. It built up its armaments to include multiple atomic bombs and sent Sputnik, the world's first man-made satellite, into orbit. In the Far East, communist North Korea's invasion of South Korea led the United States into conflict with that country. Although war was never officially declared, Congress reinstated the expired Selective Service Act for men between the ages of 18 and 25. A hefty 20 percent of the Rhinebeck men who went into service lived in Rhinecliff. Many were volunteers, reflecting younger siblings' desire to prove themselves as had their older brothers. It also reflected the restlessness born of those times.

Harry Heywood did a stint in submarine salvage. He remembers first becoming interested in underwater diving when, as a boy, he heard talk about J. Ruppert Schalk's raising the *Philadelphia*. He trained in New York's East River, where the currents were so strong and shifting that divers' feet had to be heavily weighted to reach the level where they could work. Even then, they could remain there for only a brief time. After training, Harry was sent to Bayonne, New Jersey, to help recondition mothballed Liberty ships. During a furlough, he and Anne Cardell from Staatsburgh, who was finishing her nurses' training, were married at Rhinebeck's Church of the Good Shepherd in a hastily put together evening ceremony. (By then, St. Joseph's performed services only on Sundays, and they did not have that much time.)

After his discharge, Harry had multiple jobs. He delivered Bond's breads and, as he was free on Wednesdays, he also worked for Cardinal Farley.

During this period his father built a cesspool for the library, a job for which Harry hauled stones from the burned mansion's first story. He then buried the remainder near the site of the new administration building that was on the archdiocese's drawing boards; Harry still remembers where those stones lie. It was perhaps this work that inspired him to go into the excavating business. Gradually, he acquired equipment and a shop on the north side of the Kip homestead ruins. (The building is still there.) A fascinating attribute of that site was the many Native American arrowheads lying just below the surface of the soil. Not yet generally recognized as artifacts to be studied and preserved, Harry gave them freely to friends who expressed an interest.

During the Korean conflict, Cardinal Farley's enrollment steadily increased. Its football, basketball and soccer matches, many against local teams, drew large crowds from a wide surrounding area. So did the cadets' weekend parades and their band and glee club concerts. Older Rhinecliffers still recall how smartly the Cardinal Farley boys marched down Kelly Street to the hamlet's Memorial Day observances. Those lucky enough to witness their faultless performance in New York's St. Patrick's Day parade were doubly proud. Moreover, the tie between the community and the academy was strengthened when local boys were allowed to use its sports facilities and when Rhinecliff's own Ronald Van Etten attended the academy. (He was required to convert to Roman Catholicism in order to do so.) He is still grateful for the first-rate education he received there; he even values the school's discipline. Louis Fernandez, a student from Panama, grew so fond of Rhinecliff

Anne Cardell of Staatsburgh in her nurse's training uniform and Harry Heywood in his sailor suit before they were married. Harry was in training for submarine salvage. Photograph 1949, courtesy of Harry Heywood.

that he stayed on, later marrying Ruth Coady, the daughter of one of the academy's chefs.

The academy continued to employ local people. On the center page of an early yearbook are portraits of Rhinecliff residents Mrs. Mary Heywood, dietician, and Miss May F. O'Neill, nurse. Other Rhinecliff employees were Jim Cunningham, a chef, Martha LaPolt, in charge of the commissary, and George Cave and Harvey Holsapple, general handymen.

However, the best and most long-lasting jobs for Rhinecliff men were at IBM. In 1956 a brand-new IBM facility was opened between Rondout and Kingston. The only problem for Rhinecliffers was the commute to the other side of the river, because of the ferry's reduced schedule. As soon as the ice was out of the river, Bill Allen, who had been transferred to the Kingston plant, solved the problem as only a Rhinecliff-born man could. He hired an acquaintance to row three colleagues and himself from Slate Dock to Kingston Point in the morning. They then piled into an old car they left there for the purpose and drove to the plant. On the way home they reversed the process. Nevertheless they were relieved when the bridge to Kingston was begun. Although some Rhinecliffers were outraged when it was located on the Red Hook boundary instead of off Long Dock as had once been promised, at least its great span was within eyesight of the hamlet.

With great exertions the state formally opened the bridge on February 2, 1957, although the only guardrails were thick wooden beams. The ceremonies drew only a handful of dignitaries, for it was a cold, drizzly day. Dyed-in-the-wool opponents remarked on the inauspicious beginning, but the

Just before he died, J. Ruppert Schalk deeded Linwood to the Sisters of St. Ursula, who had established a convent and a school in Kingston. This photograph was taken in 1953 shortly after the nuns moved in. Courtesy of the Sisters of St. Ursula.

around-the-clock and throughout-the-year crossing proved irresistible.

Moreover, the town was able to buy the ferry landing at a bargain price. The newly formed Rhinecliff-Rhinebeck Boat Club was more than happy to take it. An informal, do-it-yourself organization, the club prospered. Besides boatmen's traditional camaraderie, it provided such amenities as a canvas sling for lifting boats in and out of the water at low tide. However, piling ice and swirling waters weakened the buildings. Some were actually swept away.

Estates on the Skids

Meanwhile, the estates followed their erratic courses. For the wealthy of New York City, the Hudson River Valley was still unfashionable. J. Ruppert Schalk was aging and had no blood heirs, making Linwood's future uncertain. Finally, through a young priest in Rhinebeck who had led him back to the Roman Catholic faith, he willed Linwood to the Society of St. Ursula, an uncloistered order founded in France in the early sixteenth century and focused on teaching young girls and women, especially

those who were poor. The society had already established a school for girls near Kingston Point. When the Sisters received Linwood in 1963, they set up a nursery school, a kindergarten and a summer camp. Realizing that the rambling old Ruppert house was unsuitable for public programs — among other deficiencies, it was a firetrap — they asked five fire companies to burn it as a training exercise and replaced it with pedestrian, although comfortable and well-sited, brick buildings, typical of those times.

As one of the Sisters' activating goals was to make Linwood "a sacrament of healing to a wounded world," their focus gradually shifted to developing the property as a retreat center for individuals and families seeking a more spiritual way of life. Because the Sisters also believe that the beautiful site is a wellspring of deity that should be shared, local visitors are welcome to walk or cycle on the grounds and to quietly enjoy its peaceful atmosphere and spectacular views. The only stipulation is that when a silent retreat is in progress, visitors should not speak to the participants.

Of all the estates, Wyndclyffe was the worst off. It passed from Finck's nephew through a succession of owners whose romanticism led them to buy it, then left them hanging when it came time to figure out what do with it. The mansion steadily deteriorated. Its acreage was sold off for building lots, albeit large ones. Only the land immediately surrounding the gothic hulk and an easement on the entrance road were retained. A photographer bought and remodeled the carriage house but, with no one caring for it, Miss Jones's imposing mansion began to fall apart. Second-growth trees invaded the lawns.

Most of Wyndclyffe's property had already been sold off and the mansion was fast deteriorating. A series of new owners, intrigued by its history, bought it, but none could figure out how to save it. Photograph by Tom Daley, 1990s.

Wilderstein carried its head high, but flirted with disaster. Daisy Suckley and her mother, who would die full of delusions of grandeur in 1953, scraped along by selling heirlooms to meet taxes. The widowed Betty, the only one to have married, refurbished the Wilderstein farmhouse and called it Villa Saga. Every afternoon she took tea with Daisy at Wilderstein. Her three children, the only Suckley issue, were a continuing problem. The son was a schizophrenic who, after years of devoted family

care, finally had to be institutionalized. Her daughters lived a precarious existence out of reach, and they were difficult when they visited. Betty sold the barn complex to her husband's nephew, who with his young wife, made a sort of weekend camp out of it; its salient adornment was a Caribbean sloop, which was visible in the main barn through a large windowed opening in their sitting room.

Robin, the eldest Suckley, lived in the cellar. It is said that he and Daisy did not speak, although he baked cookies and sent them upstairs via an old dumbwaiter when guests came to tea. He was, however, friendly with area young people and with professionals who answered his call when he gave up trying to fix the furnace or plumbing himself. In the artifact-packed but leaking carriage house, he entertained them with yarns of days gone by in a melodious, clipped voice that one of those men can still mimic perfectly. Arthur lived in the principality of Monaco most of the time. When he occasionally returned to Wilderstein, he took over the Louis XVI salon for his "office," piling up heaps of miscellaneous papers on the onyx-topped tables and frail damask-covered chairs. Mornings he drove the gray family Packard to Schermerhorn's pharmacy and ice cream parlor in town, where he read newspapers, wrote letters, greeted acquaintances and sipped coffee as if he were in a European café. Afternoons, if the weather was favorable, he donned white flannels and played tennis at the Edgewood Club in Tivoli as he had as a young man. Katherine, having returned from Paris just before the Depression, removed herself entirely from the family circle in a huff; she lived in a remodeled schoolhouse in the neighboring town of Milan with a couple who shared her love of music. Her name was not spoken at Wilderstein.

The sad fact was that Wilderstein's long-deteriorating mansion and outbuildings had become charming storehouses for intricately fashioned recollections and their supporting memorabilia. However,

one bright spot, in addition to Daisy's good job at the new Roosevelt Library in Hyde Park and her ability to remain cheerful despite never-ending challenges, was that Julia Clarkson Hawkins, one of the "river people," rented Wildercliff as a summer home for herself and her son's family. Her grandson remembers as a small boy dancing with glee when school was out and he and his sisters took off for Wildercliff. The only drawback was that no other similar children of suitable age lived in the vicinity. However, that deficiency was more than made up by the fact that the Southlands riding school was nearby; in fact, the horses were often brought over to Wildercliff for lessons. John Newman, who still lived in the apartment of the Suckley's coach house, was a mainstay in the smooth running of the household. Always "polite, reserved and deferential," he met the train, drove the children to tennis and riding lessons, taught them a good deal about driving cars, got the mail and did special errands. In many ways the Hawkins's life at Wildercliff seems to have been uncannily like that experienced by Henry James when, almost a hundred years before, he had visited his aunt and uncle at neighboring Linwood. Indeed, the connection with the novelist can be said to have leaped over the years when, after over twenty years at Wildercliff, Mrs. Hawkins left it to join her sister in a family house upriver and the Suckleys sold the property to Frederick Dupee, a distinguished professor at Columbia University and the noted biographer of Henry James. Neither the Hawkinses nor the Dupees, however, formed a relationship with Rhinecliff beyond use of the train. For nearby shopping they went, via Mill Road, to the village. Their social sphere was among the estate owners and the literati.

Even Ferncliff was on the skids, but from lack of attention rather than lack of money. Vincent Astor's marriage in 1940 to Minnie Cushing, the daughter of a distinguished surgeon, had not lasted. Divorced, Astor was again at loose ends. He attempted unsuccessfully to sell the estate, as he was spending most of his time on Long Island or in the Caribbean. When at Ferncliff, he "camped out" at the Casino, or as locals called it, the Tennis Court House. In 1953 he eloped with the widowed Brooke Russell, then a writer for Condé Nast magazines. In her autobiography, *Footprints*, she gives a succinct first impression of the estate: "When I arrived at Ferncliff, they [the other guests] were playing croquet on the indoor tennis court." The following day Vincent treated her to a hair-raising ride on his miniature railroad — not her cup of tea, but apparently she did not complain. However, when squadrons of mosquitoes attacked her because the building had no screens and Vincent breezily informed her that the Hudson River aristocracy refused to admit that insects existed, she got her screens.

Despite an aversion to countrified living, Brooke Astor made Vincent happy. At his death in 1959, she inherited Ferncliff, sixty million dollars for her own use and the sixty-million-dollar Astor Foundation, whose mission was broadly "the alleviation of human suffering." Almost immediately she began to disperse the land. She gave over 170 acres at the intersection of River Road and Astor Drive to the Rhinebeck Rotary Club to establish a wilderness area called Ferncliff Forest. Then, having spent a delightful time in Rome as Cardinal Spellman's guest at Pope John XXIII's coronation, she donated the estate to the Archdiocese of New York for a nursing home, to be built on the site of the mansion. The Tennis Court House was made into quarters for the nursing sisters. (Brooke Astor died in 2007 at age 105, having expended most of Vincent's great fortune on wise support of the New York City institutions in which they both had been interested, among them the New York Public Library, the Metropolitan Museum of Art and the New York Botanical Gardens. In addition she gave considerable support to revitalizing the Apollo Theater in Harlem and to launching the Public Theater in the old Astor Library building. Thousands of smaller New York City organizations and institutions as well as needy individuals also benefited, often anonymously, from her philanthropy.)

Ankony alone seemed to prosper. Allan Ryan's fine Aberdeen Angus bulls regularly won international world championships at Chicago and, when sold, brought ever-higher prices. A three-month-old bull sold for $15,000 dollars, for instance; then a six-month-old bull sold for $58,000. Buyers from all over the United States and even from Europe flocked to Ryan's fashionable, annual auctions at Ankony, adding to the community a decided zest that the Kip founders would undoubtedly have enjoyed. Nevertheless, in 1966, Ryan suddenly decided to move a part of his herd to land he owned out west and sell the rest of it at a last grand auction. "The procession of great bulls with their brushed and braided hair, polished hooves and curled eyelashes, plodding down a red velvet carpet," an observer from an upriver estate proclaimed, "was a sight never to be forgotten." The main house was closed up and left to deteriorate.

Old-time Rhinecliffers and New

During this period of transition, old-time Rhinecliff families continued to live the life they had always led, but in a somewhat wider orbit. They constantly upgraded their houses according to their particular needs and their on-hand cash. There were fewer youngsters, but more than enough to enjoy a childhood of baseball and pickup basketball, making go-carts and bicycling, shooting dump rats, skating on Cole's pond, fishing and swimming at Slate Dock and sliding down snow-covered slopes on cast-off porcelain tabletops, all unimpeded by parental prohibitions. A new fad for the boys was to take golf balls they had picked out of a bog on the Red Hook golf course, where they caddied, and hit them over the cliff onto the ice; the fun was in seeing how far they would bounce, which was undoubtedly made into a point or a wagered contest.

The Morton Memorial was nowhere near the busy center it had been. When Helen Morton died in 1952, her bequest of $20,000 gave it only a temporary lift. In 1956, when the new Rhinebeck Central School was at last completed, the Flat Rock and Orchard Street Schools were closed and Rhinecliff elementary-school students joined the high-school students who were bused to town by the faithful Lee Wheeler. (Cardinal Farley had already closed the Ellerslie School; subsequently, it is said, the former schoolhouse became a place for romantic trysts.) As the *Gazette* stated, "Old timers missed the sound of the school bell Wednesday morning when school opened." Nevertheless, most residents soon recognized that the change made sense. In fact, Rhinecliff families, such as the Coles and the Atkins, had worked long and hard to bring it about.

One unintended consequence resulting from the closings was that the Orchard Street School was taken over by a business that supplied small parts for IBM. As many as thirty women worked there, earning what were for Rhinebeck good wages. Bernie Fitzpatrick was one of them; it gave the family budget a boost and it was within walking distance of her house. When that source of employment vanished after five years' operation, the building lay vacant until it was given to the fire company with the stipulation that the field behind it be made into a hamlet recreation area. In typical Rhinecliff fashion, the men put their shoulders to the wheel to transform the "Old Swamp" into a baseball field.

Phil Stahl's grocery store heaped with Halloween-prank junk. The boarded-up Newman building is in the background. Photograph early 1970s, courtesy of Harry Heywood.

Oran Van Etten, the town's highway superintendent, got the town to lend a bulldozer, a truck and a loader. Harry Heywood brought his backhoe and loader, and Gordon Atkins a truck. Cardinal Farley donated 3,200 yards of needed fill, along with the equipment to move it. Alan Coon, who played there as a boy, described the result as a warped configuration: uphill to first base, downhill to second, a slide into the swamp for third, then uphill to home plate. The irregularities, he remembers, added spice to the game. (As I write, the field is undergoing a second reclamation, this time as a playground for small children. Again, much of the work has been done by Rhinecliff residents.)

The hamlet did not entirely escape the turbulence of the late 1960s, during which the women's movement took hold, dress codes dramatically loosened, important strides were made in racial equality, all ages experienced infinitely greater sexual freedom, drugs permeated every level of society, and the young cast off the strict control of their parents. In fact, Rhinecliff earned a reputation for out-of-hand rowdiness. Phil Stahl, who had bought Cornwell's and had gained a reputation for

sharp business practices, became the studied target of boys' pranks. They saved up trash all year and, on Halloween, heaped it against the outside of the store. When the rusted automobiles, abandoned outhouses, tin cans and putrid junk reached to the top of the second floor, Stahl became so discouraged he closed up shop. Marion Conklin's Sugar Bowl was robbed of $135; no one believed such a thing could ever happen, but it did. And nothing seemed to stop drag racers and motorcyclists from speeding through the narrow streets. Hamlet residents complained to the town board, explaining that their youngsters had no place to congregate because the Morton Memorial was closed in the summertime and operated on a limited schedule in winter. The board was sympathetic but, in reality, the protest did no good. However, the hamlet was more successful with the disposition of the Keilly/ Newman building. Boarded up but still vandalized, it was an eyesore. At last, it was designated as a public nuisance and demolished.

The Korean conflict was followed by the even more frustrating and increasingly unpopular war against the North Vietnamese, and enrollment at

Cardinal Farley, as at military schools nationwide, dwindled. Year after year the number of students declined. Finally, it closed; the last senior class marched to its graduation exercises in 1971. After a brief pause the archdiocese transformed the school into a drug treatment center for young drug addicts from New York City.

The Town's Comprehensive Plan and Zoning Ordinance

Rhinecliff got a political boost in 1970 when Bill Allen, who had been a member of the town board since 1960, became town supervisor. Although he had moved to the south edge of the village, Rhinecliffers remembered how as a teenager he had sat night after night in the back room of the Keilly/Newman building listening intently to the talk of the men as they hashed out the issues of the day, spitting tobacco juice at the pot-bellied stove for emphasis.

One of the first things Allen did when he took office was to highlight the hamlet's importance by holding two of the town board's monthly meetings at the Rhinecliff firehouse, one in April and the other in October, a pattern still in effect. Another was joining the forces of the Town Recreation Committee with the Rhinecliff Improvement Association — Roger Van Wagner, Jack Rikert, Harry Heywood and the Volunteer Fire Company — to make a park where the Newman building had stood. For starters the town pledged $500 for trees and benches. The Holy Cross facility was prevailed upon to organize a fencing project. A healthy cooperation between town and hamlet seemed to be in the making.

The Newman building had so weakened that it could be shoved over by bulldozers. The town bought most of the property and turned it into a parking lot with a mini-park facing Charles Street. Photograph by Harriet Coon, early 1970s.

Nevertheless, it came as no surprise that the hamlet stood firmly opposed to one project Supervisor Allen had long espoused — a Comprehensive Plan and Zoning Ordinance covering the entire town. At the outset the naysayers enjoyed the support of many inland residents who opposed the proposed one-acre, three-acre and five-acre residential zoning and the control of uses, scorning them as downright restrictive and even as an unconstitutional incursion into their private lives. Moreover, they insisted that there was no market for large lots, pointing out the town-wide glut of houses for sale. As the preponderance of lots in the hamlet was far smaller than one acre, Rhinecliffers had the added fear that theirs might become nonconforming and thereby subject to still more onerous restrictions. Nevertheless, with the help of the committed Homer Staley, a widely respected real estate agent, conservationist and member of the Planning Board since its inception ten years previously, one constituency after another was won over. In February 1971, Local Law No. 1, giving the town a bare bones, yet workable, Comprehensive Plan and Zoning Ordinance, was passed.

Weekenders

Meanwhile, outsiders, mainly New Yorkers in search of affordable second homes, continued to seep in. Attracted by the railroad's remarkably frequent service, as well as by the hamlet's character, these new people were mostly weekenders and were not as effective at weaving themselves into the fabric of the community as earlier newcomers had been. Some hamlet people viewed them as intruders, although most newcomers were of modest means and as much "fixer-uppers" as were hamlet residents themselves. Other Rhinecliffers, however, received them cordially. In 1968, for instance, Pat and Marshall Hayes bought the large, vacant Milroy house on Orchard Street with its glorious views of the Kingston light-

Cardy Uzzle, Alonzo Smith, Pat Hayes and Jack Dierdorff ready for a big evening. A photograph of the late Marshall Hayes is on the cabinet in the background, far right. Photograph early 1990s, courtesy of John A. Dierdorff.

house and sunsets over the mountains. As it had been empty for some time, and possibly also because a despairing Rhinecliff man had committed suicide in the barn, they bought it for well under the asking price of $10,000; still, it was all they could afford, as she worked in the art world and he published a small literary magazine. Their new neighbors, Don and Betty Cole, immediately told the Hayes how happy they were to see lights in the house again. They also offered good advice, especially when bulldozers were carving a place for a garden on the property's steep western slope. They were as fascinated as the Hayes when this improvement uncovered an immense clamshell midden, probably, they thought, the residue of early clambakes. And they cheered Pat on when she won blue ribbons at the Dutchess County Fair for her splendid tomatoes.

One by one, more outsiders came. Most continued to live in New York City and their main interests were focused on their weekday work there. Rhinecliff was for recreation, and they tended to look to each other for company. On Friday evenings they often met, either by design or by chance, in Grand Central Terminal, from which the Amtrak train then departed, and rode up the river together playing cards, sipping sherry and telling stories as the pressures of the past week fell behind them. They would become a tight-knit and long-lasting group.

Rhinebeck Celebrates the Nation's Bicentennial

To make up for the still-unfathomable lack of celebration in honor of the nation's centennial, the town historian and president of the Rhinebeck Historical Society, Dewitt Gurnell, decided to honor the bicentennial by reenacting events important to Rhinebeck that took place during the Revolutionary War. The theme Gurnell set was the role of the Livingston family in those perilous times, the connection with them being that Colonel Henry Beekman's only child, Margaret, had married Judge Robert Livingston, thus uniting the Beekman and Livingston dynasties. The performances began in 1975, when the focus was on General Richard Montgomery, the Livingstons' eldest child's husband, who was slain storming the citadel in Quebec on December 31, 1775. Montgomery's significance to the Town of Rhinebeck, Gurnell announced, was that "he lived here when he was appointed a Brigadier General in the Continental Army and was married into Rhinebeck's famous Livingston family." On Memorial Day during the Sunday service at the Dutch Reformed church, Rhinebeckians, many dressed as colonials, remembered those who had served in the Revolution. But the principal event took place on September 30, the 200th anniversary of the day Montgomery marched off to

Quebec. According to the booklet published by the Rhinebeck Historical Society, Rhinebeck firemen, American Legionnaires, Scouts, Masons, Daughters of the American Revolution and members of the Historical Society paraded to the beat of a fife and drum corps to Montgomery House, then, as now, the headquarters of the Rhinebeck chapter of the Daughters of the American Revolution. On the way, they stopped at "God's Acre," the cemetery behind the church, to pay tribute to the town's Revolutionary War dead. That evening there was a grand ball at the Mills Mansion at which the dancers vied with each other for the most elegant period costume.

Rhinecliff's special contribution during that year was of an entirely different order. It was "A Day in Old Kipsbergen." Held on July 12 and sponsored by the Ladies Auxiliary of the Volunteer Fire Company, it started with a parade to the Rhinecliff War Memorial and went on through the day with a farmers' market selling house plants, flowers and herbs, baked goods and arts and crafts. There were children's games with prizes in the field below the Orchard Street School. A quilt exhibit was hung at the Morton Memorial Center. The day ended with a very well-attended Legion Band concert on the bluff overlooking the river.

An enduring contribution of the event was the auxiliary's excellent little tour guide of the heart of Rhinecliff. From the War Memorial triangle it takes walkers along Kelly Street to Butler Street; then it proceeds west on Butler and turns north into Grinnell Street, paralleling the river down to the Rhinecliff Hotel. Going up Shatzell Avenue, it continues, via Charles Street, up the very steep rise of Hutton Street. Turning south on the corner of Orchard Street, it returns to the War Memorial via Shatzell Avenue. The guide gives descriptions of virtually every building in the circuit, and closes by urging those driving along Rhinecliff Road to notice the old Dutch burial ground (the Kerkhoff), the Kip homestead ruins, Slate Dock and the original Dutch houses on Long Dock Road. It also recommends, if time permits, visiting Rhinebeck, "two miles north [east] with its many beautiful houses, streets and important historic sites."

In 1976 the town's festivities opened with a reenactment of George Washington's taking oath of office as president of the United States, with Chancellor Robert R. Livingston officiating. Held on Saturday afternoon, March 20, at the Dutch Reformed church, it was an impressive affair. Gurnell was able to secure the original inaugural Bible from a Masonic Lodge in New York City, and he himself impersonated President-elect Washington, to whom he bore a striking resemblance. The town's only commemoration of the signing of the Declaration of Independence itself was to pin a copy on the door of the Dutch Reformed church. Many residents were watching the Tall Ship parade in New York City on television or enjoying traditional picnics with family and friends, so not as many attended local events as were expected. Rhinebeck celebrated Chancellor Livingston again with an evening parade on July 9 to mark New York State's signing of the federal constitution in 1788.

On July 10, Rhinecliff, reaffirming its independence, mounted another successful Kipsbergen Day. Thus concluded Rhinebeck's bicentennial celebrations. Representing a great deal of hard work for those who organized them, and great fun for those who participated in them, the events gave both the inland town and Rhinecliff a fine, though still separate, sense of community. Nevertheless, the heavy focus on the Livingston family, very few of whom had agreed with the Declaration's "all men are created equal" premise, was not entirely appreciated by Rhinecliffers.

14

The Unfolding of an Entirely New Ball Game

In the course of the 1970s, Rhinecliff, like many other small communities in the country, was politically turned on its head. No longer was it permitted to remain an essentially independent settlement, going about its daily business as it saw fit with minimal interference from the town, for its waterfront had become the key to attracting federal funds for myriad town-wide projects. Seeds for this new harvest of local funding from federal sources had been sown during the Depression and further cultivated during World War II. In those earlier times, however, the federally funded local programs were regarded as specific responses to temporary, albeit grim, situations. In contrast, the mechanisms for passing down federal funds to localities in the 1970s had all the earmarks of becoming permanent. Bureaucratic and, at the same time, pliable, the programs were so bewildering to townspeople who were accustomed to politics being local, that it is questionable how many understood what was happening. Nevertheless, federal funding of projects funneled through the states and on to municipalities would have tremendous impact on the town, the hamlet, and on their relationship to each other.

The impetus came from the United States Congress, which passed a series of acts with the worthy goal of protecting and enhancing the nation's coastal waterfronts. The most important and embracing of these, the Coastal Zone Management Act of 1972, set up a voluntary federal-state partnership whose stated mission was "to preserve, protect, develop and, where possible, to restore or enhance the resources of the nation's coastal zone." The Hudson River Valley from New York City to above Albany was included in the act, because that long section of the river is tidal. Designed to encourage local communities to reinvigorate their decaying waterfronts, the act would shape such far-ranging concerns as the preservation of the natural and built environments, the protection of Native American artifacts and the comprehensive planning and zoning of municipalities. Together with the Clean Water Act, which operated in a similar way, the Coastal Zone Management Act spawned a labyrinthine concate-

nation of state agencies and organizations that set guidelines to which the communities must conform in order to receive federal funds.

This system would do immense good, but, on the local level, the complexities of fulfilling the guidelines made it difficult for ordinary citizens to participate in the decision-making process. For the system to work properly, an interactive educational process between those in the know and residents who needed to know was imperative. This process was not easy to supply. Sometimes Rhinebeck succeeded, and sometimes, especially when it came to Rhinecliff, which had the town's only public waterfront, it did not.

Quite on their own, Rhinecliffers Bill Cotting and Harry Heywood, members of the boat club, decided that it was time for the town to give Rhinecliff a hand in restoring the rapidly decaying ferry landing. Fortunately, Dennis Kipp, also a Rhinecliff man, was a writer for the *Gazette* and, with his help, Cotting and Heywood got effective publicity in favor of revitalizing it. That, and the possibility of latching on to some of the federal money offered through the state, spurred the town board to look upon the landing as an asset, instead of as a shunned eyesore. As a Rhinebeck Town Board member told the *Poughkeepsie Journal*, "There was a period where we ignored the idea that we had a coast. ... We only realized it was there when stimulated by the dock project. There may be ways in which we can better utilize it for the town."

In 1979 the board established a Rhinebeck Town Landing Committee, composed of both hamlet and inland residents. The committee put on a coopera-

The siting of Rhinecliff's civic and commercial buildings as well as its houses is dictated by the up-and-down topography. This blend of the natural and built environments is one of the hamlet's major charms.

tive riverfront event to whip up support for rehabilitating the dock. This drew a huge crowd and raised some funds. As a result, the project received a $50,000 grant from a federal program that had been established to rectify damage caused by the wakes of increasingly large tankers. To celebrate this grant, the landing committee put on "A Riverfront Festival at Rhinecliff" in 1981. The festival featured music on the bluff by various performers throughout the day and included aerobic demonstrations, roving musicians, plus a circus and concerts by the Legion Band in front of the hotel and concerts by the Hudson Valley Folk Singers Guild and a group of classical musicians in the Morton Library. A delicious breakfast and a roast beef dinner were offered. Take-away food was available all day long at several locations. Recognizing that parking would be a problem with the great numbers expected, a temporary parking lot was set up on the northern periphery of the hamlet off the Rhinecliff Road with jitney service to the waterfront. The festival was an entirely successful affair.

The federal money, together with donated materials and Rhinecliff residents' time-honored sweat-equity, was enough to complete the first stage of the project — stabilizing the landing. The second and third stages, which involved adding fifty feet to the north end of the dock to deflect ice and flotsam, and fixing the ramp leading to the landing and fitting it with protection against the pileup of ice and debris, awaited future funding and an army of volunteers. As it turned out, the project ran out of momentum and those forward-looking stages became moribund.

The ferry landing was bought by the town, which allowed the Rhinecliff-Rhinebeck Boat Club to use the ferry building for its clubhouse. Photograph by Tom Daley, 1970.

Preservation of Architectural Heritage

At the same time, the preservation of historic architecture had become increasingly popular throughout the Hudson River Valley. As a result, a committee was formed to study the historic properties in a sixteen-mile corridor between Hyde Park and the Columbia County line. Its mission was to list as many sites as possible on the National Register of Historic Places. The Register, a preservation effort with roots in the Franklin D. Roosevelt administration, had been established by Congress in 1966. It offered special protections to individual properties deemed to possess historic value. The criteria for inclusion in the list were: 1) significant contribution to the broad patterns of state history; 2) association with significant historical personages; 3) a significant *and* distinguishable entity whose components might lack individual distinction; or 4) illumination of history or Native American prehistory.

In 1979 the Sixteen Mile Historic District was accepted by the National Register. It contained approximately 270 historic structures, most of which were connected in some way with the thirty great estates within the district. The Clermont Estates Historic District, an extension to the north in Columbia County, registered fifty more significant structures, and the Rhinebeck Village Historic District registered 340 properties dating from 1760 to 1940. Preservationists received the establishment of these districts with great fanfare. However, they were interesting to Rhinecliff only because it had been deliberately carved out of the Sixteen Mile Historic District, even though the hamlet might have qualified under all of the criteria. Limiting the hamlet's boundaries to Charles H. Russell's 1851 subdivision, the preservationists' stated reason was that the hamlet was merely "a popular steamboat landing in the early/mid-nineteenth century and an important rail stop on the Hudson River Railroad,"

with housing stock "composed of scattered modern and extensively altered older dwellings." Ignored was the fact that Rhinecliff began as Kipsbergen and was established well before Beekman's settlement on the Flatts — indeed, thousands of years before with Native American encampments, the remains of which still abound. The list did include the Jacob and Abraham Kip houses and the federal house in between. The Amtrak station was registered as well. However, these properties were not considered to be a part of Rhinecliff. Instead of being recognized as an integral part of that community's heritage, they were assigned to an indistinct limbo zone.

The reasons for Rhinecliff's exclusion were multiple. To preservationists' eyes, the hamlet was merely the shabby part of town; their focus was squarely on the estates, the village and the inland town's German Palatinate heritage. This was, of course, a complex social matter with very deep roots. Nevertheless, confining the hamlet to the 1851 subdivision presented an untrue picture of Rhinecliff's history that is only now tentatively showing cracks and beginning to flake.

Perhaps to make amends, a Town Multiple Resource area soon added the Heermance House (1803) and its little bracketed law office (1885) at the head of Long Dock Road to this "limbo" area. The Hendrickus Kip homestead ruins opposite Slate Dock Road were listed as the Kip-Beekman-Heermance Archaeological Site. (Uncharacteristically, Henry Beekman Livingston's long ownership of the property was left out, perhaps because of his reputation as a rotter.) Within the 1851 subdivision, the Rhinecliff Hotel (1855), the O'Brien General Store and Post Office (c.1863, more recently Cornwell's, then Stahl's), the Riverside Methodist Church and parsonage (1859), and the Episcopal parsonage (c.1867) were also added. (The Episcopal church had already been pulled down.) The Morton Memorial Center (1908) joined the roster, too. But among the many historic buildings not included were: St. Joseph's Church (designed by George Veitch, among whose estate credentials was Wyndclyffe) and its cemetery, a "mother" Roman Catholic church with very wide outreach; the remaining one of a pair of circa 1827 houses on Kelly Street; the three schoolhouses (the Ellerslie school was almost certainly designed by Alexander Jackson Davis, and the Orchard Street School was another of George Veitch's projects); the ruins of Long and Slate Docks, without which Rhinebeck village and the surrounding upstreet town would never have enjoyed the prosperity it did; and the extraordinarily rich Native American remains. The happy interplay of natural and built environments also seems worthy of mention.

The Mid-Hudson Historic Shorelands Scenic District

The Mid-Hudson Historic Shorelands Scenic District reinforced this perhaps unconscious, but certainly narrow approach. Established by the new state Department of Environmental Conservation (DEC) in 1980, the scenic district's ultimate mission was to create a local management plan that would balance competing land and waterfront issues and respond to the needs and desires of local residents, as well as those of federal and state agencies as laid out by the Coastal Zone Management Act. In the Town of Rhinebeck, the scenic district's boundaries were essentially the same as those of the Sixteen Mile Historic District, except that this time Rhinecliff was included in the magic kingdom.

Emphasizing the district's regional scope, the task force created to produce the plan was recruited from each of the five municipalities within the district and was funded by a private New York City-based foundation. In late 1982 a draft management plan was submitted to federal, state and local agen-

cies and organizations. While many applauded the plan, it was also strongly criticized for its unclear organization, undefined terminology and sketchily described recommendations. Few approved of the vehicle devised to oversee implementation of the plan — a state-created and state-funded Scenic District Commission. The common refrain was, "Why add another layer of government?" One of the Dutchess County Commissioners of Planning commented, "I believe it would be more to the area's advantage to have the management concept developed and implemented by the communities as the result of their own convictions." A public hearing was held in Rhinebeck. It was very difficult for ordinary residents to obtain copies of the draft plan, and the comments of only one are recorded in the final report. The resident warned prophetically that, if accepted, the plan would become an authority for future action. Requests for a second hearing, to take place after the public had time to read and digest the document, were denied.

The final report, published in 1983, was striking in many ways. Its scope was truly grand. Its major flaw, especially for Rhinecliff, but for the six other hamlets as well, was that its focus was even more attached than the Sixteen Mile district had been to the romantic heritage of significant estates and their designed ornamental grounds. Uniting picture-book imagery with the romantic illusions created by early-nineteenth-century landscape painters beginning with Thomas Cole and Asher Durand, the final report failed to address contemporary issues head-on. "For the most part, man's impact on this shoreline has been serene," it stated in its introduction. "There are gracious old estates, tiny and tranquil river hamlets and parklands. Despite the frantic pace of change on all sides, the same wildly noble and pastoral scene that has moved generations of Hudson River residents remains today." Again and again the final report emphasized the area's "unblemished pastoral landscape" without acknowledging that real farms (as opposed to tax havens) were in sharp decline. It is difficult to believe that the framers knew how hard it was to make a living from farming.

The hamlets seem to have baffled the task force. Labeling the hamlets "Townscapes," the report admitted that each was "a complex mosaic" in need of more study, but its major finding was that they "represent settlement patterns that retain the general character of their historic development" without illuminating readers as to what they thought that character or history might be. The report's favorite phrases for describing the hamlets were "diminutive scale" and "cottage character." The pastoral landscape surrounding them — mainly the estates — was stressed as their most valuable asset. Furthermore, the maps lacked topographic markings and, aside from diagrammatic sketches explaining general concepts, the few illustrations were idyllic nineteenth-century scenes. It is difficult to imagine from the report what the 1983 landscape that was to be preserved looked like.

Rhinecliff fared far worse than the other waterfront hamlets. It was described as "a fragile visual composition" and economically dependent on Rhinebeck for more than 250 years. Not a word about its long, separate history as a vital transportation hub or its origin as a liberal Dutch settlement. "Perhaps more than any other element, incongruous architectural construction detracts from the townscape character," the report went on to declare. Unrecognized was the fact that Rhinecliff was — and still is — a unique blend of the built and the natural environments, that its houses and commercial area are sited according to the dictates of its topography. Although in no way comparable in grandeur to the estate mansions, Rhinecliff's dwellings are just as historic — in several cases more historic — than they or even the many houses in the village. Moreover, each is an authentic expression of the generations who have lived in them. Finally, alone among the hamlets, the label the report attached to Rhinecliff tied it to the inland town and village. Not simply Rhinecliff or, more accurately, Kipsbergen/Rhinecliff, it was labeled Rhinebeck/Rhinecliff. Unfortunately, the report was not shelved as a curious artifact, but became a pillar of future planning, ever cited, but seldom read.

Rhinebeck Entertainments

In a happier interaction between the town and the hamlet, the new Rhinebeck Theater Society made arrangements to use the Morton Memorial for rehearsals. They began with Noel Coward's *Nude with Violin*. Soon, the members found the space so attractive that they staged their performances there. The large hall was transformed into a theater seating sixty people on benches steeply rising over the hall's raised platform. The play stage area was at the west end of the room. This meant that the sets, some simple, some lavish, had to be ingeniously designed to accommodate the fact that there was only a sliver of back stage. Rising again and again to the challenge, such winners as *A Funny Thing Happened on the Way to the Forum*, *The Importance of Being Ernest*, *Carousel*, *Inherit the Wind* and *A Midsummer Night's Dream*, as well as such less-well-known but equally riveting works as *Working*, *Rashomon* and *Arcadia*, were presented.

The renaissance of the Morton Memorial Center was further fueled when volunteers under the direction of local street performance designer Jeanne Fleming made huge papier-mâché puppets there for the reenacting in the village of St. Nicholas Day, December 6, as it was celebrated in old Holland. A rare tribute to the Kipsbergen patentees' heritage, and that of the Beekmans', too, the goal was to bring back the creative spirit of the season. Children were designated kings and queens for the day. They

St. George's white horse, made by volunteers in the Morton Memorial Library, makes a friend. Photograph 1984, courtesy of Jeanne Fleming.

wore paper crowns and carried decorated boughs for scepters that they had created themselves. Each child made three wishes and gave them to a Wish Lady, who recorded them in a book. One wish was for the child, one was for the child's family, one was for the whole town. There were pony rides, a teddy bear beauty contest and storytellers. Student musicians and dancers performed in Town Hall. Madrigal singers roamed the streets. The event culminated with a great candle and flashlight parade. Its main feature was St. George riding a papier-mâché horse pursuing a huge two-headed grisly green papier-mâché dragon, both of which, together with other beasties, were made at the Morton. Dutch Christmas was the focus of the holiday season for four more years, during which the number of participants rose to 15,000. Then, storekeepers, perceiving that clogging the sidewalks for a whole day decreased their sales, ended the festival, but it was not forgotten. It was revived for the 2007 holiday season, with Jeanne Fleming still at the helm. Called SinterKlaas, it has been transformed into an ethnically diverse ecumenical event.

Meanwhile, the lending library in the Morton possessed a wonderfully soothing atmosphere. Ruth Boyd, the librarian, played good classical music low on her little radio. She was not talkative. In fact, her few utterances were often sardonic, but they were to the point. Her native wit and her intelligence always poked through. The acquisitions program was sleepy, thanks to budget constraints, but patrons could get almost any book they desired through the Mid-Hudson library exchange system, albeit not, in those pre-Internet times, as speedily as they can today. It was an inviting place for readers.

Rhinebeck's Tercentennial

The celebration of the Town and Village of Rhinebeck's tercentennial took place over three years. The grand opening event was on June 8, 1986. It was called Founders' Day. Once more Rhinecliff residents were disappointed to find that the Kipsbergen patentees, whom it should have celebrated, were brushed aside. The focus was on the later Palatine tenant farmers' settlement at Wey's Corners and on the Beekman family, who did not live on the east side of the river until 1726 when Colonel Henry Beekman took over the Kip homestead. Even then, it was not his principal residence. A journalist tried to fill the gap, but all he could come up with was little better than a feeble greeting card vision: "the hamlet, a few miles away, lies quiet in the increasingly oppressive heat, except for the waves lapping. … A red neon light flicks on at the hotel, the postmaster picks up mail."

The next year, a group of area artists and their friends, again led by Fleming, conducted a week-long Arts in Education program, called "Let the River Connect Us," at the Chancellor Livingston Elementary School. Its aim was to bring Rhinebeck's neglected Native American heritage to life for the children, and through them to their parents, and to present the river as the source of the area's plentitude from time immemorial. The week culminated with a blessing of the river at the Rhinecliff Landing, during which a well-crafted papier-mâché canoe, filled with little papers on which residents of all ages had written wishes for the future of Rhinebeck and the Hudson, was floated into the river. Well attended, the ceremony brought the lapsed attention of the town to the landing and its ties with pre-Kipsbergen history, at least for a fleeting moment.

In 1988, the 300th anniversary of the Kipsbergen partners' receipt of their signed patents from the British crown, the same group staged the final tercentennial event, an outdoor community party called "Heyday." Patterned on a nineteenth-century country fair, the party was scheduled for the fairgrounds. All the tents were up. But at the

last moment, the Dutchess County Agricultural Society, which owns the fairgrounds, decreed that rain had made the ground too slippery. Undaunted, "Heyday" changed its location to the welcoming Chancellor Livingston schoolyard. Entertainments ranged from puppet shows, to turtle races, to an old-time baseball game and a magic show. The band and chorus from Rheinbach, Germany, in town for their yearly exchange with Rhinebeck students, offered a fine musical program. Huge quilts made of cotton squares, painted with scenes and icons of the town by children and sewn together by women in nursing homes, were a central attraction. (The quilts hang in the Chancellor Livingston auditorium, where they silently teach and are admired today.) There was a gala potluck supper with Miss Margaret "Daisy" Suckley of Wilderstein, then a perky ninety-six years old, as the honored guest. A fine display of fireworks concluded the festivities just before the rain came down in drenching sheets. It was a grand bringing together of the hamlet, the village and the inland town.

However, in typical fashion, the handsome 261-page profusely illustrated book that grew out of the tercentennial relegates Rhinecliff to a scant ten-page chapter sandwiched in towards the end, plus a few

To bring Rhinebeck's neglected Native American heritage to life, Jeanne Fleming created a program called "Let the River Connect Us" for Chancellor Livingston Elementary School children. Part of the tercentenary celebrations, it culminated with the launching at the Rhinecliff Landing of a papier-mâché canoe filled with wishes for the town and the river. Photograph 1987, courtesy of Jeanne Fleming.

The squares of this birthday cake celebrating the town's tercentennial were made and decorated by volunteers. The crowd is blowing out its 300 candles. Photograph 1988, courtesy of Jeanne Fleming.

references and pictures scattered throughout the text. The Rhinecliff chapter's opening paragraph reads: "A small hamlet exists in the corridor of magnificent Rhinebeck estates along the Hudson River. Surrounded by these former country seats, lies the river landing known as Rhinecliff — a small community enclave within the town of Rhinebeck."

Development Hits Rhinebeck

During this time, the housing developments the town had so long feared hit the former estate lands of Rhinebeck. In 1977, Allan A. Ryan Jr. had sold Ankony Farms to Edwin Creed, a Connecticut River tool-manufacturing magnate whom he had met a few weeks before on a Florida golf course. (Another story is that Ryan lost it to Creed in a golf course bet.) Apparently by prearrangement, Creed immediately razed the great house as too costly to keep up. Like the destruction of Pennsylvania Station in New York City, this loss gave impetus to the mid-Hudson Valley architectural preservation movement. Creed also developed breeding cattle, only his were Simmentals, a species of Swiss heavy milkers. With two sons to help him manage the enterprise, the farm prospered. However, the Creeds' role in the area was limited; the property had all the earmarks of being a trophy and a tax haven for them. They continued to increase their holdings. When, in 1981, the Cole brothers decided it was time for them to stop growing anemones, they sold the bulbs to a competent competitor and put the rest of the equipment, including the greenhouses, up for auction. That done, they sold their 171 acres to the Creeds.

In the late 1980s, Edwin Creed put forward a plan for a twenty-seven-hole international golf course on the 535 acres he had by then accumulated south of the Rhinecliff Road. The design called for 192 single-family homes and 56 attached townhouses tightly bordering the links, as well as a 45,000-square-foot clubhouse with a 240-space parking lot and a driving range illuminated for nighttime practice. One alarmed Rhinecliff newcomer described it as "Levittown-on-the-Hudson." Worried that such a large development would totally change the character of the hamlet, an informal group of residents, most of whom had lived in the community less than ten years, formed Concerned Citizens of Rhinecliff. Its goal was to persuade the town board to designate the hamlet a Critical Environment Area (CEA), a program fostered by the state Department of Environmental Conservation that would bring actions affecting a CEA under the thorough review set forth in the State Environmental Quality Review Act, familiarly called SEQRA (pronounced Seek-Rah). An innovative and powerful tool, the act triggers close community examination of the impacts developments might make on their locality.

Almost sixty residents attended the town board meeting held in the Rhinecliff Firehouse when the need for the CEA designation was presented. The request described the hamlet as a cohesive and vital community, rooted in its history and still socially, architecturally and topographically intact. Descendants of the original settlers still lived there. It underscored the diverse population that represented a full range of age, interests and income. Two school buses took children to the Rhinebeck Central schools. At the other end of the age spectrum was a large group of retirees. Most residents traveled to their place of business by automobile, but a sizable group, many of them outsiders,

Edwin Creed hoped to build a twenty-seven-hole golf course surrounded by houses on the east border of Rhinecliff. Map late 1980s, Horn Landscape Architects, Lehigh Valley, PA, collection of the author.

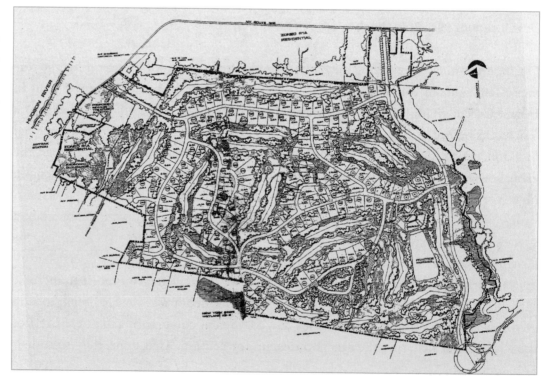

commuted via Amtrak to their offices in New York City. Weekends drew varying numbers of people from the wider area to events at the hotel or library; more were anticipated with the growth in tourism.

The CEA designation received strong support from prestigious preservationists. Scenic Hudson, an important nonprofit organization born of the decades-long fight to prevent Consolidated Edison from building a large power plant on Storm King Mountain in the Highlands section of the Hudson River, wrote that the designation would assure that the hamlet would be protected from adverse activity that would impair the very quality of life its residents were most desirous of preserving. Hudson River Heritage agreed that Rhinecliff had "managed to preserve largely intact a distinctive architectural mode, topographic features and a sense of community which should be saved from haphazard destruction and the pressures of development. ... Our environment and the subtle matter of quality of life," it went on to say, "involve fragile things which we must identify and protect lest they be accidentally, but nonetheless irretrievably, lost." Wilderstein Preservation, the group set up by Miss Suckley to manage and eventually take over her property, stressed the intertwining of the Suckleys' history with that of Rhinecliff, stating that Wilderstein's success "would be closely related to the preservation of the integrity and attractiveness of its wider surrounds." The Dutchess County Planning Department cited hamlet protection as a key component of its future planning. Later, at another public hearing, its chairman would call Rhinecliff "the most beautiful hamlet in the county."

Proud of what they had accomplished, the newcomers felt comfortable enough to put on an "I Love Rhinecliff Day" at the Morton Memorial, in part as an endeavor to bridge the gap with old-timers. The date chosen was Valentine's Day, which conveniently fell on a weekend that year. There were a puppet show and refreshments to draw area people, but the backbone of the event was an impressive exhibition of photographs and other memorabilia loaned by Rhinecliff old-timers, many of whom had not been inside the center since they were children. The show brought back good memories. A building block to unity had been planted, but there remained a long way to go to close the gap between old-timers and newcomers on a broad basis.

Concerned Citizens of Rhinecliff then asked Edwin Creed to come from Connecticut to discuss his proposed golf course with Rhinecliff residents. He did. The meeting was well attended, and the dialogue seemed fruitful. (Just as one Rhinecliffer was pointing out that the hamlet was a walking community, two little girls could be seen through the windows wheeling their dolly carriages down the hill towards Shatzell Avenue.) But nothing changed. When the public hearing for the CEA was held, almost every old-timer was solidly against the designation, for they feared new limitations on their ability to handle their property as they individually saw fit. In addition, they loyally supported Creed's agent, a young man who was a descendant of one of the old families. Those who knew Creed were certain that nothing he proposed would harm the hamlet. They organized well, and the CEA designation was defeated. This was not surprising. Old-timers distrusted the power that federal and state governments were wielding at the local level and linked the newcomers to it. That the newcomers were steadily increasing in number made them even more cautious.

One classic Rhinecliffian episode enlivened the interchange. The Creeds' agent bought a large piece of property off Russell Avenue that he wished to develop. However, he suddenly discovered that the proposed entrance to his property overlapped that of the property to the west of it. Rather than negotiate with its owner, he heaped a pile of dirt across her driveway. The person who plowed snow for her removed the dirt. Early the next morning, the agent returned with his caterpillar tractor and pushed up a twelve-foot barrier of dirt. That accomplished, he parked the tractor on top of the pile and removed the keys. Somehow the controversy was settled. The agent took off for a ranch in the West and eventually sold that land, and its one unfinished house deep in the woods, to a weekending family that built its own driveway.

Heartened by the defeat of the CEA, the Creed development pushed forward by applying for a Planned Residential Development, a new zoning instrument that gave developers higher densities in exchange for open space. This triggered the SEQRA process with its environmental safeguards. The hearings were crowded and spirited. The general consensus was that Creed's Draft Environmental Impact Statement (DEIS), listing potential impacts, was incomplete as well as misleading. In addition to poor overall design, the impacts of pesticides, herbicides and fertilizers needed to maintain the golf course, and the runoff of polluted rainwater from the proposed road system were not raised. Moreover, the clubhouse was too big. In fact, with its restaurants, bars and sales areas, it might well be categorized as a commercial space. Nor were light pollution from the parking lots and nighttime use of the driving range addressed. In addition, there were only a few units of affordable housing — important to the town and the state — and these were intended for the development's maintenance workers. Public access to the open space had not been considered. There was no provision for proper traffic studies or for estimating the need for extra police and firefighters. The Town Board sent the DEIS back for more work.

Concurrently, the town was embroiled in a long-standing confrontation with the owners of the eastern section of Ferncliff property — around 1,600 acres between Route 9 and River Road, some of it in the village and some in the town. The owners had completed one condominium complex of "townhouses," named The Woods, on the north side of the old entrance to Ferncliff, now Astor Drive. Developer friends were in the process of laying out a somewhat less upscale complex filling the fields on the south side of Astor Drive. There they planned to put 600 units with access from both Astor Drive and Rhinecliff Road. Called The Gardens, this development would have even greater impact on Rhinecliff, not only because it would generate traffic, but also because the owners agreed to cooperate with Creed on an extensive sewer system capable of servicing the hamlet, which town planners had made clear they thought Rhinecliff should have. That idea came to grief over the fact that the sewer line would run under Creed's land on the waterfront side of River Road, yet he would not be allowed to tap into it. Negotiations dragged on with many strong words. The owners threatened to sue the town. No satisfactory conclusion was in sight.

The Town and Village of Rhinebeck's Local Waterfront Revitalization Program

Meanwhile, the New York State Division of Local Government Services granted funds from the State Coastal Management Program to enable towns along the river to prepare Local Waterfront Revitalization Programs (LWRP). The first step the Town of Rhinebeck took in drafting so important a document was novel and forward-thinking. It formed a partnership with the village so that it would reflect the needs of the village as well as those of the town. The LWRP progressed slowly, but, at last, in 1987, the document was ready to be reviewed by the state. It promised to be powerful, for it stipulated that all actions proposed for Rhinebeck by local, state and federal agencies should be consistent with the policies of the LWRP. For further elucidation, it explained, "All policies once included in the Town and Village LWRP … whether of State or local origin, [will] become Rhinebeck's policies." (It is still not clear whether the LWRP, when adopted, and the town laws work together, or whether one has precedence over the other.)

The policies in the drafted LWRP that had the greatest impact on Rhinecliff were centered on extending use of the town landing for residents and for tourists. It advocated renovation of the landing's deteriorated over-the-tracks access, as well as extensive development of its dock, its passive recreation area and its support facilities, including adding boat sewerage disposal, snack bars and a first-aid station. The goal was to make the landing a regional marina for private and excursion boats. On the east side of the track would be restaurants, parking lots and even boat construction and repair businesses, "all on a limited scale." Further development of the waterfront by means of over-the-tracks access to Slate and Long docks (owned by Conrail) and to the former Ellerslie dock was expressed as a hope. At the same time the LWRP advocated increased opportunities for commercial fishing, even though commercial shad fishing was virtually at an end and the state was about to outlaw commercial bass fishing because of contamination from PCBs, a nondegradable chemical pollutant flushed into the river by upstream General Electric manufacturing plants.

As far as Rhinecliff was concerned, the LWRP was a grand potpourri of wishes, not entirely connected to reality. However, the hamlet was treated with marginally greater accuracy and respect than previously. For instance, the LWRP stated that "water dependent uses must be consistent with the capacity of the land to accommodate such uses and the compatibility with the natural and built environment of the community." Moreover, parking problems at the railroad station were recognized, as was

the near impossibility of improving hamlet roads to absorb significant increases of traffic. Nevertheless, while the LWRP admitted that linking the hamlet to the village sewer system would be costly to hamlet residents, it strongly hoped that, despite the rockbound subsurface and the narrow roadways, that feat would be accomplished. Interestingly, the draft LWRP referred, albeit briefly, to problems of rising Hudson River water levels caused by global warming, an advanced topic at that time.

Overall, the LWRP gave top priority to preserving the great estates' cultivated agricultural land, rolling fallow meadows and designed landscapes, as exhibited in the Shorelands Management Plan, for these lands provided open space, although principally visual and restricted to owners and their friends. Good views of the great houses from boats on the river were also sought.

What would ultimately prevent the state from accepting the LWRP was embedded in the forty-four general policies the state expected municipalities to follow. Called Historic and Scenic Resources, it set forth guidelines to insure that new and restored buildings would be compatible with historic buildings. To implement this policy it prohibited the "Demolition or removal in whole or in part of a building, structure, or earthworks that is a recognized historic, cultural, or archeological resource or component thereof," unless certified dangerous to life and public health. The state expected that municipalities would have passed a law to cover this provision. Rhinebeck had not yet done so, and approval was denied.

The town board assigned the job of writing a local law embodying the needed protections to a Historic Structures Committee. It failed to do so, mainly because property owners, when given a chance to express their opinions at a public hearing, resisted the law's provisions as unclear and overreaching. For instance, the provisions covered not only changes to a whole building, but to a part of a building, raising the valid question of how big a part — the modification of a window or a doorway, or much more? Moreover, the public believed the law would put owners through too many hoops, adding significant expense to a simple alteration. The struggle between the state and the town, and the planners and property owners, would continue in varying degrees of intensity for the next twenty years.

An LWRP for the Town of Rhinebeck — the village had dropped out of the partnership — containing an acceptable demolition law was not sent to Albany for approval until the fall of 2006. This time the state signed the Rhinebeck LWRP. As of this writing the LWRP has been placed in the hands of the federal government for printing. No date has been given as to when it will be available in hard copy. It is, however, available on the Internet.

15

Rhinecliff Renaissance

Meanwhile, the hamlet was changing, but only bit by bit. The fire company remained a bastion of old-timers. It dedicated a memorial at the firehouse to all deceased members with a touching ceremony that spoke of those who had passed as "in their minds and hearts all the year." It upgraded its equipment with a General Motors thousand-gallon pumper and an International Harvester pumper of the same capacity, as well as a new ambulance.

The post office, still in the Trowbridge building, was under the cheerful stewardship of Harriet Talmadge Coon, one of the rooted Talmadge family — her Talmadge forebearer was cited as a path master in 1816 for the road from Long Dock to the village. Harriet had had a perfect attendance and fine marks at the Orchard Street School, so as postmaster — and she was firm about that title — it was not surprising that she received top awards. Dressed every day in a carefully color-coordinated costume, her hair perfectly upswept and fixed with a velvet ribbon, she popped the mail merrily into the old-fashioned combination lock boxes. Behind the scenes she was a tigress at defending the Rhinecliff Post Office against continual threats to close it down. At home on Kelly Street, she was a mean tractor driver when, with hair no less meticulously groomed than at work, she shared with her husband the upkeep of their rolling yard. It was no easy job, for the yard was studded with such interesting artifacts as a sleigh and a buggy, huge milk cans, a handsome nineteenth-century iron urn and a gazebo. (Some newcomers living in one of the old Ellerslie houses took a stroll downtown one day and, thinking the Coons' yard a pubic park, enjoyed a refreshing interlude in the gazebo.) Don Coon, tall, slim and stylish in his blue beret, was from a multigenerational family in Columbia County whose surname was originally spelled Kuhn. He drove an immense

tractor trailer, and Harriet often rode halfway across the country with him before she took the post office job. Getting the mail was never the quite same after Harriet retired in 1992. However, she did not stray very far away. She found a perfect part-time job — selling antiques in the village. When she died seven years later, there was not a dry eye as her handsome coffin with a plaque stating her full name, Harriet Rosalia Talmadge Coon, was lowered into its grave.

The bar in the Rhinecliff Hotel remained a local magnet, although a minor one in comparison with its earlier days. The few rooms that were rented were mainly for interim housing. For a while, young newcomers played pool downstairs in the evenings, and over the course of one winter two of the women offered Sunday afternoon teas in the upstairs dining room. The world-renowned Hudson River folk singer Pete Seeger visited periodically to delight with his sea chanteys and to arouse enthusiasm for cleaning up the polluted river. Irish musicians gave popular concerts in the increasingly musty downstairs back room on Sunday afternoons.

Across the street, the delicatessen that had taken over from Benson's bar went out of business. It was soon reopened as a vegetarian eatery, wittily called the Cannibal Café. Its coffee and pastries were delicious, but it did not last long because of problems with permits and sewage, and also because there were not as yet enough patrons for that sort of fare. (One of the women who ran the café later opened the excellent Chinese restaurant called the China Rose in the completely redecorated and properly sewered space. It has been a great success, drawing patrons from a very large area.)

Harriet Talmadge Coon, daughter of Minnie Talmadge, was a first-rate postmaster and an equally first-rate tractor driver. Photograph mid-1980s, courtesy of Alan Coon.

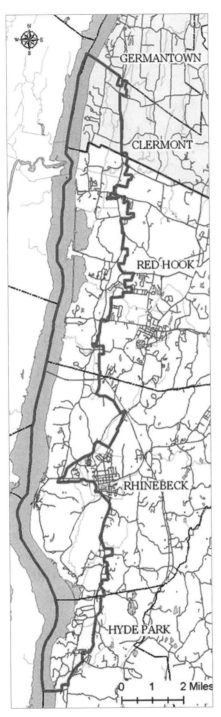

The Hudson River National Historic Landmark District, established in 1990, finally included Rhinecliff, but it did nothing to change planners' emphasis on the great estates. Courtesy of Hudson River Heritage.

Holy Cross

The Archdiocese of New York, not needing so grand a facility to deal with teenage drug problems, sold a vast tract of its riverfront property on the west side of Morton Road to its advisor/lawyer, who also bought the Astor Casino property from them. He subdivided his new Ellerslie land into twenty-acre lots and gradually resold them to wealthy outsiders. A few of those buyers further subdivided the land, but all who bought lots put up large handsome houses. This was not a major concern to newcomers to the hamlet, or even to many long-time Rhinecliffers, because many of the new owners were no more than weekenders and their impact on the hamlet was low. Besides, many residents had grown accustomed to thinking, as the planners had done for years, that the hamlet was confined to the 1851 subdivision. However, the informality of the countryside surrounding the densely settled core of the hamlet was beginning to disappear. A ramble along the bluff to experience the vitality of the great Hudson River flowing below was now a thing of the past.

The Hudson River National Historic Landmark District

The Hudson River National Historic Landmark District, which included the Livingstons' Clermont estate, a very popular state park, was registered in 1990. It was the largest such district in the country. Hudson River Heritage became its steward. Again, the aim was to preserve the district's historic architecture, rural landscapes and scenic view sheds, making them eligible for federal grants and tax breaks. As backup for the designation, Hudson River Heritage made an inventory of over 2,000 properties, complete with photographs of the individual buildings. It was an immense and useful achievement, although some categorizations of buildings, especially in Rhinecliff, are off the mark. Moreover, the hamlet would have to wait a long time before either the district or the inventory gave it significant leverage in a preservation world still so strongly oriented towards great estates.

Revision of the Comprehensive Plan and Zoning Ordinance

Worried again that it would be soon overcome by development, the town placed a moratorium on new building. Just as the moratorium was about to expire, the New York State Supreme Court delivered the awful news that the procedures for the 1970s zoning ordinance had not been properly followed, which meant that Rhinebeck might have no zoning ordinance at all. This placed the Town Comprehensive Plan and Zoning Ordinance Committee under tremendous pressure to speed acceptance of a revised plan and ordinance. Based on community values gleaned from a loosely constructed survey of town and village residents, the plan the committee devised placed preservation of open space and natural features high on its values list. At the same time, priority was given to housing variety, a moderate percentage of which was to be the still undefined category

of "affordable." Circumscribed business, office and light industry districts were established to expand the town's tax base. Tourism was to be encouraged, and the village was to remain the town's commercial center. Rhinecliff's historic fabric was to be preserved and, at the same time, modernized by being tied to a central sewer, either that of the village or of one of the developers. Thus, higher densities would be feasible at the edges of the hamlet. The Rhinecliff landing was to be developed as a regional, as well as a town, recreation facility. Additional access to the Hudson River was to be pursued at Wilderstein and at Slate and Long docks. Prehistoric archaeological sites, of special interest to the state, were to be protected.

The Zoning Ordinance, the implementing teeth of the Comprehensive Plan, provided for one-, three- and five-acre zoning and for special districts that yielded greater flexibility than straight acreage zoning could do. To bring property owners up-to-date, the plan and ordinance were published with detailed explanations in the *Gazette*. Then, the committee pushed for a vote. In its hurry to beat the expiration of the moratorium, it let stand the former one-acre zoning in Rhinecliff, with a promise to study the matter further when it had more time. The hamlet was comfortable living with the one-acre designation because it knew that, even though the designation did not reflect the hamlet's true densities, very few buildable lots existed. At the last moment, the committee reduced the size of the special Rhinecliff business district and restricted its commercial uses to small-scale enterprises designed

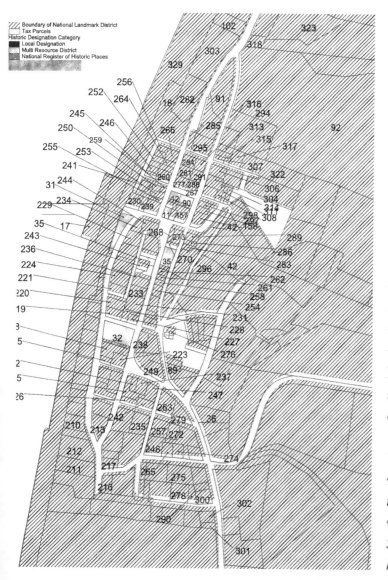

This map related to the Historic Landmark District was created by planning consultants with the assistance of the town historian. It shows how packed with buildings of historic significance Rhinecliff is. Still, preservationists continued to ignore the hamlet's long history.

to serve the needs of the hamlet instead of the wide-area uses, such as banks and furniture sales rooms, that had unwittingly slipped in.

Special provisions that would affect Rhinecliff were the "Planned Residential District," designed to give higher densities for clustering that provided open space, and the "Planned Residential Development Overlay District," devised for "areas with strong potential for provision of water and sewage through a cooperative private and public development program." Their specifics seemed so vague, they did not raise serious alarm. Nor did the provision that any alteration or new building would be subject to site and architectural review so as to conform to "the overall historic character of the Village and Town of Rhinebeck." Rushed through, the zoning law was adopted with little opposition, a result, in part, of the complexity of the task and of the real fear of threatening large developments, and, in part, because this was what the planners had long wanted to do.

Town planners were relieved that both their zoning ordinance and comprehensive plan seemed to be working. Rhinecliffers were happy that the physical and cultural cohesion of the hamlet had been deemed worthy of protecting. They were not at all perturbed that, as the years rolled by, town planners failed to scrutinize its one-acre zoning. For more than a decade, building and zoning variances would be given out with a liberal hand, the prevailing attitude of town enforcement officers being that if neighbors did not object, owners in Rhinecliff could do more or less what they liked. The ability of Rhinecliff roads to handle potentially great increases in traffic brought by tourism and development was never carefully explored, but even that did not seem vital at the time.

Moreover, as the months went by it became evident that neither the Creed nor The Gardens proposal would soon go forward, for IBM pulled out of both Kingston and Poughkeepsie, causing the local real estate market to plummet. With many IBMers moving away, houses for sale abounded. Soaring heating oil prices only made matters worse. Thus, both developments slid into a quiescent mode, hoping for a more promising day. Later, however, The Gardens went bankrupt; its five nearly finished houses were eventually declared "a hazard to the community" and were razed.

Sewerage Happens

One item, however, remained a thorn in Rhinecliff's flesh — its sewers. A few homes were known to have malfunctioning cesspools or septic tanks. Worse, some were suspected of disposing their effluent into what were euphemistically called "covered drains," but were simply ditches tied into storm drains. However, Rhinecliff's steep slopes and omnipresent rock ledge made the cost of building and operating a central sewer system prohibitive. Homeowners would have preferred to ignore the situation, for their seemingly haphazard sewer system had never caused real trouble.

However, aware that development follows infrastructure like the night the day, a group of residents — mostly newcomers — formed the Rhinecliff Wastewater Committee to investigate solutions to the problem. Dye tests were made. The sewers of a handful of houses near Shatzell Avenue were found deficient. The findings, presented in a pamphlet entitled "Sewage Happens: The Rhinecliff Wastewater Problem … and What You Can Do About It" and a vastly entertaining thirteen-minute film called *The Effluent Society*, explained in clear terms why the suggested conventional approach — connecting to a development's treatment plant — was more likely to produce noise and strong odors than the desired results. (The Woods, in fact, was already plagued by a smelly wastewater system, as was Wells Manor, the just-finished residential complex for the elderly.)

Most important, the pamphlet and film presented new techniques and equipment that would provide satisfactory on-site sewage treatment. The town was persuaded. The houses with inadequate sewer systems were brought up to code with funds received from a federal Housing and Urban Development program that helped low-income areas like Rhinecliff upgrade their infrastructure. That accomplished, Rhinecliff sewage problems faded from the picture for the next fifteen years.

Greenway

Pressure for change continued to emanate from such organizations as Greenway, a state-sponsored organization whose far-reaching policies and programs would have great power. Set in motion by the Hudson River Valley Greenway Act, passed with the blessings of the DEC in 1991, its broad mission was to protect and enhance the unique heritage of the counties and municipalities along the tidal river, as well as the river itself. Its jurisdiction extended from Saratoga County north of Albany down to lower Manhattan, but its vision was solidly regional. Recognizing that enticing municipalities to be sensitive to their neighbors' interests in such tough issues as land use would require a dramatic shift in local thinking, Greenway evolved policies and programs to lure towns and villages into cooperating with each other; one might fairly describe Greenway as a friendly, but determined, octopus. Its initial priority was to make tourism a durable part of the region's economy. If existing attractions, such as the estates, wineries and music festivals, formed a network, it reasoned, visitors might be enticed to remain not one, but two or three days and even as much as a week in the area.

Next, Greenway segued into hiking and water trails. Created for local residents as well as for tourists, the hiking trails would form segments of a continuous pathway from

Pete Seeger's sloop Clearwater *sailing into the Town Landing. Photograph circa 1990, courtesy of John A. Dierdorff.*

the Battery in New York City to Troy just north of Albany, with spurs to inland communities as well. A water trail would complement the land trails with appropriately sized landings at every riverfront settlement. This was the aspect of Greenway's envisioning that would have the most immediate impact on Rhinecliff, for the hamlet's landing provided the only existing public, over-the-tracks access to the Hudson River between Staatsburg's Norrie Point to the south and the landing at Germantown in Columbia County. Moreover, it was strategically located in the middle of the Hudson River National Historic Landmark District's stretch of waterfront. Greenway's long-range plan for the Rhinecliff landing echoed the LWRP's — that it would become a center for touring as well as local boating. It would include launch sites for canoes, kayaks, rowboats and motorboats, and docking for river cruise boats and large sailboats such as Pete Seeger's sloop *Clearwater*. The access ramp to the landing and the Amtrak station were

viewed as keys to its development as a regional recreational center. Given the small area of the landing and the limitations imposed on peripheral parking by the hamlet's narrow roads and steep topography, these visions would prove a tall order to fulfill.

Another of Greenway's key offerings was its "Compact Program" for municipalities. Encouraging preservation and such enhancements as the creation of sidewalk systems along tree-lined main streets, protected country roads through farmlands, and safe, pleasant bike routes, its thrust was, as always, to induce local communities "to pull together towards common goals." Through this program Greenway hoped to persuade municipalities to coordinate their zoning and subdivision regulations. For those that signed on, Greenway offered matching grants up to $5,000 for community planning projects and 100-percent grants for planning and zoning changes to implement the compact, as well as staff and technical assistance. In addition, it promised local con-

The abandoned Long and Slate Docks. Photograph by Alan Coon, 2007.

trol of shoreline docks, moorings and boathouses. At first only a sprinkling of Dutchess County municipalities joined the compact, then the program caught on. However, despite continued urging by the state and the county, Rhinebeck held back. It was loath to give up its autonomy. Moreover, intimate involvement in the policies of Red Hook, Milan and Hyde Park seemed too complex a burden for it to assume.

Focus on the Rhinecliff Waterfront

Although inland Rhinebeck's active interest in the river landing ebbed and flowed depending on what

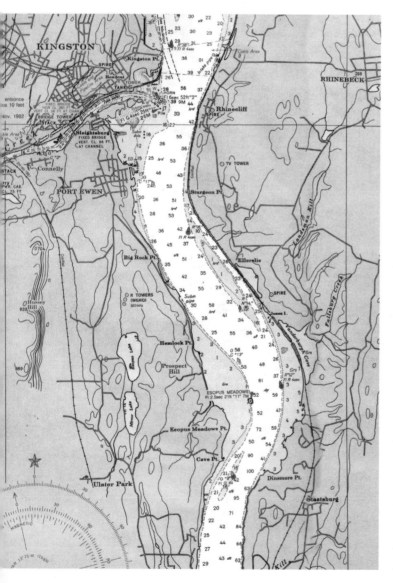

other projects claimed the town's attention, the hamlet continued to stimulate interest in improving its waterfront by holding community festivities and work projects there. A spectacular Rhinecliff Day was held on the Saturday of Columbus Day weekend in 1997 to raise money to improve the dock and, at the same time, to bring the hamlet and the inland town and village more closely together. Festivities started off at ten o'clock with the *Clearwater* taking its first load of passengers for a sail on the river and with a softball game at the old Orchard Street ball field. Throughout the day there were demonstrations of equipment at the firehouse, a presentation on hawks by the Raptor Center, a pie-baking contest, a talent show, bingo, backstage tours by the Rhinebeck Theater Society, as well as storytelling and a billiard competition at the Morton Memorial. Bands played all afternoon in front of the hotel.

This festival day was such a huge success that a second followed the next year. It began the previous evening with a *Clearwater* concert in the Morton's large hall. Ukuleles, banjos, guitars, a couple of comic instruments and the human voice in all its manifestations enticed the audience to join in with singing and laughter. On Rhinecliff Day itself the weather was miserable. Every teasing sign of clearing swiftly turned into sheets of rain. Still, people came and leapt over puddles from shelter to shelter to enjoy the games and exhibits. The *Clearwater* sold pumpkins from its decks and served pie and cider down below. The intrepid par-

The mission of Greenway, a program of the State Department of Environmental Conservation, was to unite municipalities with their waterfront. The kind of facility that would be developed in large part depended on the depth of the water. This map published by the National Oceanic and Atmospheric Administration shows the river off the Rhinecliff dock to be a good forty-two feet deep.

It poured rain on Rhinecliff's 1998 Festival Day, but leaping over puddles to get from one event to another did not discourage an intrepid band. Photograph by Cynthia Saniewski

men from Daytop (the drug rehabilitation organization), and members of AmeriCorps helped with heavy work such as dragging castoff tires from the river's edge. The next day the town highway department sent its trucks to take the piled-up debris to the landfill. It, too, was a satisfying event.

The Metro-North Extension Controversy

ticipants turned what might have been a catastrophe into a real tonic.

In the spring of 1999, the town joined Scenic Hudson's first Great River Sweep to clean up debris from the shoreline. The hamlet-organized event began with a grand parade of children and grownups carrying fluttering fish pennants. Led by Rhinebeck's prizewinning high-school jazz band, it merrily progressed from the war monument to the dock. There it was greeted by the Rhinecliff fire company's pumpers throwing streams of water high into the air. After the opening ceremonies, participants picked up bags of debris from the sides of the roads and Vanderburgh Cove. Boys from Holy Cross,

Back in the 1980s transportation experts predicted that within five years the Metropolitan Transit Authority's commuter rail service from New York's Grand Central Terminal, then terminating at Poughkeepsie, would be extended to Hyde Park or to Rhinecliff. Regional planners saw in this a way to relieve the ever-growing number of cars on the road. Nothing concrete happened, however, until June 1999, when Metro-North, as the line is called, scheduled two days of public meetings at which it expected to win the endorsement of the communities that had been designated as station stops — Hyde Park, Staatsburg, Rhinecliff, and Tivoli, its new hoped-for terminus. Metro-North's rationale for the extension, stated in a fancy brochure, was that it would reduce its overall operating costs by providing a badly needed railroad yard in which to park its trains, an equipment main-

The hamlet had better luck with the weather when it joined Scenic Hudson in its first Great River Sweep, organized to remove debris from the entire mid-Hudson waterfront. The opening parade, led by the high-school jazz band, marched from the war memorial to the Landing. Here it comes over the bridge crossing the railroad tracks. Photograph 1999, courtesy of Scenic Hudson.

tenance area and an "employee base facility." Northern Dutchess County would get a new means of commuting locally and a cheaper ride to Grand Central Terminal than the Amtrak express trains from Rhinecliff then offered to Pennsylvania Station. Convinced that commercial activity would be stimulated in the neighborhood of the stations, Metro-North predicted a big boost to the region's general economy. As soon as it received approval, Metro-North stated, it was ready to go into a study phase at a cost of $3 million, and then on to the building phase, estimated at $70 million.

The negative reaction of the communities was immediate, strong and encompassing. Urged on by the Northern Dutchess Alliance, a new consortium of municipalities and community and business organizations designed to foster long-range regional planning, the meetings were well attended and the speakers forceful. Residents' bedrock objection was that their peace and quiet would be destroyed. Another objection was, how could anyone think of spending up to three hours in an uncomfortable coach to get to New York City when Amtrak express at Rhinecliff would speed them there in plush seats with plug-ins for their computers in little more than an hour and a half, and even faster when the high-speed trains got underway? Besides, where could space be found along the bluff-strewn route for the yard, the maintenance area and the employee facility, to say nothing of parking for riders? Some questioned Metro-North's management capability, others the cost of the project, especially when they were already paying Metro-North a fee through their telephone bills and mortgage transfers. One irate Rhinebeck resident reasoned that it would make more sense to give low-income riders within Dutchess and Westchester counties a subsidy, than to spend 73 million taxpayers' dollars for such an ill-conceived scheme. Tivoli was adamantly opposed for all of the above reasons and because it was already working to gain safe access across the tracks to the river for fishing, boating and a small park, and feared the Metro-North extension would kill those plans. (It has since received a grant for an over-the-track facility.) Rhinecliff, considered as an alternate terminal, was equally opposed. There, the lack of space was even worse; the hamlet was already having a hard time finding enough additional parking for its current Amtrak riders. The final worry was that if Metro-North, which would use the same rails as Amtrak, were instituted, Amtrak service between New York and the terminus of the extended Metro-North line would be discontinued.

A few people — the owner of a small restaurant, for one — spoke in favor of the extension because they thought it would bring them clientele. What is surprising is that county officials did not take a more forceful position, at the very least because it was not a well-thought-out plan. However, for them, public transportation had long been a top priority. In the end, they did not have to take a strong stand. The outcry was so decisive and essentially so on-target that the scheme was dropped like the proverbial hot potato. But, the Metro-North extension was far from dead. It would lurk in the background ready to rise up again in the new century. So, too, would the standoff between planners and developers.

16

The Millennium

The monumental year 2000 was dubbed Y2K, for the arrival of the millennium was accompanied by a national frenzy over whether computer programs would be able to make the numerical leap or whether the country's communication system would be thrown into unimaginable chaos. Fortunately, with advanced preparation at immense expense, the computers did their jobs and the great leap forward entered with benign dignity.

Not unlinked to the reliability of computers were the stirrings of radical change in Rhinebeck's real estate market. Rhinecliff would be strongly affected. For some time, hamlet residents had noted a slow decline in the number of houses for sale and a gradual rise in the prices paid. In the previous century the convenience of the Amtrak station was the draw; now, it was the world-changing growth of computer technologies that provided myriad opportunities for conducting business from home. Fewer of the latest newcomers were weekenders. More were raising families, although with not as many children as in the days before equal employment opportunity for women. But baby carriages and strollers were becoming a common sight on the roads and on the commercial area's sidewalks. Essentially, the rise in real estate prices had to do with the simple fact that what the small community had to offer was eagerly sought after — intimacy, river views and strong historic heritage were in short supply across the country, and many people hankered for the lifestyle these amenities offered.

Generally, the current crop of "transplants" had more money and was less handy than earlier newcomers. Rather than wield hammers themselves, the new generation of fixer-uppers tended to hire contractors for serious renovations and even for mowing grass. Gardeners hastened the process of building up the rocky soil by bringing in cubic yards of prepared soil. With a careful selection of nursery-grown plants, they made riots of bloom in all seasons even on little scraps of land. Some, with diligence, also had luck with vegetables. A popular means of informal socializing became chatting with weed-pullers while walking to the post office to pick up the mail.

The post office moved from Trowbridge's to Paddy's Grill, which had been totally renovated after Annie's death by the new owner, a resident of twenty years who had accumulated a savvy portfolio of Rhinecliff real estate. The move doubled the post office's size and, equally important, gave it handicapped access. It remained the social heart of the hamlet, a place of chance, but convivial, encounters. Although no longer always a resident of the hamlet, the postmaster was a fountain of local news. The bulletin board was the place to post information about forthcoming meetings and events.

The downside of change was that old-timers were inevitably aging. When they moved to warmer climes or died, they quite simply could not be replaced by people with such deep roots. In fact, the population balance was visibly shifting to the newcomers — roughly defined as residents who had lived in the hamlet less than fifty years. Free from embedded memories of growing up in the hamlet, the newcomers tended to think more flexibly, if not less passionately, about changes. Yet, they had cho-

sen Rhinecliff for many of the same reasons old-timers continued to live there. They liked the hamlet's compact size and its steadfast character. They were proud of the hamlet's independence and were helpful when it came to volunteering both muscle and thought for community projects. Several joined the fire company, its ladies' auxiliary and its emergency medical wing, welcomed by heretofore-wary old-timers who now needed them to swell their waning ranks. In the beginning few newcomers joined the old-timers at the firehouse's Sunday breakfasts or the Women's Auxiliary's soup and bake sales, but little by little their numbers grew at these monthly events, for they offered a chance to socialize with residents they did not run into during their customary routines. Many attended the simple, but always touching, Memorial Day observances at the war monument. Although they led busy lives, some went to public meetings; one or two attended diligently, others only when drawn out by a specific issue. They brought more zest to the meetings than the old-timers, who were so tired of the town's lack of concern for the hamlet that they seldom participated at all — at least overtly.

Still, the newcomers were a different generation with different backgrounds and a good deal more money.

Revitalization of the Waterfront

The bridge and ramp that provided access over the railroad tracks to the town landing had deteriorated to the point that the State Department of Transportation (DOT) decided they should be fixed. At first the DOT thought it would be able to restore them. However, by the mid-1990s it became evident that they must be replaced. But, because Rhinecliff was a part of the Hudson River National Historic Landmark District, the new structures would have to mirror the originals as closely as possible — a very expensive job. Whether to remove the separate pedestrian overpass from the project was briefly debated. The arguments in favor of discarding it was that it obscured the spacious view of the river from Shatzell Avenue and that, since it would have to be four feet higher than the already steep originals to accommodate future high-speed trains, it probably would not be often used. The cost was great, too — around a million dollars.

The principal negotiations with the state were managed by inland Rhinebeckians who had been in charge of town planning for almost thirty years, but had not thought concretely about the hamlet's river views. They regarded the ramp and pedestrian overpass replacement as a preservation project; that the early-twentieth-century solution might be improved upon in the twenty-first century had not occurred to them. Even the cost was not an obstacle. The federal government would ultimately pay 80 percent of the over $4 million total cost, and a special Thruway Authority fund would supply most of the remaining 20 percent. Thus, reconstructing the pedestrian overpass was brought into the program. Finally, the landing itself was added, for past efforts to stem its erosion by tides, currents, the pressure of stacked ice and the wakes of huge tankers had not been entirely successful.

The NYS DOT did a superb job. Several of the key personnel were already familiar with the site; it made them — and new workers, too — happy to be working in so beautiful a location. Thanks to careful attention and sheer luck as well, construc-

The John J. Harvey Fireboat, *built in 1931 for the New York City Fire Department, was saved from scrap by a private organization in 1991. She travels the Hudson bringing attention to the important work such vessels do. Here, she is at Rhinecliff's 2006 Waterfront Festival Day. Photograph by Cynthia Saniewski.*

tion went according to plan, although mimicking the old structures proved tough to carry out. For example, virtually every segment of steel for the pedestrian bridge had to be individually detailed to represent its original look. Even laying the historic-sized brick surface on the ramp — which required an artful ninety-degree turn that went from a running bond into a herringbone pattern and then back again — went smoothly. Great care was taken to get just the right fencing; round-headed bolts were devised to simulate welded rivets.

Although not in the original contract, the job was extended to landscaping the dock area. After the bulkheads were shored up, truckloads of top soil were brought in to make lawns. Finally, almost two hundred wind- and water-worthy shrubs were planted. All that remained for the town to do was bring the old ferry slip up to date for large motor-boat launchings and provide launch platforms for canoes, kayaks and other small craft. Planning for passive recreation was already underway. Benches and tables were soon installed. Cooking grills and a shelter were on order. To celebrate the public opening of the town landing as a public park and boat-launching site, the town board declared June 30, 2002, to be Rhinebeck Town Landing Festival Day.

The festivities began at noon with the ceremonial cutting of a ribbon and ended with viewing the fireworks at Ulster Park from the riverbank, a traditional event for both town and hamlet. Special highlights were a photo contest and a special pictorial stamp offered by the post office. But the expected stampede to use the facilities was slow to materialize. Weeds grew in the shrubbery.

A real change in the hamlet took place when the aged Rhinecliff Hotel was put up for sale. It had become a destination for rowdy gatherings of young people, many under the legal drinking age. On weekends, loud music and rampant drunkenness infected the whole downtown area and beyond. The scene became so manic that even three bouncers could not manage the crowds. Finally, owner Ed Tybus, by then advanced in age, came to realize that the time had come to sell. On the night of June 29, 2003, the nearly 150-year-old hotel closed its doors.

Fortunately, a group of buyers was not long in coming. Their plan was to make the hotel into a high-class country inn with a limited number of guest rooms on the top two floors, a large hall for special parties on the floor below and a pub-like restaurant on the ground floor offering meals priced to attract locals. Unfortunately, the building was far less stable than the new owners had at first thought. For instance, when workmen started to replace the deteriorating porch overlooking the river, the entire wall began to slither towards the rail-

Both Ed Tybus and his hotel were aging and, in the summer of 2003, he sold it. The new owners had hoped to renovate it, but they soon realized it would have to be largely rebuilt. However, they saved as much as they could. Photograph by Alison J. Michaels, 2007.

road track. All those years of absorbing groundwater, along with the clay subsoil, had rotted its underpinnings. Nevertheless, the owners persisted. They saved as much as possible of the old building, such as the fine old mirrored bar that graces the pub restaurant. Still, the hotel was virtually rebuilt.

Parking was another problem the hotel faced. It was solved by leasing land between the railroad tracks and the hotel from CSX, owners of the railroad right-of-way. Still, the potential overloading of nearby roads by guests arriving all at once for private parties and the restaurant worried many Rhinecliff residents. The perfect solution has yet to be found.

The Morton Library and Community House bustled with new programs for all ages and tastes. The library was elegantly refurbished out of the endowment and offered more books and continually expanding services, such as a computer terminal and a special time for reading aloud to preschool children. Piano and tango lessons, book discussions, novel-writing and play-reading groups, as well as monthly acoustic music evenings, art exhibits and harvest suppers found enthusiastic participants and audiences. Levi P. Morton's birth date was celebrated every year with a collation and a fundraising art auction. Civic groups, such as the Town Landing Committee, held meetings there. Individuals could hire the hall for private parties. Its most recent new amenity is a huge screen with state-of-the-art equipment to run films, power-point lectures and an extraordinary variety of games.

A grant was secured to install long-overdue handicapped access. A second grant, to renovate the ground floor, followed. That will yield a concrete floor with radiant heat, a handicapped-accessible toilet room and a vastly improved lighting system. Just what the renovated space will be used for has not yet been determined. Rental as a nursery school is among the options. The final decision will depend on the level of building code required. The atmo-sphere at the Morton differs from that of its early days, but it is humming happily again as a focal point of the community.

High-Class Real Estate

The cost of real estate throughout Rhinecliff continued to increase until it was estimated to possess the highest-priced property in Rhinebeck, acre for acre — or more appropriately, foot for foot. Knowing that the awaited "promised time" had at last come, owners of the former estate lands surrounding Rhinecliff laid plans to develop them. The Gardens project off the Rhinecliff Road resurrected its approved plans for comparatively tight-packed blocks of condominium townhouses. Finishing the abandoned first phase in record time, the homes were soon sold, although some were still incomplete. Immediately, the developers went into the second phase. All those houses were nearing completion when a stop order put a halt to construction because of violations of the building code. The developers filed for bankruptcy. No one yet knows how it will turn out.

The former Pope Pius XII–Holy Cross facility was added to the roster of potential developments. It had always been troubled with both budgetary and behavioral problems, which the archdiocese tried to solve by changing the mix of youngsters. The facility became coeducational and took on increasingly difficult cases. Then, it limited its enrollment to around one hundred seriously troubled boys, aged ten to eighteen. The fire company was beset both with false alarms and real, but fortunately small, set fires. Youngsters ran away — mainly by hopping the next train out of the hamlet. Two boys tragically drowned in the lake. The carcasses of a bull and fifteen mutilated small animals were found hanging in trees in the woods. The culprit turned out to be a trapper who pled that he was returning the bodies to the earth after he stripped the pelts; he believed the flesh would nourish scavengers such as crows, and the strung-up skeletons would provide nesting places for small birds. It might have seemed a reasonable explanation to the perpetrator, but hamlet residents were spooked. The facility's administration held public information sessions to alleviate fears, but the sessions did no lasting good. Then, suddenly, in 2002, the facility was shut down, apparently because of improper social relations between an employee and one of the youngsters. The public was never informed of exactly what happened, but it was clear that supervision by the archdiocese had been lax.

The Rhinecliff community was relieved when the facility closed. However, the vacant, fast-decaying buildings and property, by now reduced to 112 acres, presented a serious challenge. Although getting rid of the contaminated debris left by both the military academy and the drug rehabilitation facility has been estimated to cost several million dollars, real estate interests intent on doing so were on hand. To make development feasible, however, they want vastly increased housing densities to help pay the costs. This has not been forthcoming, and the property is currently being offered by the present owners to a Hassidic group that, it is believed, wishes to establish a residential school there. The only certainty is that rumors continue to fly.

In 2004 the young Kibel/Dicola family bought the land surrounding Holy Cross that extends from the Creed property on the north to Mill Road on the south— 538 acres now called Goomer Hollow, LLC. Its road frontage (except for Holy Cross) runs from just south of the densely settled section of the hamlet along Morton Road for almost two miles, then turns east on Mill Road for a mile. The Kibel/Dicolas have begun reclaiming and fencing the extensive fields with the intention of establishing a horse farm on the property. They intend to develop it with a limited number of estate-type houses and an 80-to-100-house development.

Comprehensive Plan and Zoning Ordinance

Aroused by so much actual and threatened development on what was estate land, the town put a moratorium on new building and established a committee to overhaul its Comprehensive Plan and Zoning Ordinance, then over ten years old. Originally composed of twenty-five diverse town residents, the committee worked diligently to fashion a new set of laws that would respond to changed times. However, its knowledge of Rhinecliff remained scant, as few members of the committee visited Rhinecliff beyond occasional trips to the railroad station or the landing. Moreover, some of the members lived in the village, which has its own plan and zoning ordinance and, therefore, would not have to live under the regulations adopted by the Town of Rhinebeck.

Early on, the committee's response to development pressure was to raise the zoning requirements from one, three and five acres to six, ten and twenty acres in order to preserve open space. This meant that, to maintain the diversity of housing mandated by the state, the committee had to make an effort to incorporate affordable housing into its plan.

The committee found two ways of providing the needed affordable housing. One was popular. It permitted owners to convert accessory buildings, such as barns or substantial garages, into living spaces or to convert a large house into apartments. This had the advantage of seeding rental units throughout the community, although not necessarily at affordable prices.

The other solution was the creation of Traditional Neighborhood Developments (TNDs), a high-density cluster of small houses and apartments — described as starter or empty-nester homes — many of which would be rental units. Two such areas were mapped. One surrounded the Stop and Shop on Route 9. It was touted as enjoying the convenience of easy shopping at the supermarket and Williams Lumber, which had been adding household products and sporting clothes to its shelves. It even had its own athletic field, albeit mapped adjacent to the Stop and Shop parking lot on Route 9. The hope was that the TND would stimulate the emporia to upgrade their general appearance. That the TND site had multiple owners, any one of which might not wish to develop as a TND, was not regarded as an obstacle.

The second TND was an extension of the hamlet of Rhinecliff. Located on Creed property where Orchard Street breaks off from the Rhinecliff Road and the anemone operation once was, its touted advantage was that it would put TND residents within walking distance both of Amtrak, which it was supposed they would use to commute to their jobs, and of a revived Shatzell Avenue commercial area. For entertainment, residents would have the refurbished hotel and the China Rose restaurant, the Morton Library and Community Center and

the landing, as well as the trendy shops and eateries in the nearby village.

Few Rhinecliffers believed it likely that many TND residents would work in New York City and, if some did, that they would walk to the station; the very steep hill they would have to navigate in rain and snow, heat and cold, as well as several months of dark mornings and evenings — to say nothing of haste — would strongly discourage them. Instead, even short-time residents felt sure that most would drive to work somewhere in the region. (One of the severe limitations of the new comprehensive plan was that virtually all its maps lacked clear topographic markings. Most committee members equated the hamlet with the village, which is flat, and were unaware of the hamlet's steep slopes. When they were trying to add houses to the exiting hamlet, for instance, it came as a surprise that, because of steep slopes, rock outcroppings and wetlands, only two or three houses could be shoed in, not the over twenty they had planned.) Nor did it seem likely that TND residents would

Topography has always dictated and always will dictate the siting of roads in Rhinecliff. This narrow stretch of Orchard Street is cut into the hill on its eastern side and held up by a hand-laid stone wall on its western side. Photograph by Rose Fox, 2006.

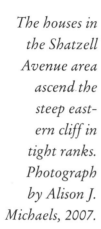

The houses in the Shatzell Avenue area ascend the steep eastern cliff in tight ranks. Photograph by Alison J. Michaels, 2007.

spend much of their free time walking in the hamlet, for they would have to do most of their daily shopping at the large stores on Route 9 or, for a wider variety of choice, in Kingston, Rhinecliff's traditional shopping place, or at other centers on their way to or from work. Nor would the site seem a good location for any but the most hardy "empty nester" retirees, one of whose major recreations is walking.

At the same time, to preserve the historic quality of Rhinecliff — required because it was part of The Hudson River National Historic Landmark District — the committee applied strict building design standards to the hamlet. Shaped to promote the hamlet's "cottage character," rather than the extraordinary variety of style that had resulted from topographic necessity and gradual adding on and sprucing up, the committee set strict rules for appearance, ranging from siting to such features as side or front porches, placement of windows and paint colors. Not only did this seem a cookie-cutter approach, the hamlet was the only part of the town to which such rigid standards were applied.

Most residents of the hamlet also believed that its historic character was as worthy of preservation as any other part of the town. This certainly had been the declared opinion of county and not-for-profit planning groups fifteen years previously when the hamlet was protesting the consequences of the proposed twenty-seven-hole golf course along its periphery. Residents were alarmed to find that the multipurpose greenbelt trail that they had strongly favored on the committee's questionnaire as a benefit to the entire town, as well as essential to the preservation of the intimacy of the hamlet, was given a very low priority.

Although the planners insisted that Rhinecliffers would get to like the TND, many residents believed that it offered such a different type of living that it would become a separate enclave, essentially unrelated to the hamlet. Their opposition to the TND was, of course, labeled as a disguised form of "not in my backyard." Indeed, a few may have been moved by such sentiments, but the large majority was simply reacting to what they saw as the committee's lack of understanding of Rhinecliff's special problems. At the very least, residents insisted, long-range traffic, drainage, demographic and marketing studies should be undertaken to test the TND's impact on the hamlet. Extensive archaeology studies would also be needed, for the TND site was known to be rich in Native American artifacts, still a high priority with the state. The committee replied that those concerns would be met during the SEQRA public hearings. But to Rhinecliffers it seemed foolish to pin a vital part of the comprehensive plan and zoning ordinance on such uncertain ground.

To replace the concept of the TND, a group of technically knowledgeable and mainly recently arrived Rhinecliff residents put together an innovative Fourteen Point Plan. In essence, the plan recognized that the densely settled area was already built out. In addition, the Fourteen Point Plan strongly favored the multi-use greenbelt that would define the historic hamlet and, at the same time, provide the multipurpose trail connection between the hamlet and the village. It also took a firm stand against sewering the hamlet, extending the commercial area and casting the landing as a major destination point.

For the well over 1,000 acres of estate land threatened by development (it has now grown to 4,500 acres), the plan presented a Four Step Process that it believed would achieve the goals of open space and agricultural soil preservation desired by the Comprehensive Plan Committee. Worked out by a globally prominent planner and subject to public SEQRA

Rhinecliff firefighters: (left to right) Henry Behrens, Craig Bassett, Kevin Denu, Jim Stone, Jeff Hicks, Harry Heywood, Bob Fitzpatrick with Adam, Christine Conklin, Cynthia Baer with Kinna Kipp, Susan Silverman, Jim Conklin, Mark Denchek with Noah. The rescue truck was bought in 2001. It is a pumper with a 1,000-gallon capacity. Its special feature is a top-mounted gun that is powerful enough to throw 1,250 gallons of water 160 feet in one minute. Photograph by Alison J. Michaels, 2008.

review, the four steps were: 1) identification of physical constraints, such as steep slopes and wet lands; 2) identification of conservation areas, such as the borders of streams, good agricultural soils and sites rich in Native American artifacts; 3) protection of these areas by making them green space; and 4) reduction of the need for roads by clustering the building lots. Although the presentation was first-class, the Fourteen Point Plan and the Four Step Process fell on deaf ears.

Political Turnarounds

The term of office for the town supervisor is two years. Board members serve four-year staggered terms. The 2005 election was a shocker to the Republicans who had held power for 104 years. A Democrat and former weekender, whose work as an educational administrator for the City of Newark, New Jersey, had made him familiar with what it takes to govern, became the supervisor. Two new town board members, both Democrats, were elected. One, a woman, was an administrator at the steadily expanding local hospital; the other was a man whose work was providing computer software for small municipalities. The two holdover board members were a woman with extensive financial experience, a Democrat, and a lone Republican man, a former IBM employee. This gave the Democrats a strong majority. Having promised to bring town government into the twenty-first century, they proceeded to follow through. The new supervisor was retired and therefore able to work full time at his town job. The other board members put their shoulders to the wheel as well. They set up committees staffed by volunteers to deal with such challenges as the high percentage of elderly people in the community, the lack of facilities beyond school athletics for teenagers, and greater transparency in the budgeting process. They also worked to enhance interchange among the town, the village and the schools.

To give a stronger voice to the hamlet, the board established the Rhinecliff Hamlet Advisory Council, a group of nine volunteers representative of that community. Its purpose was "to provide residents of Rhinecliff an opportunity to identify problems and issues of particular and unique relevance to community life in the hamlet and to have a representative forum for considering and proposing solutions to the Town Board." It was an auspicious beginning.

By far the most difficult issue that the new town board was called on to tackle was moving the Comprehensive Plan and Zoning Ordinance forward. However, when a draft of the plan was submitted to the public for comment in June 2006 with the full expectation that it would be accepted as law that year, it proved so confusing and so long (well over 550 pages with maps, photographs, drawings and unnumbered appendices) to those few in the town who attempted to understand it, that it was taken back by the committee for rewriting. As the plan was already over two years in the making, owners throughout the town wishing to subdivide, as well as large-scale developers, became increasingly restive. The board extended the moratorium on building and hired extra consultants to aid the committee. The moratorium did its job, at least temporarily, but the consultants failed to speed the process. Some criticized the Comprehensive Plan and Zoning Ordinance leadership — the same people who had masterminded virtually all previous planning efforts in the town — for causing delay through obfuscation. Others criticized the town board for not being able to see the forest for the trees. When the committee put a draft zoning ordinance before the board for comment, it was obvious that even they found grasping its complicated provisions extremely difficult.

The planning situation became even more complicated when the town board appointed an Open Space/Affordable Housing Committee to produce a document that could be worked into or appended to the Comprehensive Plan and Zoning Ordinance. Surprisingly, both co-chairs, one a village resident, the other a Rhinecliff resident, and both planners in their work lives, were ardent supporters of the Draft Comprehensive Plan's TND. They, too, prepared a long and remarkably complex document, one controversial facet of which was that developers were offered the opportunity either to transfer their affordable housing requirements to other areas of town, or to pay an equivalent in money for an agency of the town to develop affordable housing elsewhere. To some critics the very connection between open space and affordable housing was false.

Meanwhile, the operation of the Rhinecliff Hamlet Advisory Council was erratic. Convinced that their sole obligation was to the town board, they did nothing to bring the wider hamlet into the loop. Hamlet residents could attend their meetings, held twice a month, but as agendas were seldom available in advance and too often not even available at the meetings, very few did. On the other hand, in an imaginative response to the Draft Comprehensive Plan prepared for the town board, the council recommended removing the Rhinecliff TND from the plan on the grounds that it was neither walkable because of steep slopes and narrow hemmed-in streets, nor near enough to civic and commercial destinations to be viable. Instead, the council urged the planning committee to consider rehabilitating the buildings and infrastructure of the Holy Cross property by means of a private/public partnership and turning them into much-needed affordable housing and public athletic facilities. The property could also provide a site for an expansion of the school system, should that become necessary. The council also pressed for the creation of a multiuse Rhinecliff Greenway that would connect the town's residential communities, and it supported the draft plan's intention to designate Rhinecliff a Critical Environmental Area with development sub-ject to SEQRA review. At the same time, the council bewailed the hamlet's description as "a smaller version of the Village." It saw significant expansion of commercial activity in Rhinecliff as neither practicable nor desirable, and the development of the waterfront to its "highest use" as troubling.

Intent on recapturing their control of the town board, the Republicans prepared a harsh but politically astute campaign to win back the position of supervisor and the two seats on the town that would be up for election in November. Essentially, the contest that evolved was between Republican old-timers who wished to return to the government of simpler days, and less deeply rooted Democrats who believed that complex times demanded a more complex approach. One of the Republicans' chief complaints was that the Democrats had not only raised the supervisor's salary from $10,000 to $25,000 plus benefits, but had shown signs of heading towards a town manager form of government. Another complaint was the mounting cost of the consultants hired by the Comprehensive Plan Committee. The Republicans won the supervisor's job and one of the board seats handily. The vote for the second board member was so close that it was recounted. The Republican candidate finally took that, too. However, as only the two hold-over board members, both Democrats, had experience in governing, the new board faced immense challenges, not only in the planning area, but also in bringing transparency to its governing as its campaign literature had promised it would do. An odd, but not insignificant, aspect of the board is that four of its five members live in the village and will not have to live under the zoning laws it passes.

The Morton Memorial Celebrates

On the bright side of things, the Morton Memorial Library and Community House celebrated its 100th anniversary together with Levi P. Morton's birthday at the end of May 2008. A special ice cream and cake party was held on May 22 for children from one to nine years old. A guitarist led them in songs especially created for the occasion, and the older children entertained parents with a little play about squirrels. All went home happily with big fat balloons and a "Catch the Reading Bug" list of books to read over the summer.

Morton Day itself, May 24, started off with an immense group photograph of hamlet residents, and continued throughout the afternoon with musical groups of all kinds, from solo guitarists to very accomplished young violinists, a rousing chorus and jazz combos. The Rhinecliff Volunteer Fire Company displayed its brightly shined fire trucks. The post office offered a special stamp cancellation. A magician and craft-making entertained children. The Butcher Boys, located in the old business section on the Rhinecliff Road north of the Kip homestead ruins, set up a kiosk in front of the post office from which they sold steak and sausage sandwiches and soda pop. The soda could be bought in dark blue glasses embellished with the rescue squad's insignia for $5.00 extra, the proceeds benefiting the squad. The celebration ended at the Morton with the annual fund-raising art auction of paintings by local artists. Always a highly amusing as well as worthwhile affair, its theme was appropriately "Rhinecliff … 100 Years Ago." The weather the whole day was gorgeous. The crowds were relaxed and happily mingling. The caring spirit of Levi P. Morton could only have been delighted with the celebration of the 100th anniversary of his signal gift to the hamlet and his own 184th birthday.

A host of hamlet residents turned out to be photographed all together to honor the Morton Library on its centennial day. Photograph by Chris Kendall, 2008.

Epilogue

It seemed right to end my tale of Kipsbergen/Rhinecliff with the celebration of the Morton Memorial Library and Community House's centennial. Along with the Rhinecliff Volunteer Fire Company it has been, and I hope will continue to be, the civic focus of the hamlet.

Still, in these days it is not possible to stand free of the wider community. For a small place like Rhinecliff that clings to its deep-rooted independence, finding common cause with the vastly larger inland town will not be easy. Its heritage as a transportation hub differs markedly from that of the inland town, whose heritage is farming, light industry, services and the Post Road.

Nor will it be easy for the inland town to forge a bond with the waterfront community whose focus has been on its historic docks and the railroad — the route that follows the river's "sea level" periphery. In contrast, the inland town has not needed to pay much attention to the river. It seldom even sees it. There has never been much to draw inlanders to the waterfront except for a trip to the train station or an occasional ferry or boat ride. As a result, the hamlet is less familiar to Rhinebeckians than the neighboring inland towns of Red Hook and Hyde Park.

Yet today the destinies of inland Rhinebeck and riverside Rhinecliff are irrevocably intertwined. Take the Rhinecliff Landing, for instance. It is one of the town's major recreational resources and, at the same time, the heart of Rhinecliff. How the landing is developed will have far less daily impact on the inland town than on the hamlet. It could be no more than another recreation venue, real-estate selling point or a tourist attraction with potential economic benefits. On the other hand, it could become a force for bringing the town and the hamlet together.

The proposed Comprehensive Plan and Zoning Ordinance that is now speeding through the state-mandated environmental review process could also work towards unifying the town and the hamlet. To date it has not. Unfortunately, the proposed plan and the zoning ordinance persistently envision Rhinecliff as a small version of the neat, tidy village that through much of its history was called the Flatts, because it is, indeed, flat. The document quite simply fails to understand that the vitality and charm of the hamlet is a consequence of its irregular terrain. Its steep slopes alternating with swales and wetlands have dictated the siting if its houses and its narrow roads, as has its prime location on the banks of the Hudson River, one of the world's greatest thoroughfares.

It was while I was mulling over these multiple disconnects between the hamlet and the inland town that I took a step forward and began to wonder if there were not some way they might be mitigated. I knew that finding answers would mean juggling a multitude of the challenges all communities share on questions such as taxes, property rights, the feasibility of a demographically diverse community, future state and local funding, and the undeniable fact that great money does not speak, it roars.

Suddenly, it came to me that the recent hotly contested town elections might provide a good starting point. Essentially the struggle was about rootedness — the value placed on the sons of families who have lived here for generations versus the value of comparative newcomers. The former think of themselves as providing stability, while the latter claim

fresh viewpoints and flexibility. I then began to ponder what it is that makes a person truly rooted.

Here is what I have come up with. There seem to be at least two kinds of rootedness — one based on special knowledge passed down through generations, the other based on commitment to the community. To me, they are but two sides of one coin. They need not be at odds. In fact, they work best in tandem.

Needless to say, to make such a vision a reality will take leadership from every level of the community and inclusive generosity on the part of individuals with diverse interests. How much more satisfying it would be to live in the Town of Rhinebeck if acknowledgment of both kinds of rootedness were the rule rather than the exception. There would be more widespread and eager volunteerism and more citizen participation, not only in programs, but in the firehouses, hospital, schools and other organizations necessary to the well-being of the community. Serving in government would be more interesting and more productive.

Should all of these good things become realities, they might even lead to closer relationships with our neighboring towns and even spread to neighboring counties, thence to the entire country and, like the sailing ships of yore, to the world beyond.

Is such a hope fantastical? Perhaps it is. But it seems no more idle a dream to me than using the bucolic illusions of nineteenth-century romantics as a mold for planning our future, or relying on established power to preserve an unattainable status quo.

Is it too much to expect? I hope not. As the old saying goes, it takes two hands to clap.

Cynthia Owen Philip
Rhinecliff, New York
November 2008

Selected Bibliography

Baker, Paul R. *Richard Morris Hunt*. Cambridge, Mass.: M.I.T. Press, 1980.

Boyle, Robert H. *The Hudson River, a Natural and Unnatural History*. New York: Norton, 1969.

Burrows, Edwin G., and Mike Wallace. *Gotham, A History of New York City to 1898*. New York: Oxford University Press, 1999.

Christman, Henry. *Tin Horns and Calico: Decisive Episode in the Emergence of Democracy*. New York: Holt, 1945.

Clarke, Marcella. *Diary of a Central School, The Story of Rhinebeck Central School*. Rhinebeck, N.Y., 2004.

Dangerfield, George. *Chancellor Robert R. Livingston of New York 1746–1813*. New York: Harcourt, Brace & Co., 1960.

Downing, Andrew Jackson. *A Treatise of the Theory and Practice of Landscape Gardening Adapted to North America*. New York: Orange-Judd & Co., 1839.

Dutchess County Planning Board. *Landmarks of Dutchess County, 1683–1867, Architecture Worth Saving*. New York: State Council on the Arts, 1969.

Eberlein, Harold Donaldson, and Cortlandt Van Dyke Hubbard. *Historic Houses of the Hudson Valley*. New York: Architectural Book Publishing Company, 1942.

The Gazette. Rhinebeck, N.Y., 1846–2008.

Hall, Edward Hagaman. *The Hudson-Fulton Celebration 1909, The Fourth Annual Report of the Hudson-Fulton Celebration Commission*. New York, 1910.

Hastings, Hugh. *Ecclesiastical Records, State of New York*. Albany, N.Y.: L.B. Lyon, 1901.

Hutton, George V. *The Great Hudson River Brick Industry*. Fleischmanns, N.Y.: Purple Mountain Press, 2003.

Kelly, Arthur C.M., compiler. *Deaths, Marriages and Much Miscellaneous from Rhinebeck, N.Y. Newspapers, 1846–1899*, 2 volumes. Rhinebeck, N.Y.: Kinship.

Kelly, Nancy V. *A Brief History of Rhinebeck: The Living Past of a Hudson Valley Community*. The Wise Family Trust and the Rhinebeck Historical Society, 2001.

Klein, Milton M. *The Empire State, A History of New York*. Ithaca, N.Y.: Cornell University Press, 2001.

Kouwenhoven, John A. *The Columbia Historical Portrait of New York, An Essay in Graphic History*. New York: Harper and Row, 1953.

Ladies Auxiliary of the Rhinecliff Volunteer Fire Company. *A Walking Tour of Rhinecliff*. Rhinecliff, N.Y., 1975.

McElroy, Robert McNutt. *Levi P. Morton, Banker, Diplomat and Statesman*. New York: Putnam, 1930.

Moffett, Glendon L. *The Old Skillypot and Other Ferryboats of Rondout, Kingston and Rhinecliff*. Fleischmanns, N.Y.: Purple Mountain Press, 1997.

Morse, Howard H. *Historic Old Rhinebeck, Echoes of Two Centuries of a Hudson River and Post Road Town*. Rhinebeck, N.Y., 1909.

Morton, Levi P. Papers. Manuscripts and Archives, New York Public Library.

Moulton, Joseph W. *History of the State of New-York, Part II: Novum Belgium*. New York: E. Bliss and E. White, 1826.

The Museum of Rhinebeck History, ed. *World War II, Military Home Front*. Rhinebeck, N.Y., 2000.

———. *The 150th Regiment, New York Volunteer*

Infantry. Rhinebeck, N.Y., n.d.

O'Callaghan, E. B. *The Documentary History of the State of New-York*. Albany, N.Y.: Weed Parsons & Co., 1849–1850.

Philip, Cynthia Owen. *Robert Fulton, a Biography*. New York: Franklin Watts, 1985.

———. *Wilderstein and the Suckleys, A Hudson River Legacy*. Rhinebeck, N.Y.: Wilderstein Preservation, 2001.

Reynolds, Helen Wilkinson. *Dutch Houses in the Hudson Valley before 1776*. 1929. Reprint, New York: Dover Publications, 1965.

Rhinebeck Historical Society. *A Rhinebeck Album, 1776 – 1876 – 1976*. Rhinebeck, N.Y., 1984.

Rhoads, William B. *Kingston, New York, the Architectural Guide*. Hensonville, N.Y.: Black Dome Press, 2003.

Ringwald, Donald C. *History of the Kingston-Rhinecliff Ferry*. Reprinted from the Kingston *Daily Freeman* by the magazine *Steamboat Bill*, n.d.

———. *Hudson River Day Line*. Berkeley, Calif.: Howell-North Books, 1965.

Rudberg, Bernard L. *CNE Spring Tour 2005*. A copious loose-leaf notebook given to tour members. Wappingers Falls, N.Y., 2005.

Shorto, Russell. *Island at the Center of the World*. New York: Doubleday, 2003.

Smith, Edward M. *Documentary History of Rhinebeck in Dutchess Co., N.Y.* 1881. Reprint, Rhinebeck, N.Y.: Kinship, 1974.

———. *Kipsbergen in Dutchess Co., Its History, Location and Boundaries, Its Founders and Their Families through Many Generations*. 1894. Reprint, Rhinebeck, N.Y.: Kinship, 1992.

Steuding, Bob. *Rondout: A Hudson River Port*. Fleischmanns, N.Y.: Purple Mountain Press, 1995.

Strickland, William. *Journal of a Tour of the United States of America 1794–1795*. New York: New-York Historical Society, 1971.

Tietjen, Sari B. *Rhinebeck, Portrait of a Town*. Rhinebeck, N.Y.: The River Press, 1990.

Vaux, Calvert. *Villas and Cottages*. New York: Harper & Brothers Publishers, 1857.

Verplanck, William E., and Moses W. Collyer. *The Sloops of the Hudson*. 1908. Reprint, Fleischmanns, N.Y.: Purple Mountain Press, 1984.

Ward, Geoffrey C., ed. *Closest Companion, The Unknown Story of the Intimate Friendship between Franklin Roosevelt and Margaret Suckley*. New York: Houghton Mifflin Company, 1995.

White, Philip L. *The Beekmans of New York in Politics and Commerce 1647–1877*. New York: New-York Historical Society, 1956.

About the Author

Cynthia Owen Philip is an independent historian who has written extensively on the Hudson River Valley. She is the author of *Robert Fulton: A Biography* and the prize-winning *Wilderstein and the Suckleys: A Hudson River Legacy*. Her wide array of articles and essays has appeared in national and local magazines.

Index